Brighter Futures

Everlief Child Psychology

FREE ASSOCIATION BOOKS

First published in 2018 by
Free Association Books

A CIP Catalogue of this book is available from
the British Library

ISBN: 978-1-9113831-3-0

Illustrated by Mia Vaughan-Smith

Typeset by
www.chandlerbookdesign.co.uk

Printed and bound in Great Britain by
4 Edge Limited

CONTENTS

Introduction to the team   1
Dr Lucy Russell

How to get the most out of this book   16

1. Anxiety   25
When Worries Take Control
Dr Susan Wimshurst, clinical psychologist

2. Friendships and Bullying   71
'Friends are like squiggly lines; they are hard to get straight'
Dr Liz Dawes, clinical psychologist

3. Self-Esteem   129
Building your child's confidence in a challenging world
Nicola Gorringe, clinical psychologist

4. Anger and Frustration   187
Helping your child to 'tame that temper'
Dr Jennifer Swanston, clinical psychologist

5. School related Stress   229
"Maths is Impossible!"
Dr Katherine Hodson, clinical psychologist

6. Concentration and motivation   277
Attention, listening and concentration
Dr Lucy Russell, clinical psychologist

Biographies   347

Introduction to the team

Dr Lucy Russell

Who are we and why have we written this book?

We are a group of six clinical psychologists, all of whom work with children and families. We try to resolve difficulties they are facing in their lives, listening and understanding, and finding ways to break free from those difficulties.

Just as importantly, we are all parents. We have all faced our own parenting challenges, and made our own parenting mistakes! Our take on problems children face is: There is no one-size-fits-all, perfect approach, and what works for you may not work for another parent. If we think and plan carefully we can find a helpful solution for your child.

You may have heard of the word "epidemic" being used to describe the enormous increase in children with mental health problems in the UK. 1 in 10 children and young people aged 5 - 16 suffer from a diagnosable mental health disorder -- that is around three children in every class. About half of adult mental health problems begin before the age of 14.

At our independent clinic in Buckinghamshire, Everlief, we are seeing overwhelming demand for our services. We have worked with over 1800 children and families since we opened our doors in 2012.

We want this book to help parents before a child's difficulty reaches crisis point. We want to spread the message that prevention is the key to happy children. We believe that small changes can make a big difference to the way a child's future pans out.

This book is not about academic achievement. It is about having a happy, settled child at primary school. This is a solution-focussed book. It aims to be realistic and positive. Some of the suggested solutions may involve you, or your child's school, developing a new way of thinking about the problem. We have seen for ourselves that such ideas can make big differences.

HOW YOU CAN USE THIS BOOK

There are many ways of reading this book. You could read it from cover to cover, out of general interest or in order to prevent difficulties developing. You may wish to read just the chapter that is relevant to your situation. We would advise that you read this core chapter first, and follow the **SUPER** steps in each chapter. You may achieve some success by jumping a few steps and going straight to the action planning section but the plans you make are likely to be more effective if you have a deeper understanding about why you are doing what you are doing, and the root causes.

SEVEN BASIC BELIEFS

This book will give you lots of ideas and practical suggestions. The authors share some essential beliefs about childhood, and all the practical ideas will be based on these beliefs. So what are they?

 Nurturing (love, warmth, respect and a strong bond of attachment with at least one adult) is hugely important

The early months and years of a child's life can shape the way she responds to the world. A baby needs to have at least one adult who is there whenever they feel scared or anxious, angry or frustrated. These emotions are so big, a child needs an adult to help soothe them, otherwise the world can seem a terrifying place.

If a parent is consistently available for the child whenever she feels unsafe or scared, the parent provides physical soothing and comfort to help a child feel safe again. Being a role-model like this allows the child to learn how to calm themselves. This can take several years however. The child will still need to return to her "secure base" (mum, dad, grandma etc.) for comfort if they face a new or bigger fear.

Gradually, a child builds confidence and roams further and further from their "secure base", but knows there is always a safe place to return to (even in the teenage years). Through this constant process of comfort and reassurance-seeking, the child gains the view that she is safe, and eventually learns to "self-soothe" every time.

Sometimes, for many reasons, a child does not have such a positive experience. A parent can't, for some reason, soothe and comfort her every time she needs it. The child feels huge emotion but hasn't got a way of coping. The child may feel unsafe and fearful about every new situation, because she hasn't had an adult who can regularly say "it's okay, you're safe". This can lead to huge anxiety. The child does not learn the skills to self-soothe because no one has shown them how to do this.

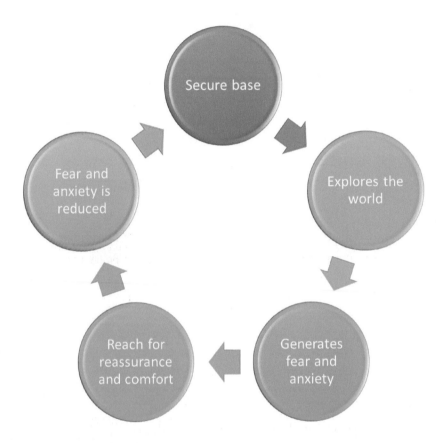

If a child starts school and doesn't have a "secure base" – the belief that they are safe and being looked after – school can feel very scary. All of a sudden, she is taken away from everything that is familiar, and put in a classroom with strange adults and a crowd of other children. Rules and expectations are completely different, and she has to gain multiple skills very quickly. Her senses can be easily overwhelmed, for example by the noisy classroom. Feeling safe helps a child cope with these demands, but if she doesn't feel safe, the anxiety will be huge. She may show it by "acting out" (difficult behaviour) either at school or at home, or by withdrawing into herself. If a child doesn't have this secure base and feel nurtured and safe, dealing with not only school but other challenges will be more difficult. But it is never too late. A child can be helped to feel safe even if they have missed out on this stage as a baby and toddler.

Karina, aged 5 years.

Karina is in year one. In reception, teachers found her quiet and a little anxious, but with a bit of encouragement she took part in all school activities and seemed to be getting on well. In year one, she had a sudden change of teacher, and had to cope with a supply teacher for two weeks while a permanent teacher was found. She started to come home and tell her mum, Stephanie, a single parent, that school was too hard. Stephanie noticed that Karina, who used to be a good sleeper, suddenly needed her mum in the room at night, otherwise she couldn't sleep. She began to have nightmares. She was exhausted at school.

When Karina began to wet herself at school, Stephanie took her to see a psychologist. The psychologist heard that Karina's big sister Elena has severe food allergies. When Karina was little, Elena was hospitalised on several occasions and Stephanie was very worried about her safety. The family moved house, in order to be closer to the hospital, in case further medical emergencies happened. Much of Stephanie's time was devoted to Elena's care. On one occasion Karina had to be left with a neighbour when Elena was rushed to hospital.

Despite Stephanie's best efforts, Karina had found all this terrifying, and as Stephanie had been focussed on keeping Elena safe, she realised she had not been able to comfort and soothe Karina as much as she would have liked.

First of all, the psychologist sent Karina to see a paediatrician to make sure there weren't any medical causes for her toileting problems. Nothing was found.

The psychologist suggested that Karina hadn't been able to develop a secure base, owing to the family's difficult experiences. This meant that she saw the world as a place where danger or threat could be around the next corner. She didn't know how to comfort herself, as she had not had an adult who could consistently help her with this.

Stephanie was encouraged to help Karina develop a secure base. This meant that Karina "regressed" a little for a while – became babyish once more and started sleeping with her mum and sucking her thumb. This gave Stephanie a chance to give extra cuddles and comfort to Karina, something she had missed out on when Elena was ill. She also had special play time each day, their chance to spend quality 1-1 time together and for Stephanie to show Karina that her mum can be her "rock" – a strong and stable parent who can comfort and support Karina when needed. At school, Karina attended a nurture group which offered extra support and attention to anxious children. A teaching assistant, Miss Pike, was also given the job of providing extra support to Karina at difficult times of the day, such as the beginning of the day and at lunch time. Miss Pike simply chatted to Karina and gave extra nurturing to help her feel safe – such as helping her put her coat on and talking through who Karina would play with at lunch time. This was offered even if Karina appeared to be coping okay, as an important step in learning that "adults can help us when we are feeling scared or worried". Karina's school focussed on giving Karina as much of a predictable and stable routine as possible.

By the end of the school year, Karina was no longer wetting herself and was much happier to go to school. Her sleep improved and she went to sleep by herself again.

2   Small changes can have a big impact

Psychologists believe firmly that small changes can make a big difference, and can even change a child's future. You may not be able to solve all your child's problems, but you may be able to make a small change which could make a big difference!

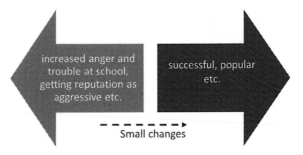

increased anger and trouble at school, getting reputation as aggressive etc.

successful, popular etc.

Small changes

Here is a case example to illustrate the point.

CASE STUDY

Ben, aged 7 years.

Ben struggles to keep friendships. He is a confident and likeable child but he likes to be in charge, and this causes problems. If another child tries to change the rules of a game, Ben refuses to allow it. He may also storm off and refuse to continue with the game. Other children have begun to avoid him, not inviting him to join in with their games. Ben has started to notice this and becomes angry when he is excluded. This has caused him to get into a fight at school and receive a "warning" for his behaviour.

Ben and his mum met with a psychologist and they identified that Ben has many strengths in his friendships (he is likeable and has the skills to start a game), but needs to be "skilled up" in:

* Allowing others to take turns in deciding how a game is played.

* Letting others take the lead sometimes.

* Learning to apologise and repair conflict.

Following "friendship skills" training in these specific areas, Ben began to play with others and repair conflict much more successfully. Others began to approach rather than avoid him at play times. His confidence was boosted and he was able to build on these skills as he got older, becoming a popular member of his year-group.

CONTINUED ON PAGE 7

BEN, *CONTINUED.*

Friendship skills training can involve many approaches such as:

- Problem-solving with an adult: looking at the desired outcome for the child, and talking through possible ways of achieving this, then choosing the best strategy.

- Role-playing with an adult: practising aspects of communication such as getting the most helpful tone of voice, making eye contact and using positive body language.

- Use of a "social story" – a personalised story for the child, explaining a specific social rule or skill in a concrete and understandable way.

3 Sometimes it's the environment which needs to change, not the child

Sometimes, the child needs to be taught skills which will help them manage the areas of difficulty. Other times, it is not the child but the environment that needs to change. One of a psychologist's key jobs is to work out which: skill up the child, change the environment to support the child or both?

Maddy, aged 7 years.

Maddy is a well-behaved and quiet child. Teachers have not noticed any problems. However, after school her parents have noticed that she appears fraught and agitated, showing aggression towards her twin brother Marcus. She has said school is too loud, and everyone is too noisy. She has started to get upset every morning before school, and tell her parents she doesn't want to go. Although she is doing fine academically, her parents feel she is capable of much more.

Maddy has just started year 3, and the class groupings have changed. On speaking to the teacher, the psychologist discovers that this year Maddy is in a class with an unusually high number of challenging children. The noise level is higher than in previous years and much of the teacher's attention has to be spent managing the children with obvious difficulties.

CONTINUED ON PAGE 8

The noise level and challenging children appear to be causing Maddy, an introvert, to feel overwhelmed and threatened. Together, the following plan is devised:

- Maddy will be allowed to go to a "quiet space" in an area outside the classroom whenever she shows her special "green card" to the teacher.

- Maddy is offered the chance to wear headphones during noisier periods in the classroom.

- Maddy is sent on regular errands to give her a break from the classroom.

- Staff agree to give Maddy extra support during large or noisy group activities.

- Maddy is encouraged to be as active as possible during break times, to "burn off" stress chemicals that have built up in her system.

- After school, Maddy is given some time and space to be quiet and calm down. Her mum and dad provide extra special calming treats, such as hot chocolate and a board game, to help her recover from her day.

Within a few weeks, Maddy is noticeably calmer and happier.

4   Problems are normal, and great for a child's development

It is normal for a child to struggle at certain points in time. It doesn't mean there's something wrong with them or with your parenting. It may be the demands and expectations of the world around the child which are causing her to struggle. The important thing is to sort out problems before they escalate and gather a life of their own, impacting on a child's well-being and self-esteem.

Jenna, aged 8 years.

Jenna had a soft and gentle teacher in year 1, and thrived. When she started year 2, Jenna showed a marked increase in anxiety, and was regularly tearful about school. The new teacher, who was very experienced but had a different approach, wanted to "toughen up" her class to be ready to go into key stage 2 the following year. She was enthusiastic about their learning and wanted to focus on preparing her class for the SATs in the summer term, so she introduced more demanding activities such as regular mental maths "quick-fire" questions. Sometimes these would make Jenna cry. Jenna began to worry at night-time about being told off, and her sleep went downhill.

Jenna had been a happy child, and there did not seem to be any other reasons for her change in mood. Gradually, Jenna's parents used her classroom situation to help increase her sense of resilience. They worked with her each evening to identify her specific worries about school, and used strategies to help her gently challenge her scary thoughts, such as "I will be told off if I can't answer the maths questions in 5 seconds". Jenna learned that she could problem-solve and see situations in new ways; she became more resilient. In tandem, Jenna's parents spoke with her class teacher and made her aware of Jenna's anxiety. The class teacher adapted her approach slightly and was more attuned to signs of anxiety in Jenna. By the summer term, Jenna was sleeping better and her anxiety symptoms had gone away. She said year 2 at school had been "the best year ever" and she would miss her teacher very much.

Balance is essential

Our view is that too much of anything is not a good idea, but everything in moderation is fine. We have all heard about the "dangers" of technology being reported in the media. Without a doubt, many hours each day spent on electronic devices is going to impact a child in many ways including the following:

- Takes away from opportunities for face to face social contact and learning/practising social skills.

- Takes away from time which could be spent engaging in physical activity (especially outdoor activity).

- Research studies show that the short-term buzzes/rewards provided by computer games and social media actually change the way the brain works; in particular, the dopamine reward system in the brain changes so that the child increasingly seeks short-term buzzes and is less able to wait for rewards. Obviously, this can lead to problems because children need to learn the skills needed to wait for rewards in order to be successful in adult life (for example, learning that if you work hard at school, you are more likely to get a good job later on).

At the same time, some computer games teach valuable skills, and some social media applications allow introverted teens, or those with limited social skills, to meet and engage with others. Becoming expert in a game such as Minecraft can help children build self-esteem.

Of course, a more difficult question is "how much is enough?". That is a question for parents to decide individually, though psychologists often give advice based on the most up-to-date research.

Other areas of a child's life in which balance is essential are:

Routine and spontaneity: Children feel safer and more secure if they have a daily routine, and sleep better if they have a regular bedtime and wind down in the same way every night. However, it can sometimes be fun to be spontaneous, and children can benefit massively from new experiences which require a change of routine, such as holidays. If a child learns to cope with the odd late night or a change of plans, she will develop a view of herself which says "I am a strong person and I can deal with the unexpected". This will also allow her to take advantage of unexpected opportunities when they come along.

Indoor and outdoor time: There is little doubt that the majority of children spend too much time indoors. Outdoor time gives them the chance to experience a less predictable world, take more risks (see section 6 below), develop more physical confidence and develop their imaginations by inventing games and exploring the unknown. Outdoor time allows children to burn off stress, and release any pent-up emotions by being loud and crazy. Also, there is emerging evidence that we need the microscopic organisms present everywhere in the outdoor environment, to help balance our gut "flora", which has a major impact on our physical and mental health. We evolved to spend a great deal more time on the move than we currently do, hunting and gathering, and a lack of physical activity can lead to restlessness and irritability and a difficulty focussing.

Demanding activities and simplicity: In the modern Western world there is increasing pressure on children to be busy. Some argue that children, even at primary school, are facing the highest ever academic demands. It is also the norm for children to engage in clubs and activities after school. Academic achievement and extra-curricular activities can be rewarding and satisfying and allow many of the conditions which a child needs to thrive, such as risk-taking (see section 6. below!). However, too much demand can lead to overload. When a child's brain is overloaded, the brain feels under threat, and triggers the "fight or flight" system, causing stress and often anxiety. The fight or flight response can also lead to exhaustion, sleep problems and irritability/aggressiveness. Children need some time each day to experience calm and quiet. This allows the body and brain to rest and recover, and prevents overload. It also creates a freedom and "mental space" that can stimulate a child's imagination: If a child's life is 100% scheduled he will have no space to develop new ideas (such as games, plans, stories) or use his imagination.

6 Children must be allowed to take risks

These are crucially important at all ages. Children learn self-confidence by taking on a challenge and accomplishing it. Sometimes the hardest thing for a parent is letting go. Without calculated risks – auditioning for a school play, attempting a flip on the trampoline or going out of her depth in the swimming pool for the first time – a child will not progress either in their physical abilities or in mental strength. Even if things don't go to plan, as long as the risk is a calculated one and not a reckless one (in other words, you are keeping an eye, from a distance), there will be plenty to learn (I didn't manage the flip but I can cope even if I fall on my face! / I didn't get chosen for the main part in the show but I had fun and discovered that I am good at dancing). Outdoor time is crucial to this. The outdoors is so much less predictable and "managed" than the indoors, so it allows for new challenges and regular risk-taking.

CASE STUDY

Hannah, aged 9 years.

Hannah is a nine-year-old girl experiencing anxiety. She fears that she will not be able to cope if she fails. She is a highly intelligent child and a high achiever. She has a flute recital coming up, and is terrified that she will stop playing and forget the tune. She is also worried about taking her 11+ exam for secondary school, which is more than a year away. Hannah is a confident girl who has always cruised through life and has two supportive parents. They cannot understand her sudden anxiety.

Getting to know Hannah in the clinic each week, the psychologist became aware that, despite having an idyllic upbringing, Hannah had never experienced failure, and therefore had not had the chance to learn that she could cope with it. The psychologist gently taught her to challenge the belief "I won't cope", and problem-solve what she would do, if she did actually "fail". The psychologist also encouraged Hannah out of her comfort zone, getting her to take very small risks and allowing the opportunity to feel and cope with failure. The psychologist also taught Hannah relaxation strategies such as deep breathing, equipping her to confront her fears such as the flute recital.

Over a period of around 3 months, Hannah's anxiety came down significantly and no longer affected her life. She was encouraged to continue to take risks as often as possible, and her parents encouraged her to engage in new challenges such as scouts and sports, in order to build on her new-found resilience.

7 It is important to understand brains and how we have evolved.

Sometimes, a little understanding about children's brains can help us see things in a new light. Brain science has thrived over the last ten to fifteen years, with new, exciting discoveries changing our views all the time. For example, neuroscientists have only recently discovered how flexible and adaptable our brains are; what they call "plasticity". Brains can adapt and change constantly, to cope with particular situations in the environment. One classic example is London black taxi drivers. They must undertake a long training during which they are required to learn thousands of routes and street names. Studies have shown that taxi drivers have a much larger posterior hippocampus, a part of the brain which is important in learning and memory. Environments shape brains, and the good news is that if one area of our brain is not strong, we can often strengthen it through practise.

Another thing we know about brains, particularly in children, is that they were not designed to work at their best when sitting still for long periods of time. As cavemen we would have spent long periods on the move as hunter-gatherers. Movement actually helps learning. It directly encourages the growth of a substance called BDNF, which causes new cell growth. Our brains have not changed much since we were "cavemen". Many of the old caveman parts are still in place, and our brains have not had a chance to adapt to modern living. Sitting still for long periods of time, as many schools require, then, is not the best condition for learning.

A final important idea is that children are not born with adult, "finished" brains. Some areas of the brain are much less developed than others. Young children are not as good at planning or being rational as adults. This is because an important part of the brain, the prefrontal cortex, is not yet finished. If a parent expects a child to be able to think through a situation rationally, weigh up the options, and then decide on the best course of action, she may be expecting too much. The prefrontal cortex has a period of rapid development from puberty onwards, allowing teenagers to get much better at planning, organising and rationalising, as they become adults.

Alex, aged 8 years.

Alex is an 8-year-old boy. He behaves "like an angel" at school. He is popular with teachers and class-mates. However, at home his parents are finding his behaviour difficult to manage. They find him demanding and unwilling to do as he has been asked. They report that he ignores requests, and the situation becomes increasingly fraught. He refuses to come off his iPad and this in particular causes arguments. Repeated requests often cause Alex to become angry, and he will show physical and verbal aggression towards his mum. This leads to daily "meltdowns" where Alex becomes distraught and screams uncontrollably. His parents feel that if he can have such perfect behaviour at school, then he must have some level of control at home. Therefore they feel that he could choose to be better-behaved.

Following a number of sessions with the psychologist Alex's parents were able to understand that:

- Alex was desperate to be "good" and please the teachers at school, and feared being told off, so he was on his best behaviour. However, being on best behaviour is exhausting and he couldn't maintain it at home. Home is the place where Alex feels more relaxed, so all the frustrations and exhaustion from the school day which have been bottled up, come out.

- Alex's prefrontal cortex is very underdeveloped as he is so young. It will have a surge in development when he hits puberty but will not be fully developed until adulthood. Until then, he may need quite a lot of help to manage his emotions, and may go into "fight or flight" easily, especially when he is exhausted from school.

- Alex was often hungry after school. Meltdowns happened more often when he hadn't eaten all his lunch. Alex's parents made sure he had a healthy snack and drink on the way home from school. This helped balance his blood-sugar levels so he was more able to cope with demands.

- Alex's parents realised they were expecting too much of him. When he was calm, they had a talk with him about what would help him to manage his feelings at home. Together they came up with lots of helpful ideas.

- Alex was encouraged to spend 10 minutes "letting off steam" each day after school, either bouncing on his trampoline or scoring goals in his football net. After this, he had 15 minutes of quiet time where he would build Lego or colour. Alex's parents agreed they would not ask him anything about school during this period, or make any demands of him.

A simple reward system helped Alex to understand more clearly what was expected of him when a request was made. Many children are better at taking in information when it is presented visually, than verbally. Therefore, Alex's mum created a visual chart of what he needed to do each night of the week. For example, on Mondays:

CONTINUED ON PAGE 15

ALEX, *CONTINUED.*

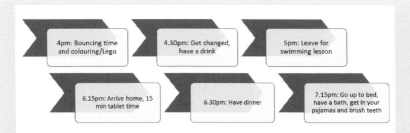

As Alex now knew exactly what was happening each day, he found it easier to follow requests. Every time he was asked to do something, if he did it first time he would immediately be given a special token. Once he had 8 tokens, he had earned enough to "win" a bike ride with his dad, or a game of badminton with his mum. Alex responded well to the new, clearer system, and responded particularly well to the exercise and "down time" straight after school, which gave his body and mind a chance to recover from school. Within 2 weeks his parents felt more in control and were able to be more patient with him, helping him to learn to manage his emotions rather than getting cross with him.

How to get the most out of this book

In the coming chapters we will look at areas which might affect your child growing up:

1. Anxiety

2. Friendships and bullying

3. Confidence and self-esteem

4. Anger and frustration

5. Academic stress

6. Concentration and motivation

Each chapter of the book will take you through from identifying and understanding what is going on, to planning and applying solutions. To help you, we take you through the "SUPER" process.

SPELL IT OUT **UNDERSTAND** **PLAN** **ENERGISE** **REVIEW**

Things may be difficult, but figuring out in words what the actual problem is can give you a sense of power over it. You may find that at first you only have a vague description, such as "my child is showing poor behaviour at school". We will help you to focus on specifics, such as for example "my child shows anger towards others when he is not chosen to be in a sports team", as this is the key to finding a solution.

Once you have pinpointed specifically what the problems are, you can seek to understand. In other words, your child is displaying anxious, disruptive or withdrawn behaviour, but what is the root cause of this?

Children, especially young children, may not be able to put into words why they are feeling distressed, worried or anxious. Therefore, many express it through difficult behaviour.

e.g. If I can't explain to you that I am lonely and feeling out of my depth at school, I will show you by throwing all my books at you and ripping out the pages of my homework diary.

When a psychologist looks at a difficulty faced by a child or family, each one is individual. We meet a child and family and gather together as much information as we possibly can, a bit like a detective. Then we develop a 'formulation'. A formulation is a diagram or piece of writing which tells the story of:

- What has caused the problem?
- What is keeping the problem going?
- We consider things from a number of perspectives.
  For example:

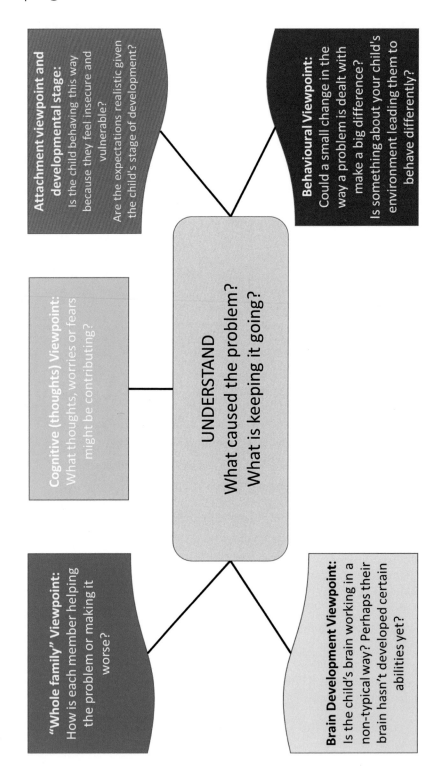

Attachment viewpoint and developmental stage:
Is the child behaving this way because they feel insecure and vulnerable?
Are the expectations realistic given the child's stage of development?

Behavioural Viewpoint:
Could a small change in the way a problem is dealt with make a big difference?
Is something about your child's environment leading them to behave differently?

Cognitive (thoughts) Viewpoint:
What thoughts, worries or fears might be contributing?

UNDERSTAND
What caused the problem?
What is keeping it going?

"Whole family" Viewpoint:
How is each member helping the problem or making it worse?

Brain Development Viewpoint:
Is the child's brain working in a non-typical way? Perhaps their brain hasn't developed certain abilities yet?

Formulation

Attachment viewpoint and developmental stage:
Is the child behaving this way because they feel insecure and vulnerable?
Are the expectations realistic given the child's stage of development?

Children need to develop a "secure base". This means they rely on a parent or important adult to reassure them and comfort them when they are scared. They explore the world a little, and then return to the "secure base" (parent) if the world feels a little scary and they need support. Gradually, a child learns that the world is (mostly) safe and learns to soothe her/himself rather than always returning to the secure base.

Behavioural Viewpoint:
Could a small change in the way a problem is dealt with make a big difference?
Is something about your child's environment leading them to behave differently?

This perspective suggests that all behaviours happen for a reason. It is important to understand the underlying reasons why a child is behaving in a certain way, as there may be very simple changes in the home, classroom, or adult's approach to the problem, which could have a positive influence on the behaviour or problem.

Brain Development Viewpoint:
Is the child's brain working in a non-typical way? Perhaps their brain hasn't developed certain abilities yet?

Children's brains are very different from adults'. This perspective involves thinking about what a child's brain would or would not, typically, be able to do at their age. It asks whether there might be an underlying difference compared with a "typical" brain, or whether the child's brain may simply need more time to mature.

"Whole family" Viewpoint:
How is each member helping the problem or making it worse?

This considers how each person might be impacting on another. Family life can be viewed as being like a group dance. If a life event, such as illness or change, causes the family to get out of step with one another, it can cause problems, but these are usually only temporary until the family finds a way of getting back in its rhythm. Other people in a child's life, such as friends and teachers, are also part of the dance. Each person can have an impact on each other person, and it can be really helpful to understand how this might be affecting a problem.

Cognitive (thoughts) Viewpoint:
What thoughts, worries or fears might be contributing?

This perspective looks at what thoughts are contributing to a particular behaviour. These may be worries or beliefs that a child is not even aware of, but are driving the child to act or feel a certain way. By understanding these, we can try to adapt them or reduce the power of unhelpful beliefs.

Which areas need to be tackled? Which are the priority areas for you? By the end of this section of each chapter, you will have a personalised chart. You will then be able to move on to "Energise" – to prioritise and put a plan into action.

In this section we will help you carry out your plan. You will be able to read case examples to help you. Problems can be overwhelming. If a child seems to have a number of difficulties, working on one thing at a time can be freeing.

This section of the chapter will consider what worked and what didn't. Should you continue with the plan as is, or does it need tweaking? We will also look at long-term changes you can make to continue with the success and progress you have achieved, and give case examples of these.

The following example will help bring this to life...

Jayden, aged 5 years.

Jayden was brought to the clinic by his mother. The main concern was that he didn't want to go to school, and would cling to his mum every day in the playground. A teaching assistant would gently peel Jayden away from his mum each morning. However, Jayden would sometimes kick the teaching assistant during the fraught 5 minutes getting him into the classroom. This had been going on for over a year, and could no longer be seen as "just a phase" which he would grow out of. Jayden's mum Bev was stressed, worried and embarrassed. Monday mornings were particularly difficult.

At the first appointment, the psychologist learned all about Jayden's family and his development, as well as exactly what happens each morning when he refuses to go to school. She discovered the following:

- Jayden was born with a heart defect which means he must be monitored regularly in hospital, and undergo surgical procedures. Until the age of one he spent up to half his time in hospital.

- Although Jayden is now much stronger, Bev is understandably protective of him, and worries about him when he is at school.

- Jayden's dad, Clive, is in the army and is away a lot. However, Bev's mum Claudia lives in the same street and is a great support.

- Jayden has a little sister, Rosa, and finds it hard to share his mum with her. He can be aggressive towards Rosa sometimes.

- Once Jayden is settled in to the school day and is kept busy, he enjoys school very much and likes his teacher, Mrs Moore.

Attachment viewpoint and developmental stage:
Is the child behaving this way because they feel insecure and vulnerable?
Are the expectations realistic given the child's stage of development?

In Jayden's case, his hospital stays may have interrupted this process. He was regularly separated from his mum to undergo procedures, which were painful and scary. Bev was unable to comfort him, on the occasions she wasn't allowed in. To Jayden, the world must seem like a scary place, because he may feel that this could happen again at any time. He has not learned how to "self-soothe" because the fear and pain he experienced in hospital were too big for him to handle.

CONTINUED ON PAGE 22

Brain Development Viewpoint:
Is the child's brain working in a non-typical way? Perhaps their brain hasn't developed certain abilities yet?

Because Jayden has had difficult experiences and feels insecure, his brain sees school as a threat (as he is away from his mum, and has to cope with new and difficult situations such as being in a class of 30). His brain takes him into "fight or flight" mode each morning. This powerful physical response floods the body with stress chemicals including cortisol and adrenaline, to help Jayden either run away from the danger (flight) or fight the danger. This means that at first Jayden has an all-consuming desire for "flight" (getting away) each morning. When the teacher takes him inside and this is no longer an option, his body instead takes him into "fight" mode and the adrenalin causes him to kick the teaching assistant.

Cognitive (thoughts) Viewpoint:
What thoughts, worries or fears might be contributing?

In Jayden's case, a dominant thought is probably "the world is a dangerous place". As he was taken away from his mum's care in hospital and didn't know when he would see her again, he may also be thinking "mummy might not come back".

Bev and Jayden's psychologist decided that the areas of priority to tackle were as follows:

1. Aim to help Jayden build a 'secure base', feeling even more relaxed and safe at home, and increasing his feeling of safety at school

2. Give Bev a break from the stress of school handover once a week

3. Increase the number of days Jayden goes in to school happily, and reduce the amount of violence towards his teaching assistant

CONTINUED ON PAGE 23

JAYDEN, CONTINUED.

"Energising" Jayden's plan: Making it happen

The psychologist, Bev and school worked on the following strategies:

Goal One: With some ideas and instructions from the psychologist, Bev worked hard to provide extra nurture at home, such as extra cuddles and special 1-1 time. This allowed Jayden to make up for lost time, building up a secure base and gradually learning how to self-soothe himself when he felt scared.

Goal Two: Jayden was allowed to take Bev's hat to school, and keep it on his peg. This helped reassure him that she would be coming back for him at the end of the day.

Goal Three: On Mondays, it was decided that Bev's mum Claudia would take Jayden to school. This meant Bev would have a break from the stress of getting Jayden in to school, and would feel less fraught when she got to work.

Goal Four: Jayden's school worked hard to provide him with extra nurture so that he could feel safer at school and wouldn't go into 'fight or flight' mode. He had a special teddy he could cuddle, and spent time with the SENCO in her special room, a calming space with soft music and colouring books, three times each week.

Goal Five: If Jayden managed to go into school without crying or getting cross, he would get a small reward when he came out of school each day (a new eraser for his collection).

Within four weeks, Jayden was going to school without complaint or anxiety on average 4 days out of 5. His parents and school continued to review and adapt the plan, and things improved still further over the next 3 months.

"Reviewing" Jayden's plan:

Bev, Mrs Moore and Jayden's psychologist reviewed the plan after 6 weeks. They could see that goals 2 and 3 (in the plan section) had been achieved. Bev wanted to keep many of the strategies in place. For example, having Claudia take Jayden to school on a Monday helped Bev to be much more relaxed, and this had a positive impact on Jayden.

Goal One, helping Jayden to build a secure base, was a long-term goal but lots of progress had taken place. Mrs Moore and the SENCO felt that having the teddy to cuddle and 'special time' with the SENCO were helping Jayden to feel safe at school, and decided to continue with these ideas.

Jayden had lost interest in his eraser collection, so Bev found a different reward to give him if he went to school calmly.

References

Gray, C. (2016). *The New Social Story Book.* Future Horizons.

Further reading:

Gerhardt, S. (2014). *Why Love Matters: How affection shapes a baby's brain.* Routledge.

Anxiety
When Worries Take Control
Dr Susan Wimshurst, clinical psychologist

*"I feel like there is a house of butterflies in my tummy -
I didn't invite them and now they won't go away"*

(Max aged 9)

As parents we like to think that our children don't have any big worries or at least feel like they *shouldn't* have at this young age. You may even find yourself saying things like "you have nothing to worry about at your age - wait till you get to my age!". But children are increasingly suffering with worries and anxieties about a whole range of issues. Anxiety is the most common problem reported by children of all ages. Furthermore, studies have estimated that between 5 and 10 per cent of children meet criteria for a diagnosis of anxiety disorder.

School in particular can be full of potential triggers for worries to develop. Friendship issues, being told off, academic performance, peer pressure, transitions, and bullying are all common issues in school aged children. There may be worries at home too with wider family issues such as financial difficulties, bereavements, family illness, sibling conflict and parent separation. Added to this, is the fact that children do not have the same understanding of anxiety as we do and are not yet equipped with the strategies to manage their worries. Regulating emotions is a skill which we develop as we mature and young children need a lot of help with this. For a parent of an anxious child, it can be both exhausting and heart-breaking to see your child worry so much and you may feel at a loss as to how best help your child. Hopefully this chapter will provide you with a better understanding of anxiety and some ideas for dealing with worry in general.

So, let's look at anxiety in more detail...

Anxiety is a normal and healthy emotion that we all feel throughout our lives. We all need a certain amount of anxiety to spur us on and motivate us - imagine if we didn't worry about what our boss said if we didn't turn up for work, or if we didn't care enough to check whether there is a car coming before we cross the road? A certain amount of anxiety can keep us safe and is good for us. It actually helps to enhance performance. See the diagram below:

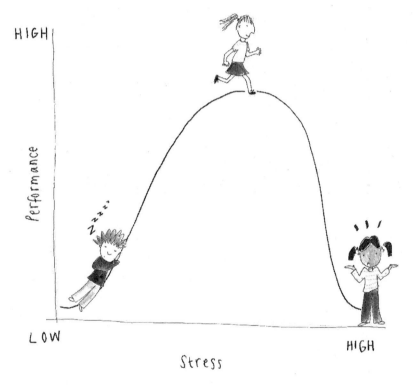

adapted from the original Yerkes-Dodson law (1908)

But what happens when our worries get too big or feel out of control? What happens when they exceed what is perceived as developmentally 'normal'? As we can see from the diagram, it starts to have a negative impact on our performance. As the stress/anxiety levels become too much and pass the 'optimal point', our ability to perform, along with our resourcefulness diminishes. It is when we think our child's anxiety levels have moved into this section that action may be needed to rein it back in.

All children experience fears and anxieties at different stages of their lives. Below is a list of common worries and fears through the different developmental stages:

Table 1-1 **Sources of anxiety by age**

Age	Main source of anxiety (adapted from Carr, 2006)
0-6 months	Loss of support, loud noises, intense sensory stimuli
Late infancy, 6-12 months	Strangers, separation
Toddler years, 2-4 years	Imaginary creatures, potential burglars, the dark.
Early childhood, 5-7 years	Natural disasters, injury, animals, media-based fears.
Middle childhood, 8-11 years	Poor academic and athletic performance.
Adolescence, 12-18 years	Peer rejection.

This table highlights the normal developmental worries children may experience. It is only when your child's anxieties appear to be having a significant impact on their day to day functioning, or they are preventing them from completing developmentally appropriate tasks such as going to school or mixing with peers, that you may need to seek professional help. It is useful to view all fears as 'normal', it is just the fact that some may become more *intense* or more *extensive* than others. Consider whether the worry is a problem for your child. If it is having a negative effect on his or her life, then it sounds like some strategies to help your child tackle their fears would be beneficial.

As a parent, you know your child better than anybody else and so you are in a good position to be able to notice and help your child act on their worries before the worries get too big and start to take control.

How does anxiety affect us?

Anxiety affects us in **four** main ways - the way we *feel*, the way we *think*, the way our *body works* and the way we *behave*. This is at the centre of something you may have heard about called 'Cognitive Behavioural Therapy' or CBT for short. CBT is a psychological approach used to help children/young people and adults overcome a wide range of issues including anxiety and low mood.

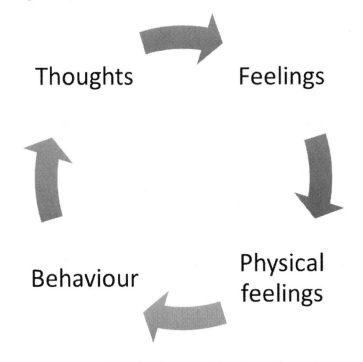

CBT is based on the idea that how we think (cognitions), how we feel (emotions) and how we act (behaviours) are all closely linked and interact with each other. Negative thoughts can cause us distress and make us worry. Often the worry we have is not in proportion or realistic to the situation. Just imagine for a moment that you are lying in bed and you hear a bang downstairs. If your thought processes are– 'Oh it's Alfie the cat again' you are likely to remain quite calm and go and check or go back to sleep. However, if you think 'oh my goodness, there must be a burglar downstairs', you are likely to feel a sense of fear and panic and may ring the police. When we are worried our thoughts tend to focus on some degree of danger or threat.

The way we think and interpret situations hugely impacts on how we feel and behave and also affects how our body reacts. In Lucy's introduction section we described the 'fight or flight' response (also sometimes referred to as the 'stress response').

The 'fight or flight' response is a primitive defence system located in our sympathetic nervous system. The 'fight or flight' response is a physiological response triggered when we feel a strong emotion like fear or anger. It is a response which evolved to enable us to react with appropriate actions when faced with danger –i.e. to run away, to fight, or sometimes freeze in order to keep ourselves safe. A series of physiological changes occur in our body when our fight or flight response is triggered:

CAN'T "SWITCH OFF" OR GET TO SLEEP

CAN'T FOCUS

MUSCLES TENSE

BRIGHT RED CHEEKS

BREATHING FAST

TINGLY HANDS/ FEET

HEART RACING

SWEATING

CAN'T FIGHT OFF COLDS / ILLNESSES

UPSET TUMMY/ "BUTTERFLIES"/ FEEL SICK

So, it is important to think of this as a normal, healthy response that can be productive in certain situations. However, our fight or flight response can be triggered too often, by things which we *perceive* to be a threat to us (such as school tests, going to a party) but are not actually dangerous. I find a helpful way of explaining it to children, is to consider a smoke alarm.

A smoke alarm is designed to alert us to a potential fire, however, it can easily be triggered by a burnt piece of toast. It is not able to distinguish between a fire (real threat) and smoke from burnt toast (false alarm). If we are thinking of or perceiving certain situations as worrying or threatening, our fight or flight response will still be triggered but the response of the alarm is the same, resulting in us feeling uncomfortable and geared up as if we are under real threat.

It is really important that children understand and 'tune in' to their own experiences of the fight or flight response and describe what they actually feel inside their bodies. As they become more aware of the symptoms of anxiety they can see them for what they really are. Symptoms of worry and anxiety can often be misinterpreted as further reasons for worry (e.g. 'My tummy hurts - something is wrong with me!').

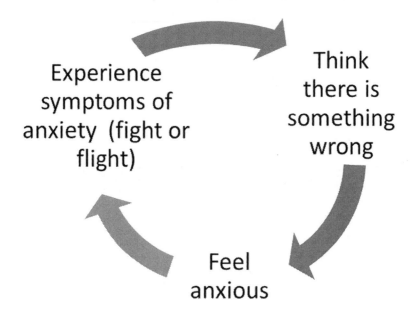

Experience symptoms of anxiety (fight or flight)

Think there is something wrong

Feel anxious

As we become more adept at recognising the early signs that our threat system has been activated, we also have a better chance of being able to 'nip the worry in the bud' before it starts to take control.

It is important to remember that anxiety can affect children's lives in different ways and no two people will have the exact same experience.

Case examples:

Max, aged 9 years.

Max had very loving parents and a good set of friends. However, Max experienced feelings of anxiety on school mornings in particular, and although he did get into school each morning, he found it a struggle and would become upset and agitated in the morning before school. This was especially the case if he had a spelling test or had to read out in class. Max also had anxiety about trying new things for fear of failing and had difficultly sticking with a task if he felt he was not good at it.

Socially, Max would also become very anxious if there were plans to do certain activities, such as going to the cinema, and his initial reaction was always that he did not want to go. Max would experience symptoms of anxiety, such as feeling sick, and then he would often worry that this meant he may actually be sick. The anticipation of certain social events triggered so much fear that he would avoid accepting social engagements. His parents found his levels of anxiety distressing and were not sure how best to respond. Consequently, they found themselves agreeing that it would be best for him to not go to social occasions that caused him stress and therefore found themselves colluding with his avoidance.

Sally, aged 7 years.

Sally was a 7 year old girl who used to love going to the park like any other child. When Sally was almost 6 years old she was accidently knocked over by her grandparents very excitable dog, Fido. Since this time, her parents noticed that she was increasingly anxious about visiting her grandparents at their house and started to avoid playdates if the friend in question had a pet dog. She would also not want to go to parks or any family outings where there was an increased chance of coming across a dog not on a lead.

This obviously impacted the whole family and limited their choice of family activities. It was also impacting Sally's friendships as she was avoiding certain playdates. Sally had also just made the transition into Year 3 which meant that she had to change schools - moving from the comfort of her familiar infant school to a larger junior school. Sally's older sister (who had just transitioned to secondary school) would get very upset and cross with her and Sally's parents felt at a loss as to how to help her. They admitted that they were quite inconsistent in the way they were responding to her (sometimes being angry with her, sometimes providing lots of reassurance). They discovered this only served to maintain her anxieties.

As highlighted in the two examples above, sometimes there is an obvious trigger for the anxiety and in other cases it may be very difficult to identify what has caused the worry to develop.

We will now explore anxiety in more detail, looking at ways to keep worries under control using our **SUPER** tool. But here are the important points to remember so far:

- Anxiety is a normal emotion experienced by children and adults alike

- Children experience common worries at different stages in their lives

- Anxiety affects people in different ways

- Anxiety affects the way we think, feel and behave

- A certain amount of anxiety is good for us and it's only when it starts to have a negative impact on functioning that it is considered a problem

- There is not always a clear trigger for anxiety

 # So.... What are you seeing in your own child? Spell It Out.

Now focussing more on the anxiety you may be seeing in your own child, you can use our '**SUPER**' tool to take some action and start to make a plan. It will help to begin with *'Spelling it out'*. What do you see in your child that makes you feel that they are worrying too much?

How might anxiety present itself in your child? Although all children are different, some common signs of stress/anxiety include:

- Sleep issues (difficultly getting off to sleep/ disturbed sleep)

- Appetite (often reduced)

- Avoidance - possible school refusing, avoiding social situations

- Physical symptoms (tummy aches, headaches)

- Poor concentration

- Clingy behaviour

- Challenging behaviour/acting out

- Repetitive behaviours /compulsions

- Anger

- Regressive behaviour such as bedwetting, thumb sucking

Try and highlight what issues you feel are interfering with your child's life, on a scale above and beyond what is expected for a child their age. Also consider: when do the worries seem to be most evident? Is there a pattern to your child's worrying? Do they worry about specific events only, or is it more generalised? Do they only worry during school times? If the worries are driven by any bullying or academic performance, it might be that you notice your child is much more relaxed during weekends and school holidays. Have school noticed any change in your child? It is always good to keep open communication between school and home as much as possible, and it may be worth asking your child's teacher if they are noticing any anxiety behaviours in your child.

Is your child feeling the need to do certain things again and again or in a certain order? Are they encouraging you to say things a certain amount of times or feeling that things just 'don't feel right' unless they complete a certain routine?

At this stage you are becoming a detective and looking for patterns that may provide you with clues as to what the anxiety is about. It may be helpful to make a log/journal of when you are seeing the signs of worry in your child so that possible connections can be made.

Have a go at filling in the box below, thinking about what's happening for your child:

Questions to ask yourself:	...Jot it down.
What do I see? How is my child outwardly behaving?	
When does it tend to happen?	
Describe any patterns I notice (e.g. Is it always before bed, school etc.?)	
Have school/friends/others commented?	
How are we as parents responding to the anxiety?	
What impact is it having on my child's life?	

Look at underlying reasons why the anxiety developed

Now focussing on the 'U' part of our '**SUPER**' tool, let's try and *understand* what might be behind your child's anxiety. If we have a better sense of understanding, it makes it much easier to be patient and less frustrated as a parent. Seeing your child avoid certain situations or clinging to us can leave us feeling helpless and quite often frustrated. Putting together the pieces of the jigsaw and identifying possible triggers and maintaining factors not only helps you as the parent understand what is going on, but will also then help your child feel more understood and hopefully more empowered to take charge of their emotions.

Although nobody knows the answer as to why some children are more anxious than others, certain factors have been shown to increase the likelihood of anxiety and possibly play a role in maintaining it. Researchers believe that anxiety is caused by a combination of innate characteristics and external situations, events and experiences.

Developmental stage:

As mentioned earlier in this chapter, there are normal worries and fears that all children go through at different developmental stages. So it's important to consider the developmental stage of your child and refer back to **Table 1-1**. This may help to normalise some of the worries your child is experiencing - but again, rather than wondering whether this worry is 'normal or abnormal', think about the extent to which it is impacting on your child's well- being.

Depending on the age of your child, they may be able to talk to you and put into words how they feel - but more often than not young children find it hard to make sense of how they are feeling and may not identify it as worry/anxiety. They may feel there is something really wrong with them and may struggle to see a way to move forward, often feeling helpless. This in turn fuels more anxiety and a vicious cycle begins. This is why it is important to help your child identify and name their emotions, but we will come on to how to do this later on.

Biological:

Our nervous system, includes our brain, spinal cord, organs, nerves and chemicals in the body. The human nervous system has two separate parts: The **Voluntary** and the **Autonomic** System.

> The Voluntary System is related to movement and sensation –
> so when we lift our hand up it's the voluntary nervous system
> coming into action and lots of nerves are moving.

The Autonomic System controls areas which we have less control over, including heart rate, digestion of food, blood pressure, etc. Basically, our nerves leave the spine to connect to our major organs and glands. The nerves either stimulate or inhibit them. There are two branches to the Autonomic nervous system – the Sympathetic and the Parasympathetic nervous system.

The sympathetic system helps to prepare the body to defend itself by activating certain glands and organs that trigger the **Fight or Flight** response, as mentioned earlier in this chapter.

If the sympathetic nervous system is constantly being activated it is not good for our bodies and if most of our energy is being used to prepare us to fight or run, we start to feel exhausted and run down. The parasympathetic nervous system on the other hand is responsible for stimulating the immune system, digestion and organs that promote wellbeing. The parasympathetic nervous system can be activated by relaxation, rest and happy/positive thoughts. Diet and exercise are both important factors too. Activation of the parasympathetic system offers benefits to both our physical and mental health.

It is important to know that the sympathetic and parasympathetic nervous systems cannot run together - it is either one or the other. So, the aim is to try and encourage your child to be able to 'switch off' the sympathetic system and 'switch on' the parasympathetic state of calm. This can be very difficult for a child who is prone to worry and faced with 'worry triggers' on a daily basis (especially if school based). But the good news is that we will be covering strategies to help with this in the upcoming sections!

Still looking at biological factors, anxiety does tend to run in families and children with higher levels of anxiety quite often have at least one parent who has a tendency to worry or possibly have more significant anxiety issues. Some children are therefore genetically predisposed to be more emotionally sensitive. This is not intended to point blame or make you feel guilty as a parent, but it is just one part of the jigsaw to consider and hopefully contribute to your understanding as a parent. We all have different temperaments and personalities and in the same way that we can vary in height and eye colour, we vary in how *emotional* we are. Anxious children tend to be more emotionally sensitive, which often makes them more caring and thoughtful, but on the downside is likely to make them feel more worried and fearful.

Neurological (brain development):

As you may read in other chapters the part of the brain responsible for regulating emotions is known as the 'pre-frontal cortex'. This part of the brain helps us to control our emotional responses, along with planning and organisational skills. Although these abilities start to develop during the toddler years, they do not fully develop until our early twenties. The prefrontal cortex is one of the areas most sensitive to parental interaction. Children learn to use this part of their brain by watching you as parents. It has long been known that children learn more by imitation than they do by instruction – so if you as parents model good problem solving and anxiety management skills, your child is more likely to internalize calmness in the face of worry.

Cognitive (thoughts):

As we saw from earlier in this chapter, the way we think hugely impacts the way we feel and can serve to keep the anxiety going. Children who are pre-disposed to worry are more likely to interpret situations as 'threatening' and focus their attention on any possible element of danger. Your child's anxious thoughts may focus on themselves ("I am no good at school work"); other people ("everyone is judging me"); or the wider environment ("the world is a dangerous place").

Children who are prone to worry tend to focus on the bad and filter out the good and as you can anticipate, these thinking patterns maintain the anxiety. It can be easy to get caught up with thoughts that are based on our own judgments rather than based on reality. Identifying and challenging some of these negative assumptions is at the crux of much of the treatment plan and we will cover this later on.

Behavioural:

It is natural for anxious children to want to avoid things. Why wouldn't you avoid a situation if you knew it was going to make you feel uncomfortable and distressed? However, avoidance fuels the anxiety and keeps it alive. If children continue to avoid the situations they feel worried about they never give themselves the opportunity to prove that they can cope.

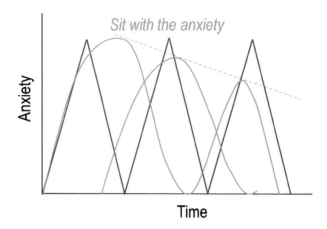

The Anxiety Curve

The red lines on the graph above highlight what happens to our anxiety levels if we continue to engage in avoidance strategies. As our stress levels peak, we tend to *avoid* the situation and in the short-term we feel better and our anxiety levels reduce. However, this is only a short-term fix as you can see the red peaks stay the same height over time. So…what we really need to do is 'sit' with the uncomfortable feelings of anxiety (rather than the tempting option of running away and avoiding) and over time we notice that our anxiety levels reduce as we begin to face our fears (illustrated by the green lines).

Anxiety can also often manifest itself as *anger*. As we know from earlier in this chapter, fear triggers the fight or flight response, and this can make us withdraw into ourselves (flight) or become agitated and angry (fight). It is therefore important as parents to try and establish whether underlying anxiety may be the cause of some angry behaviours you may be seeing. Anger is often received negatively by others, and this may reinforce their view that something is wrong with them, which in turn creates more anxiety (Anger can be better understood by reading chapter 4).

Sometimes anxiety is maintained because of the *perceived positive effect* it may have- for example more attention perhaps from a parent or main caregiver? I have worked with many young children who have issues going to sleep on their own and have fallen into a pattern of mummy or daddy cuddling/lying with them until they fall asleep. Often these children are almost scared to get better for fear of losing this 'special time' with mummy/daddy amongst a usually very busy household with other siblings.

Environmental:

There may be clear triggers or stressors in your child's environment that cause increased anxiety. Bereavement, parental separation, bullying and academic pressure are common stressors that lead to a natural level of heightened anxiety. Such events are likely to have an even bigger impact for a child who is more emotionally sensitive. It is not always the case that environmental triggers are present, but it is important to consider whether any external stressors may be playing a part.

Systemic (whole family viewpoint):

The way we as parents respond and interact with our children can also play a role in keeping the anxiety alive. Consider the role of your relationship with your child and reflect on the notion of the 'secure base' discussed in the introductory chapter. This relates to the strong bond you have with your child, which is expressed through love, affection and acceptance. This "safe-base" provides the building blocks for our children to explore the world.

As parents it is only normal and healthy to want to protect our children from distress and rush to their aid. However, it can sometimes be the case that this helping behaviour is actually allowing the child to avoid…and we know that avoidance is not good for anxiety! As a parent, you know your child better than anyone else and therefore you are probably quite in tune with what might make your child feel worried. You also may find yourself anticipating this and helping your child even when it's not necessary. Again, this is understandably done out of love, but can sometimes inadvertently reinforce the message for your child that they cannot cope on their own and that 'the world really is a dangerous place'. Thinking back to the fundamental beliefs discussed in the section on 'How to get the most out of this book', it is important to let children take some risks, to empower them and encourage independence in a safe way.

In a similar vein, we know that children learn by observing and imitation and therefore the behaviour you model as a parent is another important factor. If a parent deals with anxiety by avoiding situations, then it is fair to expect the child to copy this and internalise the view that this is the best way to deal with fear. Again, this is not about pointing blame at parents, but it may be one piece of the jigsaw and if your child already has some anxious tendencies, these may be strengthened by your own anxiety management style.

So, do you remember Sally from earlier in this chapter, who had developed anxiety around dogs? Let's use the factors above to help us understand more about Sally's anxieties.

Developmental: Looking back at **Table 1-1**, it can be seen that Sally is at an age where it is not uncommon to have some anxieties centred around animals. The incident wherein Sally was knocked over by her grandparents dog, Fido, served to compound this fear. Only being 5 years old when this happened, Sally would have been unlikely to have understood that the dog was just excited to see her and perceived the situation as a threatening one.

Around the age of seven, children become more socially aware, thinking more about the world around them. With this, there may be a stronger desire to be perfect and self-criticism may be more prevalent. Self-esteem tends to be more fragile and Sally may feel cross with herself for having the anxieties she has, feeling different to her peers.

Biological: As we know, temperament plays an important role. Sally's parents reported that she has always been 'more of a worrier', compared to her sister. Sally's mother also explained that anxiety runs in her side of the family and so Sally may be genetically predisposed to be vulnerable to anxiety. The incident with Fido led to Sally's 'fight or flight' response being triggered as her brain perceived a real threat. Sally likely experienced a range of physiological symptoms such as increased heart rate and muscle tension but was not able to make sense of them or articulate her anxieties. Sally has now made a negative association between dogs and that unpleasant experience.

Neurological (brain development): Sally is 7 years old and we know from our earlier reading that children do not fully develop the ability to regulate their emotions until early twenties. This helps to make sense of why Sally is having trouble managing her anxieties around dogs.

Cognitive: We have learnt that the way we think hugely affects the way we feel and consequently behave. We also know that children who are predisposed to anxiety are more likely to interpret situations as threatening. Sally's experience with Fido the dog left her having thoughts such as 'dogs are unpredictable and dangerous'. These negative and danger–focused thoughts have a knock-on effect on how Sally feels about dogs (scared) and her also her behaviour (avoidance).

Behavioural: Sally's natural reaction is to want to avoid dogs in an attempt to avoid the possibility of being knocked over again. In the short–term you can see how this makes sense, but as we know, avoidance of the things we are scared of only serves to fuel the fear *(refer to anxiety curve on p38)*. Sally's avoidance is not allowing her the chance to see that she will not always be knocked over by dogs and that she can cope with the situation. As time goes on Sally will believe that she is only ok as a result of her deliberately avoiding dogs.

There may also have been a perceived positive effect maintaining Sally's anxieties. With her older sister transitioning to secondary school, Sally may have felt that a lot of attention had been focused on her sister. As we know all children crave attention, positive or negative, and so the family attention given to Sally's anxieties may have been a perceived benefit.

Environmental: Sally had just made a significant transition to junior school where the classes had been mixed up and so she was having to adjust to her new class, school building and teacher. Sally's older sister had also transitioned to secondary school and so there had been some stress and anxiety in the family around this too. These factors are likely to have caused increased anxiety for Sally and given her young age she may not be able to articulate these worries, so they channelled into the anxiety around dogs.

Systemic (whole family viewpoint): Sally's parents were honest in saying that they were not always consistent in the way they dealt with Sally's anxieties. This is completely normal - as parents we are not robots and come with our own personalities, ideas, thoughts and feelings that are not always in line with our partners! When we enter parenthood, we tend to also reflect on the way we were raised by our own parents and this can obviously differ greatly within families. As parents we want to avoid seeing our children distressed and so at times Sally's parents were inadvertently reinforcing the message that dogs are dangerous by colluding with her avoidance.

Strategies to help you to tackle your child's worries.

So now you have looked at the anxiety related behaviours you are seeing in your own child and hopefully have a better understanding of what may have caused/what is maintaining the anxiety, you probably want to think about what you can do to help! This is where the planning stage comes in and we will consider child friendly strategies that will hopefully help your child understand and manage their anxiety.

Physiological - teaching your child about the fight or flight response:

I always think a good place to start is looking at the physical signs of anxiety and helping your child identify how worry affects their body. Even if young children cannot put words to their feelings, they can often describe the sensations in their body, such as 'my tummy hurts' or 'my legs feel like jelly'. It is these symptoms that can often get misinterpreted as something more worrying too and feed into their fear that something is seriously wrong with them.

So, you can start this by drawing an outline of a body on a piece of paper (you don't have to be a skilled artist for this – a gingerbread man style outline is fine!). It can be quite fun to actually ask your child to lie down on a huge piece of paper and draw around them. Then ask your child to use colours and arrows to illustrate where in their body they feel different sensations. It may also be helpful for you to sit with your child and do your own version. This can help to open up a dialogue about how different people may experience slightly different symptoms of anxiety, but also to share similar feelings. Some children may also benefit from some prompts if they are struggling to identify physiological sensations... so you could say "mummy sometimes feels stress and worry in her tummy and it feels like a fluttering feeling – do you ever feel anything like that?"

These body pictures can be done to help look at other emotions too, such as anger and excitement.

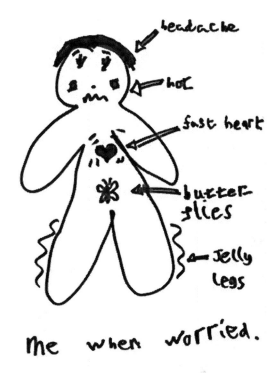

headache

hot

fast heart

butter-flies

Jelly Legs

me when worried.

Once you have your pictures, describe the fight or flight response and its purpose. I often explain to children that when we were all cave men and women, if we were suddenly faced with a big bear our brain would be clever and tell our bodies that we need to prepare to fight the bear (fight) or run away as fast as we can (flight). We go into survival mode and we are lucky really that our bodies are so clever! All the physiological responses are productive and enable us to act quickly for the best chance of survival *(you can refer back to the picture on page29)*. However, in this day and age we are not often faced by big scary bears, but day-to day stresses such as school work, exams and friendship issues can still trigger our alarm system and set off all the bodily symptoms described. A lot of children quite like learning the science behind it all and this in itself can be calming for the child, reassuring them that what they experience is normal. You can use the 'smoke alarm' analogy we discussed earlier on to illustrate how our survival alarm system can go off when it doesn't really need to.

Thinking back to Max, one of his worries was that he would actually be sick if he was put in an anxiety provoking situation because he really felt the churning in his stomach. Rather than seeing this as one of the normal physiological signs of stress, he took it to mean that he would literally be sick. Once he understood the science behind the 'fight or flight' response, he was able to say to himself 'I know what this feeling is' and saw it for what it really was - his body's survival alarm being triggered when it didn't need to be!

Following on from this it is important to stress that anxiety is a normal and healthy emotion that we all feel and that it's just that worries need to be reined in sometimes as they become 'cheeky' and want to take control.

Relaxation strategies for calming the fight or flight response

Do you remember back in the *biological section* of 'Understanding your child's anxiety', we got a bit more technical and talked about the sympathetic and parasympathetic nervous system? Well.... although your child does not need to necessarily know all about this, it helps you to understand that strategies which will help your child 'switch' on the more **calming system** in their body will help them to feel more comfortable and relaxed.

One easy and quick way to do this is to help your child master the skill of 'controlled breathing'. There are many different ways in which you can 'do' controlled breathing but I find the 'box breathing' method quite a nice easy one and children often like the visual imagery element to it. This is also something you can practise together - as let's face it, we could all do with coping strategies for stress!

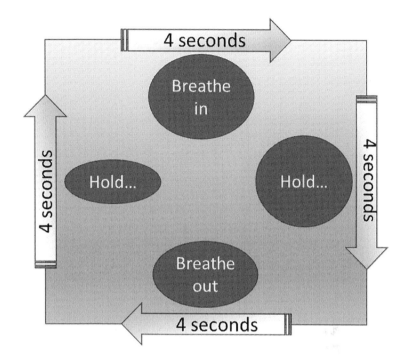

The crucial element is that you breathe in through your nose and out through your mouth. I often say to younger children, "breathe in as if you are smelling your favourite smell and breathe out as if you are blowing candles out on a cake". Also, when breathing in, encourage your child to place their hand on their tummy and watch their hand rise slightly as they breathe in. This shows that they are breathing correctly from their diaphragm rather than from their chest, which is what we tend to do when we are stressed (the more shallow rapid breathing). Introducing a bottle of bubbles and blowing different sized bubbles can also be a fun way of practicing breathing in a nice, slow, controlled way.

Progressive muscle relaxation is another useful technique to practise to help your child relax and feel a greater sense of calm in their body. The idea is to help your child identify how different their bodies feel when they are tense and stressed compared to when they completely relax. If we can keep our bodies nice and relaxed it sends the message back to our brain that we are relaxed. There are many scripts available online and I particularly like the one you can find on the website www.anxietybc. com as it pulls on visual imagery which is especially helpful for children.

Mindfulness exercises have become very popular and the evidence base for the benefits for children and adults alike is constantly growing. Mindfulness is a form of meditation. It is about paying attention to the **present moment** and learning to shift your focus of attention to the **'here and now'** rather than listening to worrying thoughts about today or tomorrow. There is not the scope to discuss mindfulness in detail here, but there are several books and websites which describe the benefits in detail and provide child –friendly techniques.

I often recommend the book 'Sitting Still like a Frog: Mindfulness Exercises for Kids (and Their Parents)' by Eline Snel. This has lots of lovely exercises to do together with your child and also comes with a 60-minute audio CD of guided exercises. A good website is annakaharris.com and this provides mindfulness exercises specifically targeted at 6 to 10 year olds. Older children and adolescents may prefer one of the many apps available to download. A lot of the young people I have worked with have found the free app - 'Headspace' helpful.

Identifying possible triggers for anxiety

Once your child has recognised how anxiety affects their own bodies they are much better placed to identify times that they feel more anxious (they might not have made the association between that *"funny feeling in their tummy"* and school tests for example). To help identify possible triggers, it can be useful to keep a **Mood Diary** for a couple of weeks to help make connections between what happened that day and your child's mood/level of worry.

Mood rating

Day			Mood rating (1–10)	What good and bad things happened today?	How did these things make you feel?
Monday	Morning / Afternoon / Evening		1 2 3 4 5 6 7 8 9 10		
Tuesday	Morning / Afternoon / Evening		1 2 3 4 5 6 7 8 9 10		
Wednesday	Morning / Afternoon / Evening		1 2 3 4 5 6 7 8 9 10		
Thursday	Morning / Afternoon / Evening		1 2 3 4 5 6 7 8 9 10		
Friday	Morning / Afternoon / Evening		1 2 3 4 5 6 7 8 9 10		
Saturday	Morning / Afternoon / Evening		1 2 3 4 5 6 7 8 9 10		
Sunday	Morning / Afternoon / Evening		1 2 3 4 5 6 7 8 9 10		

In this way you and your child are working like detectives together to see if you can spot any patterns to the worry.

Measuring worry

It is helpful for both you and your child to be able to measure your child's level of worry and this can be done using rating scales. Being able to distinguish different levels of worry is important not only to recognise that anxiety levels change depending on the situation and how long you have been in the situation, but also to monitor success over time. I think children find it reassuring when I say to them "anxiety can only go as high as 10 – it will not go higher and then it will plateau and come down naturally".

Using ratings scales also provides a common language in your household that everyone can use and you as parents can model; for example, "mummy's feeling a number 6 this morning as I have a presentation to do at work" (At this point you could provide some modelling of positive anxiety management too, such as "I know that by doing my breathing exercises I will feel calmer").

So, using a rating scale like the one below encourages your child to give their anxiety ratings in different situations and at the beginning, middle and end of certain situations. For example, asking them how they felt just before they went to the party, in the middle and when they got home. This helps children to see that often our anxiety may start high but the longer we stay with the situation, it starts to come down naturally. We can often suffer with something known as 'anticipatory anxiety' - in other words, the anticipation or thought of an event can cause much higher levels of anxiety than the *actual* anxiety rating once in the situation. Our predicted level of anxiety can be much higher than the real experienced level.

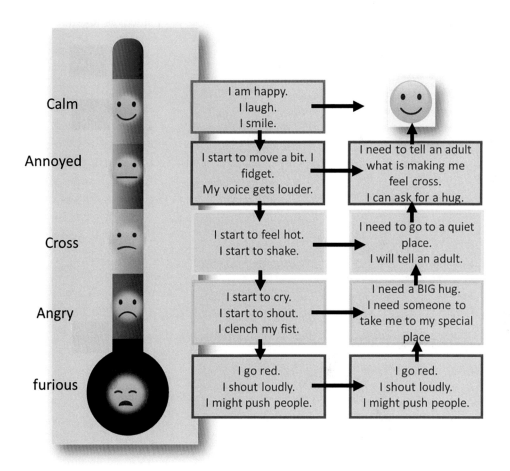

This is a generic one but feel free to tailor it to an interest for your child and they can add their own images on to it.

Helping your child identify their thoughts

Along with being more in tune with what's going on in their body, it's going to be really important for your child to tune into what's going on in their head by exploring their thoughts and beliefs.

It is useful for your child to realise that their feelings are strongly connected to how they think about things and feelings of worry usually go hand in hand with thoughts of danger and threat. I often introduce children to this idea by drawing the bus stop picture on the following page:

The bus didn't stop for these three people. They have very different feelings. Why might this be? What might they be thinking?

This helps children see that it is not the situation itself that creates the emotion but how you **perceive** it. What sort of thoughts does that particular situation or event trigger in your mind? Children often find it difficult to distinguish between thoughts and feelings and it is important to try and help them see the difference. So, when you ask your child why they are feeling worried about the party they have been invited to next week, for example, they may say "I am scared". This describes their feeling, but does not give you any detail about what they are worried about – their **worrying thought**. If your child was able to say, "I might not have anyone to play with", this gives you more of an indication of what they are worrying about.

You might find it helpful to do a small quiz with your child to help them understand the difference between thoughts, feelings and behaviour.

Ask your child to identify the following as either a **thought (T), a feeling (F) or a behaviour (B):**

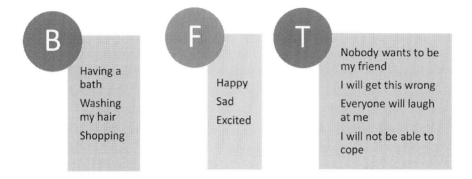

B
Having a bath

Washing my hair

Shopping

F
Happy

Sad

Excited

T
Nobody wants to be my friend

I will get this wrong

Everyone will laugh at me

I will not be able to cope

You can also help your child develop their skills with this in quite a light-hearted way by looking at pictures in magazines or characters on television and asking your child to think about how that person might be feeling and what they may be thinking. Encourage them to look at the persons face and body language and consider what thoughts might be going through that person's mind. If your child is into a particular sport for example you could ask them what they may think and feel when they win a game and similarly when they lose a game.

To help make that connection between thoughts, feelings and behaviour, you can sit with your child and ask them to think of a time they recently felt happy, sad and angry. Ask them what they were doing, what they were thinking and how they were feeling for each one.

Once your child becomes more of a master at identifying his/her thoughts, they will be more able to tell you the worrying thoughts behind their anxiety. You can then move on to encouraging your child to become a 'detective' and catch those thoughts by recording them on paper. I find it really helps children to get their thoughts out of their head and onto paper so then you can look at them together and start to **challenge** them. We have thoughts going through our minds all the time and some thoughts can be unhelpful ones which are not based on truth and can lead us to feel worried when there is no real need for us to feel anxiety. If a child is more sensitive to worry, they are likely to overestimate the likelihood of something bad happening and also believe that the consequences will be catastrophic. It is these unhelpful thoughts we need to 'fish out' and look at in more detail.

The use of a **'Worry Box'** can be helpful to have in the home to help children feel encouraged to jot down their worries and then look at them/share them with a parent. You can make a worry box with your child by using an old shoe box with a slot in the top. Your child may enjoy decorating the box with stickers, pictures, wrapping paper etc. This must be kept somewhere safe that your child is happy with (maybe away from prying eyes of siblings!). Next to the box you would have some small pieces of coloured card so that your child can write down any worries they may have. They then put the card in the box and are encouraged to not think about the worry until the set 'Worry time' you have agreed, which should be the same time each day.

The idea is that you are helping your child to see that all problems can be looked at in a systematic way and problem-solved. You are working as a team to *shrink the worries down* (refer to the Everlief Website for more information on the Worry Box).

In a similar vein, encouraging your child to externalise their worry by turning it into a character can be helpful. Say to your child "if you could draw your worries, what would they look like? What sort of character would they look like?". I never stop being fascinated and intrigued by the visions/images children have of what their worries look like if allowed to be given a personality. This technique is known as 'externalising' and helps the child to see that anxiety is not an integral part of them, that cannot be changed – but something external to them that they can learn to combat and conquer. It can be very empowering, and you can work alongside your child as a team to 'beat' the anxiety.

(child's image of externalising anxiety)

We know that our feelings don't just come out of the blue and there is always a thought/belief behind our emotions. Therefore, by helping your child make changes in the way they think, this will hopefully have a positive impact on their ability to control their anxiety. Reflecting back to one of the core principles discussed in the introductory section on 'How to get the most out of this book', it is all about small steps making a big difference. Although it is not possible to control our thoughts and feelings 100 per cent of the time, some shifts in thinking patterns will hopefully reduce some of your child's anxiety levels.

So...you can encourage your child to engage in detective thinking by using a sheet like the one below:

Situation - what was happening? (who, where, when)

Questions to ask yourself:	...Jot it down.
Thoughts – what thoughts or images are going through my mind?	
What is the evidence for my thought?	
What is the evidence against my thought?	
What would be a more helpful and realistic thought?	

The idea is that you are encouraging your child to look for **evidence for and against** their current worrying thought. It is not about 'positive thinking', which can be really hard to actually believe, but instead it is based on **realistic thinking**. So, based on the evidence, what would be a more realistic helpful way of viewing this situation?

If we refer back to the case example of Max, one of his worrying thoughts was *"if I try something I have not done before, I will get it wrong and everyone will laugh at me"*. By looking at this in more detail and challenging this thought, he was able to think about times he had done something for the first time and no one had laughed. He was also able to consider how he would think and react if one of his friends made a mistake and realised that he was falling into an unhelpful thinking pattern and that his worrying thoughts were not based on fact.

Helping your child think about how anxiety affects their behaviour

It is useful to think together with your child about all the ways in which worry affects the way they behave. This is likely to include some degree of avoidance.

Is it stopping them from doing something they would like to do (going to parties, sleep-overs)? As we discussed earlier in this chapter, avoiding may be helpful in the short-term as it temporarily reduces the symptoms of stress, but long-term it is not helpful and only serves to fuel the fear. I find the graph we touched on before a really useful way of explaining this in a visual way:

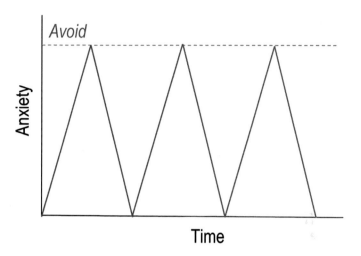

So, let's consider for a moment a child with a fear of dogs, like our case study - Sally. Each time the child sees a dog, their anxiety may reach 10/10 on the worry rating scale (the peaks on the graph), their fight or flight response is triggered which makes them feel very uncomfortable and therefore their immediate reaction is to want to avoid. They escape/ run away from the situation and their stress levels reduce significantly. Everything is okay again...Until they are faced with another dog, and then the same pattern occurs. Over time you can see the peaks continue (red lines on graph) with the long-term anxiety levels never having a chance to reduce (always staying at 10/10 when faced with a dog).

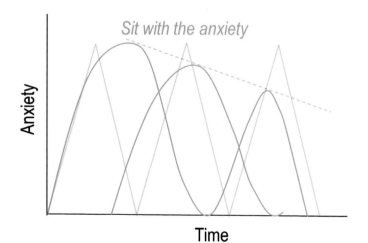

By providing the child with strategies to *stay in the anxiety-producing situation* and learn coping techniques to tolerate their levels of anxiety, over time you can see that the anxiety levels reduces (with the green lines reducing in size on graph).

This is why it is so important to help your child gradually face their fears and stay with the situation long enough to see that their anxiety levels come down naturally rather than giving into the urge to escape and avoid. I know this is easier said than done, but the best way to do this is to develop a graded exposure hierarchy or stepladder approach, which breaks the fear down into small steps. This is likely to evoke heightened anxiety in your child and it is important to stress that you will be working through this together and you only move onto the next step of the ladder when they feel comfortable. It is important to also give rewards to your child for each level successfully completed. This will help with motivation as it provides a positive experience for tackling an unpleasant experience. Remember, rewards do not have to be financial and can include fun activities or special 'mummy or daddy time'. It's also important to remember to be realistic about timescales and stick with the plan. It's easy to get disheartened if you don't see immediate results.

It is important to be realistic when setting up a stepladder and make the ultimate goal achievable and appropriate to your child's capabilities. Also remember it is not about completely freeing your child from all anxiety, but it's about bringing it down to a more tolerable level so that it is not impacting on their day to day activities.

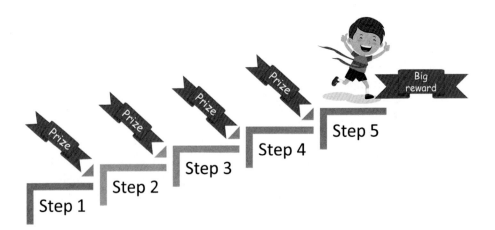

Goal	Predicted level of anxiety (0-10)	Actual level of anxiety (0-10)	Reward for facing the situation
Be able to stroke a dog	9/10		Theme park
Be in the same room as a dog off the lead	7/10		Have friend over for sleep over
Be in the same room as a dog on a lead	6/10		Go swimming
Go to our local park where there may be dogs	5/10		Choose DVD to watch together
Go to friend's house (where they have pet dog, usually kept in garden)	3/10		Choose favourite dessert

Often the anticipation of an event is a lot scarier than the actual event itself. This is why it is useful to encourage your child to consider their *predicted* level of anxiety when thinking about facing the goal in question, and then continue to rate the *real experienced* level of worry. You would start on the bottom rung of the ladder and only move on to the next step on the ladder when your child feels they have conquered the previous step and have become desensitised to it (often through a lot of repetition). This would also be used in combination with the detective thinking and relaxation skills.

Sometimes, it may be the case that a child is engaging in a particular behaviour to avoid their fear happening - for example, checking doors and windows repeatedly to avoid the fear of a someone breaking in to the house. Stepladders can be used in the same way for this sort of behaviour. The principle is the same and you want to try and encourage your child to stop those behaviours and realise that nothing bad happens, despite them not doing them. This is called **response-prevention**, as you are stopping your child doing the behaviour that offers them comfort.

This is commonly used for children with obsessive–compulsive disorder (OCD), but it is also useful for children who seek excessive reassurance or have perfectionist tendencies. If you feel your child may have OCD, seek advice from your GP as more specialist support may be necessary.

The aim with stepladders is that your child learns that even though they faced some steps that triggered anxiety, they were able to cope. The bad things they thought might happen did not occur. Reflecting on another one of the basic principles in the first chapter, it is about encouraging your child to push themselves out of their comfort zone, *take certain risks* and learn from doing this. Your child learns that they can tolerate a certain amount of anxiety – which is a great life skill as let's face it, it's impossible to go through life completely anxiety free! This sense of achievement will hopefully spur them on to try new steps.

Finally, I am aware we have been looking at specific strategies that may help your child to manage the anxiety they are feeling, but it is important not to overlook the importance of the basics such as sleep, diet and exercise. These crucial factors are all essential to positive well-being and are worthy of a chapter each, but I will just briefly touch on each one here:

Exercise is a very effective way to improve mental health and can have a profoundly positive effect on anxiety (amongst other mental health concerns). Getting your body moving is a natural and effective anti-anxiety treatment – it helps to relieve tension and stress and boosts well-being through the release of endorphins (our natural 'feel good' hormones). Your child may already be quite 'sporty' and involved in clubs which is great, but even if they are not that way inclined, going for regular family walks or having fun on the trampoline will get the same results! Or maybe you could look into certain clubs that your child maybe interested in being involved in. A team or club can help to boost general self-esteem.

Diet We all know that what we eat is important and ensuring your child has three balanced meals a day is another helpful way to limit the power of anxiety. A diet rich in whole grains, vegetables and fruits is a healthier option than eating a lot of simple carbohydrates found in processed foods. It is also important that your child does not skip meals as this may result in drops in blood sugar, which can lead to heightened anxiety symptoms. Making sure your child drinks enough and remains hydrated is also very important. I know this can be tricky when children are at school and you are not sure how much they are drinking throughout the day. Having a water bottle with them at school can help.

Sleep As parents we are well aware of the impact of sleep deprivation! Lack of sleep or disturbed sleep can leave us feeling more irritable and impatient. We feel less able to tackle the demands of the day. Getting enough sleep is important for both you as the parent and your child who may have heightened worries. Unfortunately, it is a vicious circle, as worries have a nasty habit of becoming louder at bedtime, as we are not distracted by the day's activities, and therefore they can keep us awake. Feelings of tiredness then serve to exacerbate the worries and deplete our abilities to cope in a productive manner.

If your child is having trouble sleeping, it is worth trying to tackle this first because the other strategies aimed at helping anxiety will be difficult to implement if your child is constantly tired. The following may help:

- Establishing a good bedtime routine is essential, which may involve a relaxing bath and story time.

- Ensuring the lighting and temperature in your child's bedroom is right for them is important too.

- Provide your child with an opportunity to discuss worries prior to the bedtime routine (refer back to the Worry Box idea), so that they can hopefully go to bed with the worries no longer swimming around in their heads.

- Relaxation and Mindfulness exercises may also need to become part of the bedtime routine to encourage your child to 'switch their brain off' and feel more rested.

- Avoid all digital devices at least an hour before bed. The blue light emitted from electrical devices such as iPads inhibits our body's natural melatonin levels (the substance naturally produced in our bodies which helps us sleep).

Of course, bedtime worries may be the main issue for your child and it is common for children to worry about the dark or being separated from loved ones. If this is the case the strategies discussed in this chapter can also be applied to bedtime worries.

Jump into action and carry out the plan

Now that you have *'Spelt Out'* your child's concerns, *'Understood'* more about what's keeping the anxiety going and *'Planned'* what strategies you may want to use, we need you to *'Energise'* the plan and put all of this into action. There may be, however, some things to consider before you can jump into action:

- Timing. Make sure the timing is right to tackle the anxiety. We are expecting your child to face some fears, which is no easy feat! If your child is in the middle of SATs or a school production, time may be more limited for both of you. Equally if you are away with work or have other family stresses going on (such as another child going through GCSE's), it might be better to time-table your plan in for a better time.

- Ensure that everyone involved with the care of your child is involved and aware of the plan. This is especially important for parents who are living separately as it is important that both parents are on board with the plan and willing to be consistent with rewards and consequences. This will emphasise the notion of 'team-working' for your child too.

- Support for you. Tackling your child's anxiety is going to be a journey for both you and your child. A journey that is likely to be bumpy at times! So, don't be afraid to seek extra social support from good friends and family members and have 'time-out' yourself when you feel you need it.

- Be aware of excessive reassurance seeking. As a parent we instinctively want to reassure our children and tell them it will be okay and we are here, but too much reassurance makes the child feel they cannot cope themselves and so when they find themselves in situations without us, it is no wonder they panic. It is therefore important to help your child work through the problem and come up with their own solutions to it. You are not being cruel, but adopting a more empowering approach!

- Remembering how important and effective praise is in influencing children's behaviour, it is essential that you become hypervigilant and look out for times when your child has pushed themselves and tried something, or you catch them problem-solving for themselves.

- The expectations you have of your child will influence how you interact with them. Have faith that your child can do this - children will pick up on subtle messages from parents about how capable they are, so it is important that you don't let any of your own anxieties show. Raising and looking after a child is a worry in itself as we all want the very best for our children. Having an anxious child can be even more of a worry and if you have anxieties yourself this is amplified. So, it may be important to identify any of your own personal anxieties and consider ways to overcome them.

In order to energise the plan, you need to begin by sitting down with your child and discussing the plan and the reasons behind it. Reassure them that you are with them all the way to support them. You could describe it as a 'journey or adventure' you are on together.

First, consider the goals you want to achieve - what would you like your child to be able to do (go on a sleep-over, be in a park with dogs)? It is important that you choose goals that can be achieved. We do not want to set our children up to fail and they need to be appropriate to your child's developmental level and capabilities. Once you have thought of the ultimate goal, consider some of the strategies we discussed in the **Plan** section and focus on which ones you think will help your child. Let's think back to Max and what the plan was for him. This may help you to think about what might be helpful for your own child.

Max, aged 9 years.

When Max came to see me with his mum, Rachel, the main concern was his clinginess to mum on a school morning and his anxiety levels were particularly high if he had a lesson where he may have to speak out in class. Max was very good at explaining the physical symptoms he felt when he worried and the main one for him were the 'butterflies in his tummy' and feeling sick. He would also become very anxious if he was invited to the cinema or to a friends for a sleep –over. It transpired that Max had been in the cinema once with a friend and their parents and he had that 'sick feeling' in his tummy. He feared he may be sick and he was worried about not being able to leave the cinema. He could not enjoy the film as he was so focussed on the fact he might be sick. This feeling has led him to believe it is safer not to risk doing that again. He had begun to rely on reassurance from his parents that he would not be sick and hence he did not like going on sleep-overs because his parents would not be there to offer that reassurance. Rachel admitted that they would decline offers on his behalf as they didn't like to think of him as so distressed. Their goals were for Max to feel less worried on school mornings and to be able to go on a sleep-over. Together I formed the following plan with Max and Rachel:

Max's plan

Physiological awareness:

This was particularly important for Max as he was so aware of those pesky butterflies in his tummy, but was not aware that was a 'normal' response to worry – it did not mean he was actually going to be sick. Rachel and Max had some fun drawing around his body and filling in all the other physical signs of anxiety that he experienced. He enjoyed the 'science' behind it all and this knowledge in itself seemed to calm Max down.

Relaxation strategies:

Once Max had learned about the fight or flight response and its purpose, he started to learn that his 'alarm' was going off when there was no real danger – he was not about to be eaten by a bear! It was important to teach him some strategies that would help him to switch on the calming parasympathetic nervous system (remember from the **Understand** section!). We practiced the Box Breathing exercises and Rachel and Max engaged in some Mindfulness exercises together at bed -time.

Identifying triggers:

Max devised his own anxiety rating scale (0-10) with his own smiley/sad faces depicting the varying degrees of worry he felt in different situations. He monitored how he felt over a period of a couple of weeks and was able to identify that his increased worry levels occurred on days when he had English at school as this is when he had a weekly spelling test and was more likely to have to read out loud. Unfamiliar social situations also increased his worry ratings.

Externalising his worry:

Max loved drawing and had a good imagination, so he was keen to draw what his worry looked like. He drew a wonderfully hairy monster called Mr. Sicky Pants! Max liked to think that Mr. Sicky Pants was something separate to him and something that he could potentially beat. He learned to talk back to Mr. Sicky Pants, saying things like "I'm not listening to you!"

Learning about the role of thoughts:

A lot of time was spent looking at thoughts and the effect they were having on Max's feelings and behaviour. As Max loved art, he was happy to draw lots of stick men with thought bubbles above their heads. Through doing this he was able to identify some of his negative thoughts. Max would worry that he would get his spellings wrong and the teacher would tell him off. He would also worry that he may get the words wrong in his reading out loud and other children would laugh at him. His common thought was also that if he felt sick, he would actually be sick, and he would not be able to cope if his mum was not there.

Detective thinking:

Rachel and Max would sit down together and fill in the detective work sheets, looking at each worrying thought in turn and then looking at evidence for that thought, finally reaching a more realistic and helpful way of thinking.

E.g.: **Thought:** If I get my spelling wrong, my teacher will tell me off. **Worry rating=8**

What is the evidence? My teacher has never told me off before for getting them wrong. I only need to try my best and she will be happy with me. I have got most of them right in the past.

More realistic/helpful thought: If I do my best everyone will be happy. **Worry rating=3**

Rachel would encourage Max to use the detective thinking technique whenever he noticed 'Mr. Sicky Pants' telling him he should be worried.

Facing his fears:

Time was spent looking at how anxiety affects our behaviour and how avoidance is fuelling Max's worries and actually giving more power to Mr. Sicky Pants! Max really did not want this and so was keen to show him who was boss! I also helped Max's parents understand that wanting to give lots of reassurance is a normal response as parents but that it can be counter-productive with anxiety as Max was becoming dependent on it. They soon learned to encourage Max to problem solve for himself and this was empowering for him. It meant that when his mum and dad were not with him, his confidence grew in being able to cope with the worries on his own.

Devising a stepladder:

Max and his parents devised a small stepladder for facing social situations more independently. They focussed on the ultimate goal of being able to go for a sleep –over at his best friend's house. This was something Max desperately wanted to do but 'Mr. Sicky Pants' was telling Max that he would be sick and then this would just be the worst thing ever and he would never be asked again. The ladder included steps such as watching a DVD at his friend's house, and staying at his grandparents' house on his own. Max was also involved in choosing the rewards he received for achieving each step. This helped to maintain his motivation.

By using this plan Max managed to gradually take control of his worries and squish 'Mr Sicky Pants'! With perseverance and commitment Max and his parents worked as a team and he became less worried about school days and finally got to have a sleep over at his friend's house! Once he realised he was not sick and he could cope his anxiety reduced significantly when out on other social activities too.

If your child has similar worries to Max, you may also find the chapter on self–esteem (Chapter 3) helpful as boosting general self–esteem can have a positive impact on controlling anxieties. Having a fundamental belief that we **can cope** is at the core of our overall well-being.

So, you may find it helpful to use the headings included in Max's Plan above to see which elements would be useful for your own child and start putting the plan into action!

So......Well done - You have been working hard with your child and possibly other caregivers, to tackle your child's anxiety and have implemented your well thought -out plan.

It may be time for the final step of our **SUPER** plan – which is to **Review** how things have been going. Give yourself a time frame of about 6-8 weeks so that you are giving yourself a chance to see how the plan is working. Worries and fears will not go away overnight and it really is a case of being consistent and persevering. So, keep going...but a review might be helpful.

It is useful to sit down with everyone involved to consider the following questions:

- What has worked well? What factors were involved in the success?

- What has not gone so well? Why do you think certain things have not worked so well?

- Does your child seem motivated to stick to the plan?

- Does your child understand the rationale behind the plan?

- Does anyone else need to be involved in the plan for optimum success?

- Do you have enough support as a parent?

- Are you keeping check on your own anxieties and stresses?

- Are you able to stick to the plan and be consistent?

Once you have had time to consider some of these questions, it may be necessary to look at your plan and tailor it accordingly. Remember not to be too hard on yourself if certain things are not working as this is a work in progress and it can be a case of trial and error with some of the strategies. It is a journey you and your child are both on for the first time.

I thought it would be useful to cover some common problems that families often raise when trying to tackle their child's anxiety:

We don't seem to be making any progress!

As I said before, worries do not disappear within a day, even a week or month; it can take a while to notice any significant changes. There may be times when you feel like nothing has changed, but it is important to reflect on your starting point and those notes you made at the very beginning when you were spelling out the problems that you were seeing. Compare how things are now with how they were when you first embarked on this journey. Hopefully you will notice that some changes have occurred, even if they are small changes. As long as they are in the right direction that is all that matters. If you really feel that no progress is being made, it may be that you need to re-visit the goals you set and adjust them accordingly.

Reflect on your expectations and make sure they are realistic and in line with your child's development and capabilities. It is unlikely that all the strategies mentioned will work for your child and it is helpful to note down the ones that seem to have been particularly useful so that you can refer to these in the future when you really want to boost your child's chance of success.

My child seems just too anxious at times to deal with it.

There may be times when your child is just too anxious and refuses to engage in the plan of action you have developed together. Although, you may feel a mix of frustration and helplessness, it is important to accept that as parents we cannot always take away our children's anxiety, as much as we would like to. If your child is feeling really anxious or frightened, it is important to provide a sense of security and comfort. It is also really important that you as the parent, stay calm so that you do not fuel the fear and you model a productive way of coping.

A problem-solving approach can be a structured way of helping your child reach their own solutions, so that they feel calmer, empowered and ready to take a stand against anxiety once more. The stages involved with problem–solving are as follows:

- Once you have understood the problem, encourage your child to think about whether they can change the situation or the way they are reacting to it – or both?

- Ask your child to think about all the possible ways in which their worries could be reduced. Remember to praise them for any ideas they come up with as you want to reward engagement in this process.

- For each strategy/idea your child has generated, ask them what they think the outcome will be and consider the advantages and disadvantages of each.

- Ask your child to choose the strategy they think will have the best result in terms of reducing their anxiety.

- Evaluate its success. Think about how well it worked and what they have learned for next time.

My child seems too young to be able to identify and challenge their thoughts.

A large part of the anxiety management plan does focus on identifying worrying thoughts and thinking of alternative ways of thinking. This may well be too complicated for young children, but they can still learn that there are several different ways of thinking about the same situation and at times we need to test out our beliefs to see if they come true. So, the fundamental principle is the same but you as a parent will need to take more of an active role in helping your child be aware of alternative ways of thinking and how they could be tested. You can get creative and use favourite dolls or teddies to illustrate different viewpoints and how different characters may cope with the situation.

We make some progress and then it feels like we go back to square one!

Our children are humans like us, and not robots. So, just like us they will have 'good' and 'bad' days and times where life will throw curve balls at us, knocking us off track. It is likely that you will get quite excited by any progress you see and so signs that your child is suddenly less able to cope can come as a real shock and disappointment. This can be referred to as a 'relapse' and anxiety does have a habit of creeping back in, especially at times of general stress. If this does happen, try not to panic as there really is no need to. Just go back to basics and practise the techniques that helped your child in the first place. This will hopefully help you get back on track fairly quickly. Always remember to listen to your child and encourage them to talk to you about their worries. It is important to validate your child's feelings and let them know you are there for them - you will get through this together like you have been doing.

If the set-back has been the result of another stress such as a loss or external family stress, allow time for this to be dealt with first.

We don't have enough time or motivation for stepladders.

Lack of time is a common problem, as family life tends to be generally very busy! But reducing your child's anxiety levels will require you to prioritise stepladders, detective thinking and the other anxiety-bashing skills you have acquired. As your child does start to make progress, you will not need to use them so rigidly. Remember, once you have your goal, break this down into smaller more manageable steps. Try not to have more than 10 steps in a ladder so that you and your child do not feel overwhelmed. Also, many anxieties tend to intensify within the school environment and, so you may need to enlist the help of a teacher so that the stepladders can be worked on at school as well.

Don't forget that incentives are needed to maintain motivation, not only for your child, but also for you as the parent helping your child. Reflecting on your child's successes may be reward enough to keep up the motivation levels. You may need to remind yourself of the small yet significant changes that have been made.

Sometimes it's hard to know whether my child is avoiding something because of anxiety or because they are just not interested.

Remember that you know your child better than anyone and so you are likely to be aware of the signs that your child is worried about an event. Some children may say that they are not bothered about playing in that football match or going to that party because it will be 'boring', when it is actually anxiety that is getting in the way. Look out for those early anxiety clues that you were able to identify in the 'Spell it out' section. To a certain degree, knowing how much to 'push' your child will involve trusting what your child is saying to you. Speak to your child about what is going on in their minds and problem-solving all the possible outcomes can be helpful. If there is a level of doubt about whether it is anxiety or disinterest that is leading to avoidance, it may be better to gently encourage them to face the step. Remember to reward your child for any positive steps and for pushing themselves out of their comfort zones. If it was just boredom/lack of interest - it will be an easy reward for them to achieve!

How long do we keep practising all of the techniques?

This is the 'how long is the piece of string' question! Every child and every situation is different. Some children make huge leaps in a very short time whilst others make slow but steady progress. Once you see some positive changes in your child's anxiety levels, they may not need to practise their new skills in such a formal way. However, it is important that your child keeps in mind all the new skills they have learned and views them as a set of life-long skills that can be utilised at times of stress. Whenever your child experiences heightened levels of worry, it is a good opportunity to practise the techniques.

I think we need more help!

This book focuses on common problems that primary school age children often encounter and is meant as a guide to help parents try to help their child. Having read through this chapter and tried some of the strategies, you may feel that this is not enough, and you need more specialist help. If you feel that the support your child needs in relation to their anxiety is above and beyond your capabilities, do not hesitate to seek advice from your GP as you may need some specialist support.

References

Carr, A. (2006). *The Handbook of Child and Adolescent Clinical Psychology –
A Contextual Approach (Second Edition)* London: Routledge

Yerkes RM and Dodson JD (1908). *The relation of strength of stimulus to rapidity of
habit-formation.* Journal of Comparative Neurology and Psychology. 18:459-482.

Further reading:

GOOD BOOKS:

Creswell, C and Willetts, L. (2007). *Overcoming your Child's Fears and Worries:
A Self –Help Guide using Cognitive Behavioural Techniques.* London: Robinson.

Rapee, R.M. (2008). *Helping your anxious child: A step –by-step Guide for parents.*
Oakland: New Harbinger Publications Inc.

Snel, E. (2013). *Sitting still like a Frog: Mindfulness Exercises for Kids (and Their
parents). Boston:* Shambhala publications.

Stallard, P. (2002). *Think Good, Feel Good: A Cognitive Behavioural Therapy Workbook
for Children and Young People.* Chichester: Wiley.

GOOD WEBSITES:

Annakaharris.com (Mindfulness exercises)

Anxietybc.com

Everlief.co.uk

2

Friendships and Bullying
'Friends are like squiggly lines;
they are hard to get straight'

Dr Liz Dawes, clinical psychologist

Friendships are important;
there is no denying it.
Through relationships with
others, a child learns essential
skills such as sharing, turn-taking,
compromise, negotiating and
how to communicate effectively.
A friendship allows a child to
practice skills for managing their
emotions, and understanding
and responding to the emotions
of others. Friendships enable
children to develop in their ability
to think through and problem solve
different social situations within
relationships. They can give a child a sense of belonging, bolstering
self-esteem and identity. When a child is feeling happy and secure within
their friendships, they not only feel more confident in themselves but can
actually perform better academically at school.

Sadly, when a child has difficulty making or keeping friends, this
can lead to social isolation and loneliness. For parents, this causes us
incredible concern and makes us question:

- Why isn't my child being invited on more playdates?

- Why doesn't my child get invited to parties?

- Why is my child being teased by other children?

- Why doesn't my child seem to have any friends?

Sadder still, some children will experience bullying and as a parent, this is heart-breaking to see. Bullying can have considerable long-lasting effects on the child, emotionally, physically and psychologically. Forms of bullying have become more sophisticated over time, and children can use all sorts of methods for making their targets suffer. A child in primary school may experience one or more forms of bullying including verbal bullying, emotional bullying, physical bullying or cyber bullying. As parents, we may react with anger, revenge, fear, and perhaps even denial that it is happening. Often, it is hard to keep our own feelings in check, and to know what to do to best help our child. We need to know how to spot bullying, how to manage and support our child who is being targeted, and how to face the school, the parents and the bullies themselves.

What can we do?

For any parent of a child at any age, we want our children to experience social success, to be liked by their peers and to be accepted as a friend within healthy relationships. It's heart-breaking when these friendships hit inevitable bumps in the road, or when our child has trouble making friends in the first place. We want to support our child in the best way we can. Friendship skills develop intuitively in some children, but not all. However, that doesn't mean these children miss out; they can learn new skills and ways to make and keep friends.

But as parents:

- What can we do to support our children to develop healthy friendships and learn these essential skills?

- How can we help our children to feel accepted by those around them, and to cope with and overcome rejection from others?

- How can we support our child's skills in managing arguments and teasing, and what should you do if your child is being bullied?

Ultimately, how can we as parents help our children to **make** friends, and how can we help our children to **keep** friends?

If you are worried about your child and their friendships at school, it is important to understand what aspect of the relationship is causing them difficulty. Your child might be happy and willing to talk about their difficulty. However, your child may not want to talk about or perhaps even acknowledge there is a problem. Acknowledging there is a problem may cause them embarrassment, shame, upset or guilt. Below are possible signs that things aren't OKAY.

- Perhaps they are coming home in tears everyday

- Perhaps when you ask them about who they played with today, they are consistently unable to give you a name

- Perhaps they have bruises on their body and your child is secretive about their cause

- Perhaps your child is pretending to be sick and saying they don't want to go to school more often

- Perhaps they seem more withdrawn than normal, wanting to spend time alone in their room

- Perhaps their appetite has changed recently

- Perhaps your child has started bed wetting when they have previously been dry through the night

- Perhaps they have been getting into trouble at school for fighting with or arguing with their friends

- Perhaps there have been changes to how well they have been doing in class, seeming more distracted or forgetful than normal

If your child isn't keen to talk about their difficulties with you, perhaps you could find some other way of enabling them to tell you what's up. Maybe they could draw you a picture of what has been going on, or write it down for you to read. Slightly older primary school children who are 'technology savvy' may prefer to text you or email you with something that's been bothering them. Of course, using technology in this way is not ideal for ongoing communication between you but if it gets the ball rolling, and your child feels more able to share what's been happening, it is certainly an OKAY starting point. You may find their initial reluctance to talk disappears as they start to share their concerns about their friendships.

Of course, sometimes, your child may have little awareness of what is going wrong in their friendships or may not realise that the behaviour they are receiving from others at school isn't okay within a friendship. If you can, watch your child whilst they play or interact with other children their age. What do you notice? Be as specific as possible then write down what you see.

Speak to your child's teacher and teaching assistant about what they may see and observe when your child interacts with their peers. Perhaps they have noticed something that you or child might have missed.

My child's specific friendship difficulties are

_____

_____

_____

_____

_____

_____

_____

_____

_____

Let's have a think about the kind of difficulties a child might face within their friendships at school. Below, I will introduce you to two different children struggling with different aspects of friendship. You will learn lots about these two children throughout the rest of the chapter, including how their parents helped them to learn new skills to cope with friendships.

Thomas, aged 7 years.

Thomas is 7 years old and has always been shy. At pre-school, he spent a lot of time on his own, playing with his cars and dinosaurs, and he didn't seem to enjoy being in big groups. He didn't know anyone when he started at the local primary school. He has found it hard to make friends there. His parents have tried to invite children from his class over for playdates but he never really seems to know what to do when they arrive at his house. When he first started school, he'd often receive invites to birthday parties of his classmates. When they could get him to the parties, he would rarely take part in the activities, or speak to many children. His parents would tell him 'it's okay' and take him straight home again. Thomas's now rarely gets party invitations or invited round to other people's houses to play. Thomas's parents have noticed that he has been getting upset more easily at home, wetting the bed, and complaining of stomach aches and headaches in the morning before school.

Let's SPELL IT OUT for Thomas....

When Thomas' mum went to speak to him in his room one evening to ask him what was wrong, he buried his head in his pillow and refused to speak. After seeing Thomas at parties and knowing how he was during playdates, she knew that he was having trouble making friends and that he didn't seem to quite know what to do when talking to or playing with other children. She asked Thomas to draw a picture of himself at school at break time. She asked him who was there, and where he would normally be in playground. The picture showed a drawing of Thomas, alone, whilst a group of children stood on the other side of the playground. Thomas drew a sad expression on his face on the picture.

Thomas's mum wrote down these difficulties:

- Trouble starting conversations with other children
- Trouble keeping a conversation going
- Trouble asking children to play
- Trouble joining in play with other children particularly within a group

Maggie, aged 10 years.

Maggie is 10 years old and has always wanted to 'fit in' with the girls at school. She is desperate to be popular and therefore, wants to make friends with the 'popular girls'. Recently, the 'popular girls' appeared to accept her into the gang, and invited her to sit with them at lunch time. Maggie was over the moon, and was so excited when she told her mum all about it when she came home from school that day. However, the next day, Maggie approached the lunch table where the girls sat and they appeared to ignore her. Worse still, they started laughing at her. Since then, the girls have started calling her 'loner' and 'loser', and saying 'no one likes you'. This happens during break times and at the end of school, where the girls walk behind her through the school gates and onto the bus. Maggie thinks that she has no other friends to turn to. Maggie's parents have noticed that when she comes home from school, she prefers to go straight up to her room. She says she doesn't want to go to Brownies or swimming club; activities she once really enjoyed.

Let's SPELL IT OUT for Maggie...

Maggie approached her mum one evening, in tears and desperate for help. She explained what had happened with the girls at school, and how they continue to call her names. Although Maggie's mum felt extremely sad and angry about the treatment Maggie was receiving from her 'so-called friends', she knew to stay calm and to actively listen to what her child was telling her. She made sure the television was off and put her phone aside to prevent any distractions whilst her daughter explained.

Maggie's mum wrote down these difficulties:

- Trouble dealing with bullying

- Trouble managing her feelings in reaction to bullying

- Trouble choosing friends that were right for her

- Trouble knowing how to be a good friend to herself

- Trouble being assertive

For any friendship issue that your child may have, it is important to understand **why** they might be struggling. This will help to understand:

- How did the problem become a problem?

- What caused the friendship issue in the first place?

- What might be keeping the problem being a problem?

This will also help us to understand what strategies might be best to help your child.

Let's think about the problem from a number of different perspectives;

- developmental

- neurological

- cognitive

- behavioural

- systemic

1. Developmental perspective

It is helpful to consider what a 'normal' friendship may look like for a child during primary school. It is natural for changes to occur within friendships and for challenges to happen from time to time. Many children face these challenges and cope with them alone, learning important skills such as problem solving and social communication in the process. However, other children may struggle through these developments, perhaps getting stuck at specific points, not knowing how to progress. These children need our help to feel happy and confident again within their friendships.

What are 'normal friendships'?

It is necessary to consider what is 'normal' in friendship development so we know what your child might need from you at any one time, when he or she might need it and why they might need help.

Firstly, consider, when you ask your child 'What is a friend?', what answer do they give? It is likely that their answer changes depending on their age and therefore, how you might expect them to relate to their peers will change as they grow. A child's description of what a friendship is changes over time but depends on how they view and understand the world in general. It may also depend if your child is male or female. The types of activities a child will engage in with their friend will also change according to their age and developmental stage. The table below summarises the ways children describe a friendship as they develop through primary school.

Approximate age	A friend is someone who....
2 – 5 years	- Lives near me - Likes the same toys as me - Enjoys rough and tumble play (boys) - Helps me or likes me - The same sex or age as me (more so for girls)
6 – 9 years	- Has similar interests to me - Has positive personality traits such as friendly or funny - Is fun to be around - Someone who can help me emotionally as well as practically (more so for girls) - Is my best friend
9 – 11 years	- Genuinely cares about me - Sticks up for me - I want to spend a great deal of time with - Is trustworthy and can keep secrets - I can talk to about my feelings - Accepts me within their social group

In the early stages of friendship (2-5 years), a child is largely focussed on themselves and their own needs. The child tends to be attracted to other young children who are like them, such as the same age or sex, and those who enjoy the same games as them. A friend may be sought who has the same toys as them or who has a toy which they want. Disagreements and arguments may break out relating to ownership and possession of the toys, with skills in cooperation and compromise somewhat limited at this stage. Towards the age of 5 and 6 years, children move from parallel play to game playing and learn such games cannot take place without sharing and turn-taking. During this stage, children are learning the importance of communicating through words rather than actions with their friends, and how reading body language is needed to understand friendships.

From about the age of 6 years old, a child is learning that when it comes to playing, a friend may have wishes and desires that are different to their own. Friendships are often about mutual interests and a desire to share these with another. The idea of reciprocity is important, with children becoming more aware of the need for fairness and equality within their friendship. Around the age of 8 years, a child develops a concept of a 'best friend' as someone who helps them in times of emotional and practical difficulty. Friendships at this stage are generally more stable than they have been previously and can be repaired if there is a falling out or argument. Gender differences at this age are obvious, with each gender preferring to spend more time with their own sex. For boys, they may have many different friends with whom playing and practical games are the order of the day; sharing emotions and having long conversations is not a regular occurrence. Girls, on the other hand, are beginning to share deep and meaningful conversations, spending more time talking than anything else.

From the age of 9 years old, a friend is someone who possesses desirable personality characteristics most like themselves and who the child believes genuinely cares about them. By the age of 10 years, a child may have many friends selected for sharing different things e.g. a best friend for playing football, or best friend for playing computer games. At this stage, however, group identity becomes more important and a child has a great desire to 'fit in'.

There is a tendency to see differences between boys and girls in terms of social development. It may be that as a society, we are socialising children to behave in different ways and expect different ways of behaving as a consequence. For example, competitive rivalry, such as physical or verbal aggression or joking, can be an important part of relationships particularly between boys. Girls tend to be more cooperative and relationship focussed, whereas boys are often naturally more competitive and activity focussed. Boys enjoy playing in large groups, whereas girls tend to stick to small groups or 'best friends'.

Thomas, aged 7 years.

It is 'normal' for a child of 3 or 4 years old to not know how to make friends or what to do in parties or playdates. It is also 'normal' for children at this young age not to know how to enjoy group play. Thomas's mum knew that he was a shy, reserved sort of boy who didn't take to others well. She thought that he would grow out of it. However, this didn't happen.

Thomas is behind with his friendships skills and this is preventing him from creating relationships with his peers. It seems he needs help to learn some basic social skills to enable him to cope with many aspects of friendship including initiating and reciprocating play, and managing playdates.

Maggie, aged 10 years.

Maggie has developed appropriate social skills up to this point. Her friendships have been normal and typical. Even when all the transitions through friendships have been smooth, you cannot control the often cruel and harsh behaviour of a peer group. Sadly, social hierarchies and cliques forming are typical at Maggie's age, and are part and parcel of what she will have to deal with. However, the treatment Maggie has received from the other girls goes beyond typical 'one-upmanship' in the playground. Maggie is struggling to manage teasing and bullying from other girls. She is at an age where is it important for her to feel accepted and part of a group, and likely by her peers. At Maggie's age, a significant proportion of her self-identity is established by feeling part of a social group. The apparent rejection of the group and their behaviour towards her has an incredibly detrimental effect on her self-esteem and general mood.

2. Temperament

Children are not born a 'blank slate'. Instead, your child came into the world with a set of genes that not only determined how they would look, but also how they react to the world around them and the people they meet. People refer to this as a child's 'temperament', later described as their 'personality'. You may have noticed your child's temperament from a very early age, in how they generally reacted to new situations or to new people. Perhaps they seemed outgoing and confident? Perhaps, in contrast, they were cautious and careful?

Knowing what your child's natural temperament may be is helpful for creating an environment which will support and nurture their needs. You cannot change your child's temperament, but you can work with it and perhaps adjust your parenting style in order to support their social development.

If your child seems like a naturally shy, 'inhibited' person, they may find many aspects of friendships challenging. In particular, you may have noticed them being quite unsure of visits from new people, perhaps holding onto you tightly, not wanting to let go; you may even describe them as fearful and afraid of someone different. As a child, they may tend to stand and watch their peers from the periphery rather than getting immediately involved. They may prefer others to make the first move or remain quiet, diverting eye gaze when questioned by another.

If your child seems like a strong-willed, 'uninhibited' kind of person, you may have found them somewhat of a challenge as a baby. As a growing toddler, although sociable in nature, they seemed all too often to get themselves into trouble with their peers for being too dominating and controlling. They may often get themselves into difficulty with regards to considering others' feelings. They too, can learn skills to help them relate more successfully.

A child's temperament is set from birth; innate and genetically determined. Such temperament ultimately effects how we as parents may interact with and parent our children, and their reactions will affect us as well. Arguably, the fundamental early relationship and pattern of interaction between a baby and their primary caregiver is vitally important, and becomes a template for many relationships later in life, including with their peers. Much research to date has found that the quality of the early mother-child relationship is associated with social competence during the primary school years. This means that babies described as 'securely attached' to their mother, who are more likely to successfully learn skills such as eye contact, imitating facial expressions and responding to voices, will be more confident to seek out further social interactions and therefore, learn more social skills. Conversely, those children described as 'insecurely attached', will have fewer opportunities early in life to develop key social skills, therefore leading to fewer social skills being learnt, and fewer adaptive communicative skills being used.

Thomas, aged 7 years.

Thomas sounds like his has a naturally 'inhibited' temperament. Even from birth, he found social approaches challenging and would cling to his mother to keep him safe. An inhibited temperament means he is naturally more reserved and wary when it comes to other children. His hard-wiring means he is predisposed to react to things in an inhibited way; unfamiliar situations and people, including his peers, cause him discomfort and anxiety. Thomas needs to learn to confront the anxiety and to tolerate the discomfort in social situations so he can begin to cope socially.

3. Neurological/brain development perspective

Our brains are all wired differently and in unique ways. In previous years, it was believed that a child's brain was fully mature neurologically when the child was only a few years old. Research has shown this not to be the case and in fact, the brain continues to develop neurologically well past adolescence. Therefore, the potential to learn and take on new skills continues throughout childhood, regardless of the starting neurology.

Friendships seem to come naturally to some children, whilst to others, they seem inherently difficult and fraught with challenges. For these children, it may be that they just need time to catch up. However, if problems persist despite support or help, it is also worth considering whether differences in brain neurology might account for the issue. If you are at all concerned regarding this issue, it is worth discussing it further with your GP to discuss referral routes for further assessment.

Specific neurological issues that might make friendships challenging for children include:

Neurological issue	Tick if you think it applies to your child
Not knowing how to read body language including facial expressions	
Makes impulsive, inappropriate comments	
Intrudes on others' personal space	
Difficulty processing information e.g. during a conversation	
Difficulty formulating a response to a question e.g. during a conversation, seeming slow to respond	
Difficulty understanding non-literal language	
Difficulty using empathy to guide social behaviour	
Shows an apparent 'disinterest' in other children	
Lack of understanding of what a friendship is	

4. Cognitive/thoughts and beliefs perspective

Our thoughts have a lot to answer for; they have a big impact on how we make sense of the world, ourselves and our futures. The way we think about something is influenced by many things including previous experience and messages from others. The way your child thinks about the friendship challenges they face is important and it is worth you finding out more. You can ask them questions such as:

- What goes through your head when X happens?

- What does it mean to you that X happened?

The way your child thinks about a challenge they face affects how they feel emotionally. Furthermore, it will affect how they go about facing the friendship issue and the course of action they might take. The diagram below helps to understand this.

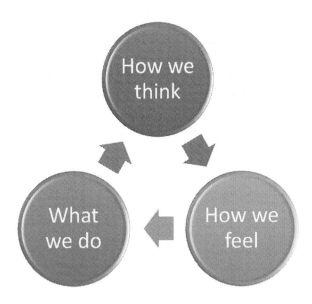

To note, younger children, before the age of 7, will really struggle to tell you what thoughts are in their head and it is not worth upsetting yourself and your child by pushing too hard.

The table below outlines the link between a child's thoughts, feelings and behaviour in different social situations.

Situation	Thought	Feeling	Behaviour
Ball not passed during a football match	I'm not much fun Other children don't like me	Anxious Sad	Withdraw from social contact Avoid playing football again
	They are not passing to me on purpose	Angry	May become aggressive Try to get them back
	They didn't see me to pass the ball to Maybe they didn't hear me when I shouted	Confident Resilient *(disappointed at first but quickly recovers)*	Next time they play football, shout louder for the ball
Friend doesn't say hello to child in the corridor at school on passing each other	She doesn't like me I've done something wrong I'm a bad person	Sad Upset	Withdraw from people at school Hide in the toilet at break time to avoid friend
	My friend must be really stressed about something and didn't notice me there	Concern for friend	Seek friend out at break time and ask if they are okay
A child in the playground approaches saying 'hey, four eyes!'	I hate my glasses. I hate how I look. Why can't I just be like everyone else? It's true what the child is saying so there is nothing I can do about it	Sad Alone Disempowered	Take self to the toilets and cry
	That kid is so mean. I hate him	Angry	Punch the child After school detention for a week
	That child is stating the obvious! Yes, I do have glasses and I need them to see	Confident	Laugh at the child Walk away to be with friends

The diagram below helps to make sense of the connection between thoughts, feelings and behaviours.

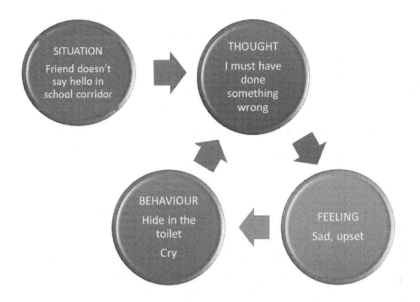

This example illustrates how the child appears to have 'jumped to conclusions' and come up with the worst possible explanation for why a friend has not said hello in the corridor. Thinking in this way has left them feeling sad and upset, perhaps feeling rejected as well by their friend. To cope with these unpleasant feelings, the child takes action and hides in the toilet at school, crying. Perhaps this course of action helps them to feel better as they are hiding away from any further instances of rejection from their so-called friend. However, the more the child hides away, the less chance they are allowing themselves to learn that there may be an alternative explanation for the friend not saying hello; perhaps the friend didn't see them, perhaps they were distracted thinking of something else, perhaps they were rushing elsewhere and not paying attention. Learning to face the problem and challenge the thought is important, not only to increase the child's positive feelings, but also to learn important social skills needed to deal with this situation should it arise again.

Maggie, aged 10 years.

When Maggie's mum spoke to her about what had been happening at school, she wrote down some of the things that she said. This included things like:

'It's all my fault that they don't like me'

'I've got no friends'

'Why can't I be more like the popular girls?'

'I hate myself'

Parental thoughts and feelings

As parents, when our child is experiencing a friendship issue, no matter what it is, this can trigger many different feelings for us including anger, frustration, guilt and sadness. We know that there is a relationship between how we think about a situation, how we feel about it and then how we behave. Therefore, the way we think and feel in reaction to our child's friendship issues will affect how we deal with the problem. As hard as it may be, it is important that we find ways to manage our unhelpful thoughts and feelings so that we are able to listen to our child's thoughts and feelings. In doing so, we are tolerating their often distressing feelings and helping them to learn ways to cope with them. For our children, this is essential; we have to allow our children to make social mistakes and to experience somewhat negative feelings in order to learn the necessary social (and emotional) skills to deal with them.

The table below shows this:

Situation	Thought	Feeling	Behaviour
Your child tells you that they have got no friends	It's my fault they have no friends. I don't get on well with people so she's just like me My child was born this way so there is nothing that can be done to help	Sad Helpless	Tell your child that it's okay, they are just like their mummy Offer no guidance on how to make the situation better Avoid taking your child into social situations which you know they don't like
	I know that isn't true. She had a friend round for tea last night and they played so well together	Concerned	Sit down with your child and explore why all of a sudden they believe they have no friends Talk about all the ways they have made friends in the past Role play ways to make friends
Your child tells you that they are being bullied at school	That must be so awful for my child. I am sorry they are having to deal with that.	Concerned	Sit down with their child and talk through what is happening at school, when and where. Talk through and role play specific ways of responding to the bullying.
	The school is doing nothing to protect them!	Angry	Storm into the school demanding they do something about it Ring the parents of the bully on the phone and demand that they punish their child

5. Behavioural perspective

Children can get stuck with behaving in ways that they believe are helpful to them. Often, this might take the form of avoidance, particularly if something is hard or difficult. It is easier to avoid a problem than it is to face it. However, in order to learn that we can cope with problems and learn ways of overcoming them, we need to face it! We as parents can also fall into ways of behaving with our children, which actually prolongs the problem; the opposite effect to what we intended. And we thought we were helping!

a) Avoidance

It is human nature to want to avoid things that we find hard, difficult or scary. However, the more we avoid something, the worse the problem seems as it becomes something more unpleasant in our minds. Furthermore, avoidance means we are not giving our children a chance to learn how to cope in a situation that they don't like.

Thomas, aged 7 years.

Thomas finds having other children round to play at the house difficult. His parents have noticed his unease, and theirs, with playdates so they have stopped asking his friends round to play. No one feels uneasy anymore but the avoidance of playdates means Thomas is missing out on opportunities to learn the skills of how to manage the situation. Furthermore, the more Thomas avoids other children, the less likely they are to want to ask him to play.

Maggie, aged 10 years.

Understandably, Maggie was feeling very low and upset about the treatment she was receiving from the girls at school. She believed she was at fault and that she had no other friends. Even though she did have other friends at school, she was avoiding them because she believed that no one liked her. She was also avoiding activities after school, not because she didn't feel like going, but because she was worried that she might experience the same treatment she'd received from the girls at school, from others she met.

b) 'Safety behaviours'

At times, to make ourselves feel better, we might use certain ways to cope in a situation. For example, if having conversations are difficult for your child, they may learn to cope by spending lots of time thinking about and writing down exactly what they might say when talking to another person. Of course, some preparation is helpful but over-preparing to the point of 'parrot repetition' can have the opposite effect to what was intended; if they forget what they are meant to say, they might not be able to recover and know how to carry on the conversation.

One way that children make themselves feel better is to ask us for reassurance. Sometimes we feel that to make our child okay we need to tell them that 'it's okay' and 'don't worry about it'. Perhaps this makes us feel better and makes us believe that we are doing something to help. However, reassurance doesn't help to make the child feel better in the long term. In fact, it keeps them dependent on us to fix their feelings and make him okay again.

c) Behaviour in reaction to bullying

Sadly, more children are having experiences of being bullied during their early years. Bullying can take many forms including verbal, physical, emotional, sexual and even more so these days, via the internet and social media (cyber-bullying). It seems our children can become victims of bullying in more ways than ever before.

Inevitably, the experience of bullying has many negative impacts on a child, not least on their emotions and how they feel about themselves. The way they behave in reaction to bullying can have quite an impact on them if the bullying continues.

Maggie, aged 10 years.

For example, Maggie is extremely hurt and upset by the behaviour of the girls at school towards her. She is struggling to manage those feelings and therefore, finds that she is more tearful at school, and wants to be by herself. Unfortunately, she is giving the bullies exactly what they want; a reaction that shows that they have got to her. Maggie needs to learn skills of how to show the bullies that what they are doing doesn't bother her. She needs to let them know through her behaviour that she is strong and confident, and their words and actions are meaningless to her; a very hard skill to learn!

Maggie's mum was feeling extremely angry about what had happened to her daughter. She desperately wanted to march into the school and demand they sort it out. She also wanted to call all the girls' parents and demand an explanation. However, she knew that this might not be very helpful and without careful consideration, she could be making the situation worse for her daughter. Instead, she needed to find a way to stay calm so she could be reactive to her child's needs and to her feelings.

4. Family and other networks/ Systemic perspective

Children don't exist in isolation but as part of many different 'networks of relationships'; at school, at home, within the wider family, at clubs. Each network can greatly influence a child's friendships including how they react to challenges that arise.

a) How do you as parents behave?

Our children take many clues as to how to behave from watching us as parents. Our influence on our children is extremely powerful and we often don't realise how strong our influence can be. If your child sees you wanting to socialise with others, and being relatively able when you do so, your child is more likely to want to do the same. If you are the kind of parent that prefers to spend time alone, finding socialising challenging, your child may see this as the normal way of doing it.

b) How do you talk about friendships?

Our influence continues...It's not just how we behave with other people and within our friendships, but how we talk about friends and the value we place on them is also extremely important. If you are quick to reject a friend after a seemingly small mistake and speak of this in front of your child, be aware that they may take on your words and internalise them, believing they too should reject a friend after a small mishap.

c) School considerations

How a school views the importance of friendships for a child will influence the kind of support they offer and their attention to social skills in general. Most primary schools understand that social development is just as important as academic development, and therefore actively encourage friendships between pupils. Many schools have Social Skills groups or Peer Mentoring programmes for children who struggle more with their social skills.

It is important for you to know as a parent what values the school places on their pupils, what their ethos to friendships and fallings-out are. Perhaps your child has observed other children having friendship issues, sought help from a teacher who was dismissive or unsupportive. This may lead to your child feeling less able to ask for help, or even acknowledge that there is a problem in the first place.

Let's summarise what you have now come to 'Understand' about your child's friendship issue.

	Tick if it could be a problem	Page number of the explanation of the issue	Page number for the possible strategies to help this issue
1. Development / stage of life			
2. Personality			
3. Neurological (brain development)			
4. Thoughts			
5. Behaviour			
6. Systemic			

 Right, let's get started on working on helping you and your child to make changes to the problem. I will now go through each of the areas listed in the 'understand' section, and discuss some ways to address each one.

1. Developmental

Let's begin by thinking about ways that we can help all children with their friendship skills.

a) Help your child to develop realistic expectations for a friendship

As mentioned earlier in the chapter, children conceptualise friendships differently depending on their age. Even so, at any age, children should appreciate the difference between friendly and unfriendly behaviours. If your child enjoys arts and crafts, you might think about making a poster together of pictures, photos, and magazine clippings of behaviours deemed 'unfriendly' and 'friendly'. Perhaps your child really enjoys a particular TV programme. Utilise this interest and spend some time together watching their programme. Make it into a game with your child shouting out when they see a friendly or an unfriendly behaviour in their chosen character.

It is equally important for children to learn that they have different kinds of relationships in their lives, and that the expectations for and how they might behave can be quite different. For example, younger children can find it more challenging to decipher between those they class as 'best friends' and those they class as 'friends'. This social naivety can lead to mistake being made when it comes to how much time they expect these 'best friends' to spend with them, or when the 'best friend' wants to play with another.

The Friendometer, as shown below, is a great way of demonstrating these differences to children. Furthermore, it introduces the fact that relationships are somewhat fluid and changeable, and you may have variance within each category e.g. you may have a friend who is nearing being a best friend, or an acquaintance who you are learning more about so they are moving more towards being a friend.

The Friendometer allows you to have a conversation about how you define each type of relationship e.g. stranger, acquaintance, friend, best friend. It can help to create a 'table of traits', made to be age appropriate to your child of course, which can become a sort of checklist for your child to measure their relationships against.

For example, you may talk about a child at school who your child says he knows their name, but doesn't know what their interests are. You can talk to your child about how you may define this relationship as an 'acquaintance' at this point, but as he learns more about the child, as per the 'friends' checklist below, this relationship may move up the Friendometer.

Together, write up a list of traits you might expect from a friend e.g. that they are kind, thoughtful, helpful. Draw pictures and discuss the specific ways that a 'real' friend might show these traits, for example, a friend could be helpful to me when I have dropped my school bag and it has emptied over the floor.

Stranger	Acquaintance	Friend	Best Friend
You don't know their name	May know their name	You know their full name	See them or have contact with them most days
You don't talk to them (though may say hello if your parents say it first)	Have seen them somewhere away from home more than once	May know when their birthday is	Spend most break times with them if they are your school
You may know where they work	You know very little information about you	Share one or two interests	Know their full name
	Don't spend any leisure time together	Likes some of the same games as you (maybe not all)	Know when their birthday is
	Recognise their face but know little about them	You may meet them in places of interest or clubs	Have play dates with them outside of school
			Share many interests with them
			Prefer to play with them over any other child

b) Observe your child's behaviour

Some parents feel that they should let their child sort out any challenges for themselves. For example, at a party, if their child is arguing with another over the use of a toy, some parents feel that they should step back, and allow their child the space to problem solve completely alone. Conversely, some parents feel they should do the opposite; that their child is too young to know what to do, so they step in at the first sign of trouble and sort things out for their child. Many children will be able to sort out many friendship challenges alone or with the help of their peers. However, some do need more help. Carefully observe a situation unfolding, being mindful of how your child and their friend appear to be feeling. If distress levels get too high, you need to step in, encouraging the children to come up with their own solutions to the problem, using questions such as 'How can you settle this?' and 'Is there any other way you guys can....?'

c) Where to meet friends

As children begin school, this becomes the greatest source of potential friends. However, there are other places where a child can meet others and make friends. Joining an after school club, especially if it is based on something your child really enjoys, is highly recommended. Such clubs enable your child to meet other children who share their interests; a natural conversation starter. Football club, martial arts club, computer club, Cubs and Brownies are great places to consider. Some children, (particularly those who are shy and unsure in social situations) really appreciate the structure and routine of a club. You may have to try out a number of different clubs to see which one your child most enjoys. Interests naturally wane so be prepared that a club once enjoyed, may soon become disinteresting!

It is worth making a special mention about the internet here. The internet is ever more present in our lives and even more so for our children; even children at primary school age. From an ever increasingly young age, children are being exposed to the internet and are using it for social purposes. This is scary for us parents as we are wary of the potential dangers of this way of interacting. Many children use the internet as a source of entertainment which they share between them. Some games allow children to verbally interact with each other, and this could be with other people on the internet, not necessarily people they have physically met before. Some may be described as 'friends'. But are these friends different to ones they make face to face?

Talk to your child about the difference between an 'internet' friend and face-to-face friend, particularly with reference to the fact that you can't always visually see the internet friend. Encourage the child to think about the negatives of an internet friend, for example that they don't really know if they are telling the truth.

On a practical level, it is always important to check that the right internet security features are installed on your family or child's personal computer.

d) Playdates

The best way for children to learn such social skills naturally is through play with other children. The more play skills a child has, the more able they are to develop positive behaviours and friendship skills. It is important to provide your child with these social opportunities like playdates and get togethers, rather than always sitting down and talking about friendships and social skills. Children mostly learn through playing and doing, rather than simply talking. Arranging times and places where your child can meet friends or potential friends is essential. It may be helpful to provide structure around the playdate and to manage your child's expectations. For example, create together a list of games to play. Perhaps help the child to think about what their friend might like to play. Put toys away which they might have a hard time sharing. Be on hand to facilitate a playdate and to give your child immediate feedback on their skills, including constructive criticism. At times, it might be helpful to reflect on how their behaviour might be affecting that of their playmate, and what they could do to change their reaction. This encourages perspective taking which is extremely important within any friendship.

Now let us consider more specific social skills that a child can learn to help them make friends.

a) Eye contact

- Show your child the importance of eye contact by "modelling" this behaviour to them.

- Play games such as the 'staring game'. Sit face to face with your child or ask a sibling/friend to pair up with them. Ask one child to speak on a topic of interest whilst the other either stares intently or looks away completely sharing no eye contact at all. Discuss how each felt to the speaker and to the listener.

b) Greetings

- Ask your child to act as a 'spy' at school who watches and listens to the way that their peers greet each other. You will need this important piece of investigative work on your child's part so you are aware of the ever changing social conventions of a child and what words are the norm!

- Together with your child, write a list of possible ways they might greet a friend at or outside of school.

c) Listening

- Create a poster together of how to be a good listener. For example, how far to stand/sit from someone who is talking, how to maintain a good listening position where the body is positioned towards the speaker, how to show interest via body language such as nodding head and saying 'yes' and 'mmm'.

- Playing the 'whisper game' is a great way for the child to learn the importance of listening. In a circle, someone starts by whispering something in their neighbours' ear. They then have to re-tell what was whispered in their ear to their neighbour. This continues in this way until the whisper reaches the final person in the circle who says the words out loud. Is it the same as the original whisper? Prizes for all if it is!

d) Turn taking

- Describe any conversation or play like a game of tennis. The ball is passed to and fro like words are exchanged between two (or more) people.

- Create a 'talking stick' which is passed between you, with the person holding the stick as the only person who is allowed to speak. Once they have spoken, pass this onto the next person to speak.

e) Conversation skills

There are many different elements to a conversation, many of which children can struggle with. A child must:

- Gain someone's attention
- Think about what they are going to say
- Alter what they say based on reactions from their conversation partner

For all the below strategies, practising the skills in as many different settings as possible is ideal – at home, at school, at clubs etc.

CONVERSATION TOPICS

- Ask your child to think about the kinds of things they like to talk about, such as hobbies, books, games, food, etc.

- Discuss with your child the importance of choosing topics that other people would find interesting. You could write a list of children's names at school, perhaps children from their class who are friends, or perhaps children who your child would like to befriend. Under each name, write 2 or 3 things that they like or which could be suitable topics of conversation.

- For each possible topic of conversation, ask your child to write 3-5 different questions related to that topic. Questions are an important aspect of any conversation and a great way of your child getting to know others.

CONVERSATION MAINTENANCE

- Conversations work well when you are able to stay on topic or on a related subject matter. Play a game of 'association' with your child. You say a word and your child has to say another word which is related to it. You then do the same. The game continues until you run out of things to say!

- Help your child to learn how to carry on conversations by role playing. Agree a list of conversation topics and write on a separate piece of paper. Pull a piece of paper out of a hat and this is the topic you will practise having a conversation about. You may like to film the role play so you can watch it back together to see how you both did!

- If your child struggles with the to and fro of conversations, you could create a 'talking stick' for practice at home. The talking stick indicates who is talking at any one time and must be passed between you as you speak.

- To practise the build-up of conversations, encourage your child to ask a question, you answer it, then ask a question back related to the topic.

f) Joining in

Knowing how and when it might be okay to join in with an already established conversation or game is challenging for anyone, let alone our children. Firstly, talk through when might be an appropriate time to attempt to join in on an activity or conversation. For example, in the middle of a board game is not always a great time to join in. Furthermore, trying to get into a conversation with a group during lesson time is also not ideal. Role playing different scenarios and enlisting the help of a sibling or friend is a great idea and really brings situations and practise to life. If your child wants to join in, encourage them to:

- Observe what the group is doing, by watching, listening or standing nearby
- Stand up close to the group who are either talking or doing an activity
- Choose a good time to interrupt such as when there is a pause in conversation or activity
- Ask to join in saying 'Would you mind if I joined in?'

g) Problem solving

When talking to your child about their friendship difficulty, try to encourage them to come up with solutions themselves, rather than giving them the answers or giving them the 'quick fix'. Try to encourage them to come up with solutions themselves, rather than giving them the answers or giving them the 'quick fix'. This will develop their feelings of empowerment. Discuss the advantages and disadvantages of decisions they make rather than giving them the answers.

Role play different scenarios. Siblings can be involved in this too. Video the role play and watch back together and reflect on non-verbal behaviours seen.

Drawing can be a really helpful way of going through a difficult problem your child may have had with their friends. You could use stick figures to represent everyone that was involved and tell a story of what happened. Try using speech bubbles to write down what each person said. It would be really helpful also to use thought bubbles for each person to encourage your child to reflect on what each person was thinking when they said and behaved as they did. Drawing it in this way, you could add in different colours to the speech bubbles to represent your child's guess at how each person is feeling and perhaps to wonder if this made them act as they did. You could change the ending of the story to play around with different ideas for coping and behaving next time.

2. Temperament

We can't change our genetics and we can't change our temperaments and personality. Let's consider what aspects of our child's personality might be causing them an issue within their friendships and how we might help them.

'Inhibited' introvert type personality

Possible Issue	Strategies
Child says they would rather play on their own	- Talk with your child about the value of friendship - Explain why friendships are important and why we need friends e.g. to help us fix problems - Enrol child in an after school or lunch time structured club based on their interests and strengths - Perhaps encourage a friendship with someone outside of school, perhaps slightly younger than your child so they are on a par socially
Reluctance to attend birthday parties	- Encourage the child to attend - Perhaps you could offer a treat or reward for them having attended - If your child has avoided parties for some time, agree ahead of time how long you could stay at the party. After they successfully attend this party, increase the amount of time they might stay at the next party
Child doesn't want to ask anyone from school over to play	- Talk to the teacher at school about which children might be patient and empathetic towards your child - Set up a date and time when that child can come over to your house by contacting the parent - Remain with the children during the playdate to reinforce and praise your child's efforts to interact - Your child might be happier to have a playdate at home rather than going to another person's house

'Uninhibited' extrovert type personality

Possible Issue	Strategies
Always wanting to pick the game played at break times	- Discuss together the importance of **compromise** - Role play how to compromise in different made up situations such as 'You have a playdate and your friend wants to play a different game to you'
Wanting the same toy as another child and pushing to get it	- This suggests a delay in skills such as sharing and turn taking. - A timer or stop watch can be used to help with sharing - Encourage your child to reflect on how it might feel to the other child when they continue to snatch the toy
Shouting and crying when s/he loses a game	- Learning ways to be a 'good loser' is important as other children will be reluctant to play with the child who reacts badly to losing - Teach your child key phrases to say such as 'Well done', 'Good job' and 'It's okay to lose, I'll get another chance to win next time we play' - At home, play games together where as a family, you deliberately change the rules and in order to win the game, you actually have to lose e.g. you have to miss all the snaps, rather than say them

3. Neurological/brain development

If your child is consistently struggling socially and has done so for some time, it may be that your child has particular strengths and weaknesses indicative of neurological developmental issues such as Autistic Spectrum Disorder (ASD). If you are at all concerned, speak to your GP. Talk with your child's school teacher to see if they share similar concerns and concur that a further investigative diagnostic assessment might be warranted.

It is worth mentioning that many traits associated with a developmental disorder such as ASD do in fact occur within the typical population also. A full diagnostic assessment is the only means to determine whether such traits are just part of typical development or due to something else.

A diagnostic assessment can be completed within the NHS or within a private setting. It is not taken lightly by professionals to consider giving a child a label and therefore, the assessments tend to be quite long and involve many professionals.

Deciding to pursue a diagnosis is a personal decision and one families make for many different reasons. It is worth considering the impact of a potential diagnosis on the child, their family and surrounding network. Perhaps a diagnosis will help the child understand more aspects about themselves, and understand why they struggle in certain areas more than their peers. It may help schools better understand what they are dealing with, to know what support is required to best meet the needs of the child. It may also help to plan for the future, and to understand how to intervene in the most helpful ways.

Regardless of the diagnosis, your child may still be struggling with many aspects of the social world and all the strategies listed within this section will be helpful. Research has shown us that social skills are best taught and most effective when instruction is given within the environment in which they are used. This means that schools are one of the best places to teach social skills. Having a member of staff available at break time who your child can come to if they are confused about a social situation or seeking instruction as to what to do is invaluable. The teacher could also set specific 'social goals' at break time with the child receiving a reward for having achieved the goal e.g. a sticker every time the child shares a toy at break time (depending on what skill you are focussing on at the time).

Children who have a difference in their neurology which accounts for differences in their social skills, need to be taught about the social world in extremely clear, concrete and specific ways. Creating a 'dictionary' of social rules is a good way for your child to remember exactly what is expected of them in different contexts e.g. you would greet your teacher by saying 'Hello Mrs/Mr *insert teacher's name*' but a friend you might just say 'Hi'.

You might like to start a 'social project' with your child where they film natural interactions between people at school (with consent from them and their parents). Together, you can discuss what you see, how people behave, what they say etc. You may also like to take static photographs of people at school to teach specific skills on facial expressions and body clues.

4. Cognitive/thoughts

Remember, how your child thinks about a problem or a friendship issue will affect how they feel and ultimately what they do to try to solve the issue. Once you have written down the kind of thoughts and beliefs your child has about the problem, it is now time to start challenging them and helping your child to see things from a different perspective; a perspective that allows them to feel more positive and to take positive action.

We are all guilty of listening to our thoughts and beliefs and taking them to mean the truth. However, if we are able to evaluate our thoughts and perhaps develop a new perspective, this will change how we feel and ultimately how we behave.

a) Thought challenging

This is a technique taken from Cognitive Behaviour Therapy (CBT) (see the book *Think Good Feel Good* by Paul Stallard for more information). This is a process of checking and testing out the thoughts, to access the validity of them. As we begin the process of searching for evidence for and against each thought, the aim is to reduce the strength of and belief of each thought, ultimately developing a newer, more balanced perspective of the problem. As the parent, you can be responsible for asking the thought challenging questions.

Helpful questions to begin challenging a thought include:

- What evidence is there for this thought?
- If it were really true, would I be able to cope? How would I cope?
- Is there another way of looking at this situation?
- If my best friend told me this thought, what would I say to him/her?
- Does it really matter what other people think?
- Am I being too hard on myself?
- Is it helpful to think in this way?

Maggie, aged 10 years.

Let's consider what thoughts Maggie had in reaction to the bullies and how we might challenge them.

Negative thought	Challenging thought questions	Answers to the questions	Alternative perspective/ thought
I've got no friends	– Is that really true? – What evidence have you got that you have no friends?	– Before I started hanging out with the girls, I did have other friends – I have stopped spending as much time with them – However I know I am capable of making friends as I have done it well before	– It is true that I have let down my old friends to be with this new group of girls. However I know that I am capable of making friends again
It's all my fault	– Are you being too hard on yourself? – Is it helpful to think in this way?	– Thinking this way isn't helpful as it makes me think I have no power over what other people do to me – I can never be 100% responsible for other people's behaviour	– It's not my fault. I am not responsible for the bullies behaviour

b) Parental thoughts

As we've discussed so far, parents are not empty vessels and the feelings and behaviours of our children can create thoughts and feelings in us too. Furthermore, these thoughts and feelings cause us to behave in certain ways; sometimes not necessarily in the most helpful ways. Remember Maggie's mum, after hearing that her daughter was being bullied? She had thoughts like 'the school isn't protecting my child' and she was feeling angry, she wanted nothing more than to storm up to the school and demand action. However, she had enough foresight to think through these actions and consider the negative impact they may have on her daughter. Maggie's mum needed to take time to balance her negative thoughts and consider if she was just 'jumping to conclusions'.

To keep your negative thoughts in check, it is important to:

- Be aware of your thoughts in any situation. You might like to write them down on a piece of paper or on your phone to remember them

- As soon as you notice the type of thought that may get in the way of you behaving in a helpful way, say to yourself 'STOP'

- Use this pause to start challenging your thought and weighing up the validity of it. For example, is it really true that the school had taken no action to help Maggie at school?

c) Developing empathy for other children

An important skill that a child needs to develop is that of empathy. Empathy requires a child to be aware of the association between thoughts, feelings and behaviour in other people. Awareness of other peoples' thoughts and feelings develops naturally during childhood, with the basic awareness of other people having a mind that thinks differently to themselves being established around the age of 4 years old.

Like conversations, there are many different elements of empathy and as such, different ways that children must learn about other people's feelings. Obviously, we can never know for sure how someone is thinking but children can learn to take a guess and to adapt their behaviour in reaction to this. Emotional empathy is where children can learn to feel other people's emotions, as if feelings were physically contagious. Finally, researchers refer to compassionate empathy where a child is so moved by the emotion, they are compelled to help and do something about it. Arguably, these skills are incredibly important in any friendship, particularly as children move into the later stages of primary schools where friendships are naturally based on more emotional sharing and support giving.

To have emotional empathy, a child needs to be attuned to their own emotions and be able to cope with their own distressing feelings. This will be discussed later when we consider a child's skills in 'Emotional regulation and control'.

An important first step for your child is noticing that other children have feelings. How do children show feelings?

5. Body Language

A child needs to learn that we communicate by other means as well as words. For example, only 30% of how we communicate comes from speech; the rest is communicated through HOW we say something, e.g. tone of voice, intonation, frequency, volume and through our bodies. Below is a diagram of places where you may look to check for clues as to how someone is feeling.

BODY POSTURE
how someone is standing

EYEBROWS

LIPS/MOUTH

GESTURES
arm movements

EYES

Play a game with your child where they are 'Body Clue Detectives'. Watch a TV programme with the volume off (I would suggest that it isn't their favourite programme!). Ask your child to guess how someone on the TV is feeling from their body clues that they can see which show this feeling.

To empathise, your child needs to wonder about how their actions impact on the other child's thoughts and feelings. Use comic strip conversations (outlined earlier) to draw together different possible thoughts and feelings for people in different social situations. Help them to develop a reportoire of responses to use should they see certain behaviours in their friends. You could talk through and/or role play their responses to the following scenarios:

Scenario 1	Your friend Maisey is crying because the teacher shouted at her. What can you do?
Scenario 2	Your friend Mario is angry because you have just won the game of Snakes and Ladders. What do you do?
Scenario 3	You see your friend Lucy is alone at break time. What do you do?
Scenario 4	You are talking to Thomas about your favourite TV programme. He starts to yawn. What do you do?

Emotional regulation

In any friendship, knowing how to stay calm and in control is important. Even more so, remaining cool and calm in reaction to something that has gone wrong, such as losing a game, or emotional response to teasing and bullying, is a hard skill to learn.

a) Where do feelings come from?

A child can learn that feelings originate from within their body, triggered by a situation and thought process or cognitive interpretation. For any emotional experience, there are associated body clues and sensations. For example, when you are sad, your body might feel heavy and lacking in energy. When you are anxious, your body is in 'fight or flight' mode with increased heart rate, high body temperature and fast breathing.

A fun activity with your child could be to get a large piece of paper and lay it onto the floor. Ask your child to lay down on the paper and you draw round their body to create an outline on the paper. Together you discuss what body clues they feel in reaction to a certain friend situation. For example, with Maggie, her mum might discuss how she feels inside when the girls call her names. Or for Thomas, his mum might ask him to draw what happens in his body when he arrives at a party and doesn't know what to do.

You may like to number the body clues in the order in which they arrive or are felt by the child. For example, for Maggie, she may notice that when the girls call her names, her heart races, then her skin gets hot. For Thomas, he first notices that his mind goes blank, and then he starts breathing quickly.

b) Thermometer

A thermometer analogy is helpful to teach children that feelings are not all or nothing, and that you can experience different levels of a feeling depending on the situation, your thoughts, and what you do about it.

Draw a thermometer together with 5 points. The lowest point on the thermometer represents the lowest level of emotion; for Maggie, this might be the lowest feeling of anxiety. Ask your child to give a label for each level of the thermometer, for example 1/5 might be 'a little bit of anxiety', and 5/5 might be 'exploding anxiety'.

Next talk together about how their body might feel inside at each level of the thermometer. When do they notice a change in heart rate? Or hands becoming sweaty?

Finally, discuss ways that they can manage their emotions at each stage of the thermometer. It might be helpful to separate strategies into 'school based strategies' and 'home based strategies'.

Strategies might include:

- Taking deep breaths
- Putting a 'safety cloud' around themselves
- Thinking happy thoughts
- Talking to someone
- Distracting self with a book or music

With consent from your child, it may be helpful to share the thermometer with your child's school teacher, so they can be attentive to changes in your child's emotions and what might be helpful for them to enable them to cope.

Below is an example of a thermometer to illustrate this for you.

	What it looks/ sounds like (to others)	What it feels like (inside my body)	What I can do/ What can other people do to help
5			
4			
3			
2			
1			

c) Be a friend to yourself

We saw earlier how Maggie told her mum that following the bullying at school, she 'hated herself'. This suggests a low self-esteem and more techniques and strategies to help a child struggling in this way can be found in the 'Self-Esteem' chapter of this book (chapter 3).

It is important for our children to learn ways to be a good friend to others, but even more so, they need to be a friend to themselves. A good friend means being kind, gentle, loyal and accepting of your friend. It means letting go of small mistakes that your friend may make and supporting them through difficult times. The same applies to your child!

Encourage your child to write down 5 things they like about themselves. Balance this with 5 things they aren't so keen about.

Ask them to write down 5 compliments they have heard people say to them. You could even start a 'Compliments diary' so that on those difficult days, your child can still remind themselves of their positive qualities.

6. Behaviour

We learnt earlier that the way our child behaves in a social situation, may inadvertently end up making the problem worse.

Thomas, aged 7 years.

For example, we say that Thomas found it easier to avoid going to parties and playdates because he found them too hard, and now he rarely receives an invite.

a) Avoidance

If situations are hard or make us feel unhappy, our natural tendency is to want to avoid it. And avoiding something is the easiest thing in the world! However, we know that the more we avoid those things, the worse they seem.

Maggie, aged 10 years.

For example, Maggie found that it was easier to avoid going to activities such as Brownies and swimming club where she thought she might experience rejection and unkindness from peers. However, the more she avoided these activities, the worse she felt. She wasn't doing anything that she once enjoyed and therefore was getting no pleasure or happiness. Her behaviour and avoidance was also working to make her belief 'I've got no friends' stronger and she had more time to think about it.

We have to teach our children that in order to make ourselves feel better, we need to stop avoiding the things we find hard. We need to teach them that although facing hard situations may make them feel unpleasant feelings like anxiety, in the long term, they are learning important ways to cope. They are also teaching themselves that their worst fears are never as bad as they think.

Thomas, aged 7 years.

For example, Thomas does not want to attend parties and will avoid them at all costs. We want him to learn the skills to cope at the party, in terms of his anxiety and in terms of his social skills. Thomas's mum could create a 'hierarchy' with him with 'going to a party' as the ultimate goal. She may start with a first step of having a playdate at home with 1 other child, before moving on to a playdate at home with 2 other children. Next, the playdate could be with 1 friend at their house, then increase the number who might attend. Next, Thomas might have a 'tea party' at his house with a few other children. Finally, Thomas could attend a party away from the house. At each step, he is learning to cope but in a controlled and step-wise manner. His mum gives him a reward at each stage to keep him motivated and trying his best.

Sue's chapter on anxiety (chapter 1) has more information on how to deal with avoidance and anxiety more generally. She explains that one way of breaking down patterns of avoidance is to start your child facing their fears, but in small, controlled ways and steps.

b) Safety behaviours

Like avoidance, safety behaviours make our children feel better in the short-term, but in the long-term, they come to believe that they need to use these strategies to cope in the same situation in the future.

First, you need to help your child identify any safety behaviours that they might be using. Ask them questions like:

- Is there anything that you do that makes you feel better?

- If you didn't do these things, what do you think might happen?

Next, you need to talk about how to stop using the safety behaviour and how they could cope without it. For example, a child who wants to learn how to have conversations with others but who over-prepares by reading and writing down numerous questions and answers, needs to learn that such preparation isn't necessary and actually might make them stilted and awkward in a conversation. Instead, you could teach them a few key phrases and a few key questions that they might use in a conversation with people at school (more can be found in the 'conversation' section of this chapter).

c) Reaction to arguments, teasing and bullying

We know that the way children react to unpleasant situations between peers such as during arguments, in reaction to teasing and bullying, can inadvertantly worsen the situation and may actually make it more likely to happen again.

Maggie, aged 10 years.

We saw earlier how Maggie, who is struggling with bullying, reacts with tears and sadness in front of her tormenters, and runs to hide away at break time. I'm sure you'd agree this is a reaction that many of us would feel like doing in this horrible situation but sadly, it is making the situation worse as the bullies see they are getting a reaction which reinforces their behaviour.

Children often come up against disagreements and arguments within their friendships. These are unpleasant to experience but important for your child's development. They are also inevitable and it is important to manage your child's expectations around the normality of them. It is natural for disagreements to occur within any friendship and they are not necessarily an indication the friendship is ending. However, if arguments and disagreements occur within your child's friendships more often than positive interaction, it may well be that the friendship is not well matched.

A. How to manage feelings in reaction to arguments and bullying

Inevitably, arguments and bullying will trigger difficult feelings in your child, not least anger and frustration. Fighting and shouting at your friend would not be helpful and will solve little. Similarly, reacting in any way to the bully will reinforce their behaviour which will more than likely keep it happening. Instead, your child needs to learn how to keep a check on their feelings, noticing that their body is becoming increasingly more frustrated, and taking action to calm it down. Being calm means being in control and being able to think clearly enough to know how to handle the situation. Refer back to the 'Emotion regulation' section in this chapter for ideas of how to help your child identify these feelings. Teach your child skills to manage these sensations such as:

- Balloon breathing – pretend there is a balloon in their chest that they must inflate with slow and steady breaths

- Muscle relaxation – starting from the toes, and moving up with body with each major muscle area, teach your child to notice the difference between tenseness and relaxation by over tensing the area for 6 seconds, followed by the slow release and relaxation

- Use a 'catch phrase' to say in their head such as 'Calm down' and 'Stay in control'

B. How to handle arguments

Ask your child to describe the argument or disagreement they had with their friend, including as many of the steps before and after the incident as possible. Encourage your child to think about who was around, what were they doing, and how they felt at each point. If talking is too difficult at this point, ask them to write down or draw what happened. This will give you an idea of the specific challenges and why they were so difficult for your child. Remember, encourage your child to come up with solutions to the problem themselves and ideas for how they might deal with it again should the situation arise at a later date.

Being assertive is a more helpful way of dealing with an argument than being aggressive, shouting or fighting.

Assertiveness is the ability to stand up for ourselves and to say how we feel when we feel we need to. It includes:

- Expressing your own opinion and feelings.

- Saying "no" without feeling guilty.

- Setting your own priorities i.e. choosing how you spend your time.

- Asking for what you want.

- Being able to take reasonable risks.

- Choosing not to assert yourself at times when you feel it would be better not to say anything.

Below are the steps to being assertive:

STEP 1

Say how you feel about the problem

'I feel................'

STEP 2

Say what the problem is

'When you.............'

STEP 3

Say what you'd prefer to happen

'I'd prefer it if............'

Encourage your child to practise being assertive during a role play with you or another family member. The role play may be re-enacting the argument they had, or it could be a new scenario such as:

> *Your parents buy you and your sister an iPod to share. Your sister tells you that she can use it during the week and you can have it on weekends. That means she gets it for 5 days a week and you only get it for 2.*

C. How to handle bullying

If you were ever bullied in school, you may remember being given advice 'Oh, just ignore them'. Perhaps you have given this advice to your child. **Ignoring the bully does not work**. Your child needs to learn other ways to stop the bullying happening.

Showing the bully that your child doesn't care (although of course inside they most definitely do) is important. Together, come up with a list of responses of minimal but strong words to use as a 'come back' to any verbal bullying. For example, statements like:

- I don't care

- Whatever

- Grow up

- Who cares?

Teach them about showing strong, controlled body language. This means head up, shoulders back, straight back, firm voice and eye contact. You may like to practice this at home where you role play giving them a mean comment, to which they must respond strongly and confidently.

Talk about where they could go at school when they are feeling threatened and afraid. Perhaps there is an office they could go to? Or to other people/friends in their class? Ideally, teach your child that being somewhere alone is not a good idea, particularly if they are victims of physical bullying and could be found and attacked, with no one to defend them.

As a parent, practically speaking, you should:

- Remain calm.

- Record your child's reports of instances of bullying including times and dates.

- Make an appointment to meet with the school head teacher. The head teacher obviously has the most influence and control over how the school reacts to bullying. The head teacher is responsible for disseminating the policy, procedure and reaction to all other staff at the school.

- At the meeting, calmly explain your concerns, giving specific times and dates when the bullying took place.

- During the meeting, agree a plan of action that the school will take to keep your child safe. You could ask for greater supervision at school particularly at break times.

- Ensure someone at the meeting is documenting the actions of the meeting and that all attendees are given a copy following the meeting.

- If the bullying continues, meet with the head teacher again to reaffirm that action should be taken.

- The school have a responsibility to react even if the bullying occurs on the journey to or from school. However, if they don't, you have the right to contact the police, especially where physical bullying is involved.

7. Family/networks

a) Model positive social skills

You are a very important role model for your child and your child will learn an immense amount of information through just watching you. This means you have to show all the important social skills that you would like your child to learn. For example, when talking to your child and to others, ensure you make good, effective eye contact. Greet people appropriately and put away your phone when you are doing it!

b) School considerations

Linking in with school is important, regardless of the friendship issue. If your child is having trouble making friends, a teacher can help to 'socially engineer' an association between your child and another peer, similar perhaps in age and interests. Meet with the teacher once a month to talk about what positive social behaviours you would like to try and increase at school and home, and set up a reward system between both settings. Your child can receive a tick/sticker on the chart every time they show this particular chosen social behaviour at school which adds up to a pre-discussed and agreed treat for your child. Each week, it is best to change the social behaviour that they need to show to get the reward, and also change the reward itself so to keep motivation high. If your child is really struggling at break time, talk to the teacher about having a 'coach' or 'supervisor' during these times, who can watch over your child, guide them towards peers they might consider initiating a friendship with and be on hand to give feedback and facilitate any issue that may arise.

c) School reaction to bullying

Especially when it comes to bullying, schools have a responsibility to react and respond. Schools should:

- Take reports of bullying seriously
- Take action to deal with the bullying
- Implement a school Anti Bullying Policy
- Make sure the Anti Bullying Policy is being implemented by all school staff
- Be aware of their legal responsibility to implement and monitor the Anti Bullying Policy

The school needs to show a 'united front' and zero tolerance when it comes to bullying to provide a culture at school that any sort of bullying will not be accepted. This starts from the top, the head teacher, who should have a clear direction and vision for keeping bullying to a minimum at school.

It may seem that your child has a lot to work on, but change takes time and effort. Therefore, let's think about what to work on first so that change doesn't feel so overwhelming.

When a problem seems quite overwhelming, we can all fall into the trap of setting general, often vague goals which just aren't helpful. Instead, let's set some specific targets that you can work towards. If we keep them simple and small, we will be able to see when we have met the goals and even small changes that have occurred.

Ask your child to think of goals, and you should too. Number them according to priority. Does your list of goals match that of your child's?

My Goals	My Child's Goals
1	1
2	2
3	3
4	4
5	5

Remember in the 'Understand' section, you wrote down a list of specific difficulties that you want to help your child with. Now, think about what strategies you will use to work on these goals:

1. _____

2. _____

3. _____

4. _____

5. _____

Do you see any challenges with the strategies you have decided to use? Perhaps you need to recruit other members of the family or involve your child's teacher at school to help?

Let's think through our case examples to see what their parents planned and tried:

Thomas, aged 7 years.

Relevant Issues	What are the issues?	Ideas to try
Developmental	Delayed skills in: - Expectations/knowledge of friendships - What is a friend - Conversation skills - Joining in with groups - Managing playdates	- Simple education about 'what is a friend' - Poster of friendly vs. unfriendly behaviour - How to greet new friends - What to say/questions to ask (through role plays) - Write down 3 possible topics of conversation that he may have with a new friend - Practice role plays for joining in the group games
Personality	Inhibited personality/naturally wary of any social interaction	- Give more encouragement for him to socialise - Offer rewards as an incentive to get him motivated to try - Enrol him in a structured after school club, 'Bug Club', which she knew he'd enjoy so he could meet others with the same interest
Neurological	Mum wasn't concerned	Not addressed
Cognitive	Thomas wasn't able to identify any thoughts	Not addressed

Relevant Issues	What are the issues?	Ideas to try
Behaviour	- Avoids playdates - Avoids parties	- Thomas and mum creates a 'hierarchy' with parties at the top - Each step on the hierarchy represented something that he had avoided - Slowly he works through the stages with reinforcement and reward from mum - When Thomas finally agreed to having a playdate, he starts with it at home. Before his friend arrived, Thomas and mum agreed what activities they could do, therefore structuring the date. Mum agreed to keep the playdate short and remained nearby so that she could facilitate if problems arose
Family/systemic networks	- Mum accepted that he is just shy - School haven't intervened yet	- Mum to reflect on her expectations for Thomas and believe that he is capable of changing his social behaviour - Mum to realise that boys and girls are different, and Thomas might not want to talk to his peers as much as a girl might - Mum talked to the school about them supporting Thomas' social skills. Each week, she emailed through a different 'goal' for him to work on during break time and the playground staff facilitated this. Each time he showed a particular skill, he got a sticker on his chart and a reward from his mum at the end of the day

Maggie, aged 10 years.

Relevant Issues	What are the issues?	Ideas to try
Developmental	Wanting to be accepted by peers Rejected/bullied by peers	Normalise, support and empathise Develop resilience and optimism
Personality	Inhibited personality	Mum to reflect on her expectations for Maggie's friendships. - Given Maggie's temperament and age, her relationships are generally normative and as expected. - Maggie's reaction to the bullies mimics her natural tendency to pull away from social situations especially if they get tough. - Put Maggie in control of what she wants from her friendships (don't push to take control from her)
Neurological	Mum wasn't concerned	Not addressed
Cognitive	I've got no friends It's my fault that this is happening to me	- Help her consider evidence that people do like her and that she has many other friends - Challenge thoughts with questions to help break down their validity - Increase Maggie's time spent enjoying the things she likes e.g. interests - Encourage Maggie to write down things that she likes about herself, perhaps even keep a compliments diary. Write down 'evidence' for each positive quality

MAGGIE, *CONTINUED.*

Relevant Issues	What are the issues?	Ideas to try
Behaviour	Avoids going to after school clubs Spends time alone at break time	- Encourage her to try and go back to an after school club. Perhaps there is a new one she would like to try - Encourage her to seek out new people at school to associate with - Map out her body symptoms in reaction to the bullying. Teach her Balloon Breathing and Relaxation to deal with the emotions in the here and now - Teach her assertive body language and key phrases to say when the girls call her names
Family/systemic networks	No response from school regarding the bullying as yet	- Maggie's mum to arrange to meet with the head teacher to discuss bullying and their response to it

Here's a chart for you to start filing in
to help you to energise into action!

Relevant Issues	What are the issues?	Ideas to try
Developmental		
Personality		
Neurological		
Cognitive/ thoughts		
Behaviour		
Family/systemic networks		

Let's take stock of how things are going so far. Give yourself at least a month of trying various different friendship skills strategies and then ask yourself the following questions:

- What went well?

- What didn't go so well?

- What strategies will you continue to use/practise?

- Which strategies might you stop using altogether? Which need "tweaking"?

The table below will help you to reflect on all that you have tried so far:

What social skill am I hoping to develop/support change in my child?	What have I tried?	How did my child react to what we tried?	How do I feel about what we tried?

Perhaps you feel that you and your child have made great progress with their social skills and/or friendship issue. However, you may reflect that things haven't changed much.

It may be helpful to refer back to the **Understand** section to make sure you have considered all angles of the problem. It may be that you have missed something, and perhaps a different plan should be considered.

Perhaps your child hasn't responded well to you in particular being the one to help them with their friendship issue or their social skills. Many children don't like the feeling of being 'taught' something by their parents and might not listen to them. 'Oh mum, I don't want to talk about that anymore'; sound familiar? If so, it would be helpful to enlist the help of key members of staff in your child's school such as a teaching assistant or a favourite teacher. Discuss with them your concerns and key areas where you feel your child needs support, and share this chapter with them to consider particular strategies and ideas that may help. The staff may be able to work with them at break times, perhaps even in the playground, facilitating the use of key skills in situations as they arise. They may be able to offer specific social skills groups or lessons to help also.

If you feel that the help you have provided, and perhaps school has provided too, have not made a difference in your child's life, it would be worth considering the help of a professional such as a clinical psychologist. They would be able to work with your child around particular friendship skills, teaching key skills and strategies to cope, as well as exploring and supporting the impact of these issues on the child's emotional world. An independent child psychology service, such as Everlief (our clinic in Buckinghamshire) will also be able to support children with anxiety. You can find independent child clinical psychologists by looking at the British Psychological Society's "Find a Psychologist" page: http://www.bps.org.uk/bpslegacy/dcp, or by searching on the ACHiPPP (Association for Child Psychologists in Private Practice) website: https://www.achippp.org.uk/directory.

References

Dunn Buron, K. & Curtis, M. (2012). *The Incredible 5-Point Scale*. AAPC.

Gray, C. (1994). *Comic Strip Conversations*. Jenison Public Schools.

Stallard, P. (2002) *Think Good-Feel Good: A Cognitive Behaviour Therapy Workbook for Children and Young People*. Wiley.

Further Reading

Alexander, J. (2006). *Bullies, Bigmouths, and So called Friends*. Hodder Children's Books.

Brown, L. K., & Brown, M. (1998). *How to be a friend*. Little, Brown, and Company.

Carter, M., & Santomauro, J. (2010). *Friendly Facts*. AAPC Publishing.

Diamond, D. (2011). Social Rules for Kids. AAPC Publishing.

Elman, N. M., & Moore, E. K. (2004). *The Unwritten Rules of Friendship*. Little, Brown, and Company.

Mayer, C. (2008) *Making Friends*. Raintree.

Meiners, C. J. (2003). *Share and Take Turns*. Free Spirit Publishing.

Meiners, C. J. (2004). *Join in and Play*. Free Spirit Publishing.

Rubin, K. (2002). *The Friendship Factor*. Skylight Press.

Schroeder, A. (2008). *The Friendship Formula*. LDA.

Shea, D. & Brigg, N. (2010). *How to make and keep friends*. Createspace Independent Publishing Platform.

Winner, M. G., & Crooke, P. (2010). *You are a social detective; Explaining social thinking to kids.* North River Press Publishing.

Self-Esteem
Building your child's confidence in a challenging world
Nicola Gorringe, clinical psychologist

"I don't think I can do that."

Alisha, aged 9.

Thinking back to when I first had my children, I clearly remember making a wish – I wished for each of them to be happy, confident and healthy. I know that is what we all want for our children: we have hopes and dreams for their futures and want the very best for them. We most likely all hope our beautiful babies will grow up to be happy, confident, sociable and successful. We want them to feel good about themselves. We want them to feel positive and optimistic and know they can achieve anything if they want to – in brief, we want them to develop confidence and have a strong, positive belief in themselves as individuals.

Yet the sad reality is this; one of the most common concerns parents express is the worry that their child has low self-esteem. Parents may notice their child seems anxious, or low in mood and energy, or easily upset and angered, or is having difficulties at school or with friendships. Whatever signs of unhappiness are apparent, parents will nearly always say "She has no confidence", or "What can I do to build her self-esteem?" or "He just doesn't believe in himself".

What is going wrong?

Over the past two to three decades there has been a huge focus on promoting self-esteem in the western world. Schools have developed numerous targeted programmes to boost self-esteem; children are helped by psychologists and counsellors, with the aim of building up confidence and as parents we have encouraged, praised and "bigged-up" our children's achievements in an attempt to help them feel good about themselves. We try to support our children when they do something, praising them, telling them they are clever or funny or sporty. Often children are praised for very little – even the tiniest achievement is applauded and celebrated, and we constantly try to tell our children how great they are. Our attempts to stop children losing confidence have even extended to the school sports day, where many schools don't reward winners, but applaud everyone equally for taking part.

We also try hard to protect our children when they struggle or don't do well at something. It is natural to feel upset with teachers when our children get told off for misbehaving, or worry about them if they get anxious about an upcoming test, or sad following an argument with friends. When these things happen, we generally want our children to stop feeling unhappy and are keen to sort out the problem. We might tell them their friends are in the wrong, or speak with their teacher or finish their homework for them – all with the aim of helping them feel better. Most of us find it really painful to see our children upset and we try very hard to protect them, solve their problems and build them back up.

This is very natural and certainly feels like the obvious and right thing to do. However, it is very interesting to look at the research. It seems that ever since we have been consciously trying to improve our children's self-esteem in this way, we have never had so many children experiencing anxiety, depression and feelings of low self-worth. It really has become a big problem. Research clearly identifies that children and teenagers are suffering with increased feelings of low self-esteem, and we are often made aware of this in the news. Over recent years, scientists and psychologists have been trying to work out why this should be.

Many people now think that although it is absolutely right to want our children to feel positive about themselves, and it is certainly right for parents to support and help children cope with the challenges they face, trying to boost self-esteem in this rather "false" way has come at an unintended price. Professor Martin Seligman is one of the leading experts and writers in this area. His research has led him to turn our thinking and understanding on its head. He thinks that one of the reasons our attempts to boost self-esteem has been unhelpful stems from the fact that we have prioritised "how children **feel** over what they **do**." (Seligman 2007)

In other words, we have tried too hard to protect children from experiencing negative feelings or having negative experiences while *at the same time*, we have not sufficiently focussed on what our children are actively *doing* or learning from their experiences. Professor Seligman suggests that in protecting our children from difficult situations and feelings, we have hindered their ability to learn how to cope with challenges and left them feeling under-equipped to handle life's ups and downs. Paradoxically, our children have never had it so good or so easy, yet they seem to feel more powerless and less confident than ever.

So, it seems that low self-esteem is a pervasive problem in the western world. Despite all our efforts to support and nurture, praise and reward, many children seem to struggle to develop confidence, and many of their social, emotional and behavioural problems are attributed to having low self-esteem.

In this chapter I have summarised what the current experts and practicing psychologists are now thinking about self-esteem and give you some ideas to help your children develop a healthy view of themselves and their place in the world. For those of you who are interested to read about this in more depth, there are some really great books around. Two of the main game changers in this field are Professor Martin Seligman and Dr Carol Dweck, who go into much more detail in their respective books. I have recommended some further reading at the end of this book for those of you who are keen to know more.

First, some interesting ideas

I mentioned earlier that we all try to help our children feel good about themselves. We praise when they do well, encourage them to love themselves (we've all heard the phrase "you can't love others until you love yourself"), we try not to criticise them, protect them as much as possible from experiencing failure and are very quick to sort out their problems or take them out of a difficult situation. Compare this to the way our grandparents and parents were raised – you have probably heard stories of them being left to their own devices all day. Grandparents often recall going out in the morning with a crust of bread and an apple, aged 5, and coming home for tea. Our grandparents or great-grandparents would most likely not have known what their children were doing or where they were. Children certainly didn't get lots of praise and attention, and no one worried much about children's feelings.

It was a very different time, and I am certainly **not** saying we should go back to that kind of fairly passive (even neglectful) parenting, or that we shouldn't praise and encourage our children. However, we do know there is something about the kinds of things we are doing now that seems to be having a negative impact on our children's well-being, and there is something about what happened to our parents and grandparents that meant they seemed to have had fewer emotional problems like depression, and appeared to be happier.

If we look at the effect of our modern parenting strategies, we can see a number of unintended problems that might occur when we try to directly "fix" or "boost" self-esteem by trying to protect our children from feeling bad.

The table opposite shows how our efforts may unintentionally backfire.

Parenting Strategy	Unintended Problems
1. Giving constant praise for very little achievement or effort	1. Self-esteem is based on nothing real and children may feel a "fraud". Deep down they don't really believe they are worthy of the praise. 2. Children become overly reliant on how they are viewed by others and may need constant rewards or praise to feel good about themselves. 3. Children may assume they don't have to try to earn respect or praise and so they don't learn to try hard. They think it is their right. 4. When they don't receive praise for something, they may feel quite upset and angry.
2. Protecting our children from constructive criticism	1. Any negative comments feel a huge deal. 2. Children become highly sensitive to even slight criticism and can't cope with it. 3. Children don't know how to put things in perspective, or learn and grow from healthy feedback.
3. Protecting our children from ever experiencing failure	1. Children find failure unbearable, as they have not learned ways to cope with it. 2. They avoid doing things they might fail at and so won't challenge themselves. 3. Children give up easily when things get difficult.
4. Focussing too much on "self-love" and "self-importance"	1. Children may develop an overly inflated view of themselves, which easily bursts with the harsher realities of life. 2. There is a risk of extreme self-centredness – putting oneself first at the expense of loving relationships with others. 3. Selfishness can make secure and loving relationships more difficult, thereby increasing insecurity and feelings of isolation. 4. Children can develop fixed ideas about themselves (e.g. sporty, clever, beautiful), which may not be helpful or accurate.
5. Taking over and solving their problems for them rather than with them	1. Children don't learn the skills to fight their own battles and have to rely on others. 2. They don't develop confidence to try things on their own. 3. They may lack confidence in dealing with situations they are unfamiliar with. 4. They may blame others for things that go wrong and find it hard to take responsibility for their own actions. 5. They may expect and assume others will do everything for them.

It is counter-intuitive, but attempts to boost self-esteem by constantly praising, protecting from negative experiences and telling children they are the centre of the universe may be having an unintentional negative impact. It may be causing the very problems we are trying to solve. It is interesting that when I ask parents why they think their child has low self-esteem, they will often say things like "he gives up easily" or "she's not confident trying new things" or "he is very sensitive to criticism" (in fact, many of the things in the unintended problems column).

To summarise

It seems that by trying to protect our children from negative feelings and experiences, we may be preventing them from developing a number of crucial skills that are necessary to cope in the world. It is the experience of *coping, persevering, overcoming and mastering difficult situations,* that is the basis of *real* and **enduring** confidence. Psychologists and scientists are now beginning to look more closely at the underlying skills that are necessary for people to develop confidence and have a true and *accurate* sense of their abilities and their worth. They are moving away from general and complicated ideas like "Self-Esteem" and thinking more about concepts like **competence, resilience and optimism, in the context of secure and loving relationships.**

Psychologists think that a large part of self-esteem or confidence comes from a combination of these three ideas:

Competence: *How skilled and effective a person perceives him/ herself to be in a particular situation.*

Children need to develop feelings of competence in different areas of life (that might be sport, creative writing, making friends, cooking, art – in fact any area of life). People are not generally good at everything, but as long as we feel sufficiently competent in a number of different areas of life, we usually feel okay about our ability to function in the world.

Resilience: *The ability to adapt successfully in the face of life's challenges.*

Children need help to develop resilience so that they can cope with life's ups and downs, understand the importance of persevering and know how to "get back in the saddle" when things go wrong, without seeing difficulties as a reflection on their own value or self-worth.

Optimism: *The tendency to be hopeful that difficult situations can have a positive outcome.*

Children need to develop a sense of optimism. This refers to the way they think about and make sense of situations, including difficult challenges in their lives. It means helping your child recognise the positive aspects of a situation rather than focussing only on the bad, developing a belief that with hard work and determination, they can improve or change a situation, as well as believing that things are more likely to go well than not (this is not the same as just thinking positive thoughts, which I will explain later on).

It is also helpful to remember that people develop confidence in different ways. We all have completely different temperaments, strengths and weaknesses. It is unrealistic to think that anyone, adult or child, is confident in all circumstances. Some situations are more of a challenge to some than others. For example, a child who is naturally rather quiet and doesn't like to be the centre of attention may be labelled under-confident, when they may be perfectly confident in many other aspects of their personality. Similarly, someone who is happy to stand on stage and perform, may not be confident in other situations. What's important is gradually helping our children to work out who they are, what they enjoy, how to keep learning and growing and how to feel comfortable about their place in the world despite life's ups and downs.

It is also important to accept that growing up involves many, many changes and challenges. It is perfectly normal and healthy for children to go through both over confident and under confident phases. When a child begins to show under confidence in most areas of life, stops trying and believes they can't change things for the better, they may be genuinely struggling and need help. Dr Russell's 5th fundamental principle from the introduction is helpful to remember here: Problems are normal and great for a child's development. Don't always assume a wobble is a general problem with self-esteem. Remember confidence develops gradually, and it is unreasonable (and actually unhealthy) to expect children to feel supremely confident. Most adults will remember feeling under confident in many situations as teenagers, but with experience, determination and perseverance, as well as love and support from family and friends, most adults have found things they feel more or less confident in. This is normal and healthy.

Hold these ideas in mind while you think about how this might relate to your own child. The next section will help you to think more clearly about your particular concerns and identify some ways to help your child begin to build real inner confidence.

SPELL IT OUT

If you are worried that your child is lacking confidence or seems to have low self-esteem, spend a moment thinking about exactly what concerns you.

"Self-esteem" and "confidence" are a bit too general. We need to think about what we are seeing in our children that is making us worry, so we can pin down more clearly what the real problem is.

In clinic, when I ask parents why they think their child has low self-esteem, they will often say things like:

- "he won't try anything new", or
- "he gives up as soon as it gets tough", or
- "he's so self-conscious, he takes everything personally".

Have a go at describing exactly:

1. What your child does (describe their behaviour) and

2. What your child says and thinks (listen to the words they say)

You may find that there are a number of different things that your child does. That's okay, you can write them all down and it will help you decide what you want to work on first.

Here are some common difficulties that spell out the problem and may indicate feelings of low self-esteem:

Common difficulties might include:

☑ My child can't take a compliment – he never believes them.

☑ Even though he does well, he still thinks he's no good.

☑ My child is always worried about what others think of him.

☑ My child can't cope with criticism.

☑ My child over-reacts if I say anything negative.

☑ My child gets really upset if she makes a small mistake.

☑ My child avoids doing things that might be difficult.

☑ My child gives up if he can't do something first time.

☑ My child thinks everyone is against him/her.

☑ My child doesn't think she is good at anything.

☑ My child is very hard on herself.

Meet Harry and Belinda below. They will help you to see how to put the ideas that follow into practice, so you can try it with your own children.

Harry, aged 9 years.

Harry is 9 years old, and when he was very little he showed a keen interest and ability for football. Harry joined the school football team when he was in Year 1, and over the next few years, was often captain of the team and would win "Man of the Match" quite regularly. He loved playing football. However, when a new teacher took over football practice in Year 4, Harry seemed to lose his confidence very quickly. His new coach was much stricter, and challenged Harry's skills with some complicated drills and practice exercises. Harry told his mum he didn't like football because he wasn't any good at it. When his mum disputed this, Harry said that the drills were too hard and his coach was always telling him he should practice more. Harry said that he obviously wasn't as good as everyone thought and didn't want to go anymore. He was very down and hard on himself, and it really seemed to knock his confidence. His parents couldn't understand why he gave up so easily when he was one of the best players, and why his confidence was so low when he had experienced so many successes in the past.

In this example, it would be accurate to say that *Harry gave up easily when things got hard. He says and thinks he's not as good as everyone thinks he is.*

Belinda, aged 11 years.

Belinda is 11 years old. She has always been a capable girl, and her teachers would describe her as friendly and pleasant. Recently her parents have noticed that she is being more critical of herself. She is quite easily upset, and anything her parents say to her is interpreted as a criticism. Belinda has started to say things like: "I hate my nose" and "I'm fat" as well as "no one likes me". She is actually perfectly pretty and has some nice friends, but no one can convince her of this. Belinda has started to avoid going out with friends, and when she does, she seems convinced that people are criticising and judging her harshly.

In this example, it would be helpful to say that *Belinda is worried that others will think badly of her and doesn't want to go out as much. Also, Belinda is very critical of herself. She says she doesn't like the way she looks.*

Now you have a clearer description of what your child does, you will

1. know exactly what you are going to try and change, and

2. have a better idea of whether your child is improving following your support.

The next step is to start understanding the reasons **why** your child is struggling so you know what to do to help. In Harry's example, **why** has his confidence been knocked despite all of his early success? Why is he prepared to give up football when he has always loved it so much?

This is the time to work out what might be causing this behaviour and you need to look underneath the behaviour to think about what might have led your child to behave and think like this as well as what could make them continue to behave and think like this.

In Belinda's case, **why** has she started to feel bad about herself, and **why** is she struggling to believe she is likeable and pretty?

Now, consider your child's difficulties from each of the different psychological perspectives outlined in the introductory chapter: Attachment and Developmental Stage, Brain development, Cognitive (thoughts), Behavioural, and "Whole Family" perspectives. Are there particular issues within each of these areas that might be contributing to your child's current lack of confidence?

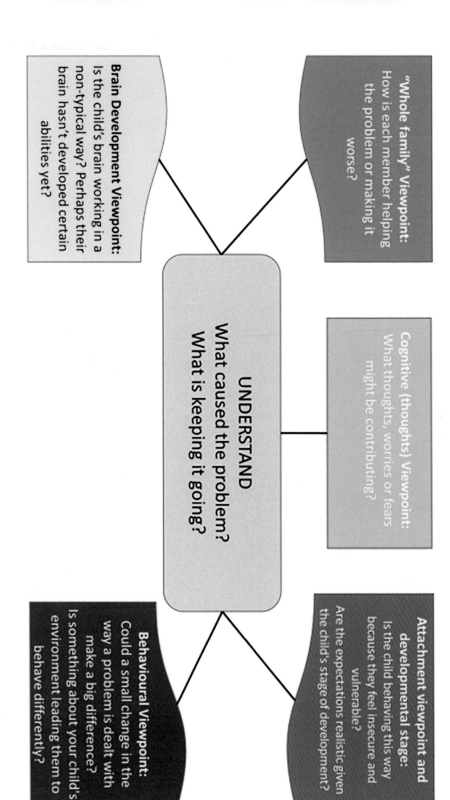

"Whole family" Viewpoint: How is each member helping the problem or making it worse?

Brain Development Viewpoint: Is the child's brain working in a non-typical way? Perhaps their brain hasn't developed certain abilities yet?

UNDERSTAND
What caused the problem?
What is keeping it going?

Cognitive (thoughts) Viewpoint: What thoughts, worries or fears might be contributing?

Attachment viewpoint and developmental stage: Is the child behaving this way because they feel insecure and vulnerable?
Are the expectations realistic given the child's stage of development?

Behavioural Viewpoint: Could a small change in the way a problem is dealt with make a big difference? Is something about your child's environment leading them to behave differently?

1. Developmental stages

It is helpful to remember that there are lots of normal challenges and changes that occur throughout childhood as brains and bodies develop and children have new experiences and begin to think differently. All changes cause a wobble in confidence (think about yourself when you start a new job, move to a new area etc.). With time and support, children usually work out how to adapt and overcome these normal stages, but sometimes they may need a little help from you.

Consider these developmental questions when thinking about your child's self-esteem:

a) Are you expecting too much?

Sometimes we expect a lot from our children, and forget they may not have developed the skills or understanding necessary to cope with the demands we are placing on them. If we are expecting too much, then our children will also have unrealistic expectations for themselves and feel they are missing the mark. This is different from setting your sights high, which means working towards an end goal, with realistic small steps on the way to reaching it. Expecting too much means expecting them to be doing more, or doing better than they are ready or able to do right now. Think realistically about what is reasonable *for your child*. Give them opportunities to develop feelings of competence, but let them develop at their own pace. Go to the section on developing competence if you think your child is struggling to meet your expectations.

b) Are there any developmental changes going on that are normal for their age?

I have summarised below some of the developmental changes that occur in the primary school years.

- It is normal for children aged 7-10 to develop new and unexpected fears about the world as they begin to understand the news and understand more about the dangers in the world. Typical fears include worries about family members' health, burglars, fire, illness and war. If they are a little fearful at this age, and reluctant to go to sleep with the door shut, or express a lot of worries about the world, this is not necessarily a lack of confidence. It is completely normal, and your child probably just needs some gentle handling and support to cope with their worries. See the chapter on anxiety for more help with this if you think their fears are getting out of hand.

- Girls especially (but also boys) often go through a naturally difficult stage with friends in Year 5 and 6. They are developing their opinions and discriminate between the people they do and don't like. Consider this a normal stage, and try not to get too involved. Let them try and solve disputes themselves. They will benefit hugely from dealing with difficulties without your obvious intervening. In these cases, it is much more helpful to support them indirectly by encouraging them to develop resilience and optimism (Go to these sections to read more about this). If the problem does not resolve and your child is increasingly unhappy, or you suspect real targeted bullying, you should speak with the class teacher, and have a look at chapter 2 on developing friendships.

- It is also very normal in the latter primary school years for children to develop a better sense of their own identity as they begin to understand their strengths and their weaknesses, their personal qualities and their physical traits. They naturally start comparing themselves with their peers. Help them understand that everyone develops differently and has different strengths and talents. Read the section on developing a Growth Mindset in the resilience section below to learn how to help them keep trying, even if they are finding things hard.

- Many girls have a surge of oestrogen as they begin puberty around the age of 9-10, often causing a short-term weight-gain, and of course mood-swings. They may need reassurance that this is normal and that they will grow out of it (unless your child is overweight due to unhealthy eating and low exercise levels). Let them know that it is part of growing up, and that you know it is not their fault that they feel tearful for no reason. This is well-known in the teens, but the first pubertal changes usually occur in the last couple of primary school years and often take parents by surprise.

- Rapid physical changes also lead to tiredness, irritability, increased hunger and clumsiness. Clumsiness is often forgotten, but when your feet or legs grow, it is hard to judge exactly where they are. Remember what it's like to put a new pair of shoes on, perhaps with a pointy toe. You will often trip over the ends a little until you get used to them. Your growing children can go through clumsy phases, and temporarily find activities more difficult – normalise, explain, support and accept this. Ensure they get plenty of sleep and rest, and eat a healthy diet.

- Pubertal changes may occur very early for some children – this may mark them out as different from their peers (some girls may develop breast tissue early and start periods in year 5 or 6, or boys may grow facial hair). More often it is subtle, and you only see the emotional fallout. This is normal, but they will need reassurance and understanding, and they will benefit from developing resilience and optimism.

- Other children may be slower to develop, and seem more immature or less independent than others. Again, this is temporary, as children generally catch up and your job is to help them build some resilience so they can cope with the difficult feelings, and optimism so they know and understand that it is temporary.

These are some of the normal variations in children's developmental pathways. Help them develop an understanding about what is happening to them, cut them a little slack and focus on developing their resilience and optimism.

c) Is your child at a natural transition or change point?

This will knock their confidence for a little while and is again perfectly normal (e.g. change of class teacher, moving up into a harder class with older or different children, change of school, getting used to more demands). Every time your child faces a new challenge, they have new things to learn, there are new expectations and they have moved out of their comfort zone. The key is to recognise that they are going through a transitional period, and help them to stay optimistic, be resilient and continue to develop their competence.

What developmental issues might be relevant for Harry and Belinda?

Belinda, aged 11 years.

In Belinda's case, she is just moving into puberty and has possibly put on a little weight before she grows. She is also likely to feel quite sensitive and emotional, and she is at the stage where girls can be quite unkind to each other. She is also facing a move up to secondary school. There are lots of developmental reasons why Belinda might be struggling at this point. Her parents need to be sensitive and supportive, but they can't take all her worries away – instead they need to help her to cope better with what is happening.

Harry, aged 9 years.

Harry is struggling to cope with new challenges that are different from before. He has a new teacher who perhaps hasn't yet acknowledged he knows Harry is good at football. Harry is missing his old teacher, with whom he had a strong and positive relationship. He is angry and sad that his old teacher has gone. His new teacher has a different approach, and is developing skills that are new for Harry. He isn't automatically good at them, as he has never done them before. It is natural that Harry would be feeling a little wobbly and lose some confidence, but Harry is finding it more difficult because he has never had to cope with not doing well before. Harry needs help to develop his resilience and belief that with hard work and practice, he will overcome this wobble.

2. Neurological (Brain Development) Differences

Although there are typical stages of development, children are unique and have their own individual strengths and weaknesses. Many children have specific "neurodevelopmental" difficulties or differences that make some aspects of school and home life much more challenging for them and it is always worth considering whether your child might be struggling in this way. Sometimes these are just slight developmental differences and time will help them catch up, but for others, these kinds of difficulties may be having more of an impact than you realise. Consider whether there are any issues of brain development that might be having an impact on your child's ability to keep up in class, or experience competence and success in different areas of their life. I have outlined some of the things that can be quite common, and if you think your child has some unrecognised needs like these, you should speak first with your child's teacher or your GP to discuss potential assessment and more specific ways of supporting them.

Neurodevelopmental issues that can make things harder for children include:

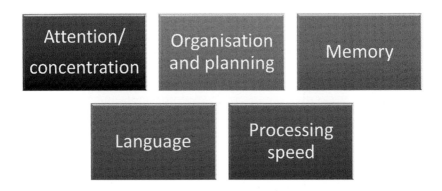

If you think your child has any of these kinds of difficulties, your role is to help your child understand him/herself better by talking about their strengths as well as the reason they find some things difficult. They may need appropriate supports in place to help them. You can refer to the chapter on concentration and focus (chapter 6) for more ideas of how to support your child in this way. Your role is then to help them cope with these difficulties by teaching them to persevere, praising effort and determination rather than achievement, and teaching them optimism. Ensure they experience a wide range of activities and interests to find their strengths and help them develop competence in areas outside school. This will protect them from feeling they are struggling in all areas of life.

3. Cognitive or Thinking Styles

When things go wrong or we face challenges in life, we have to find a way to make sense of them, and we tell ourselves a story about what and why things happen. This section will help you begin to understand the way your child thinks about things when they face difficulties. Listen to the things they say to get an idea of how they currently think when they are struggling with a particular challenge. Help them to tell you what they are thinking when things go wrong by talking with them and being interested in their views or thoughts about what happened.

Not only does our thinking have an impact on how we understand what happens in our lives, but it also affects how we choose to face a challenge, and it has a huge impact on our mood. For example, if we tend to think everything always goes wrong for us, we will feel sad and hopeless and probably won't think it is worth trying very hard. Whereas, if we think that with a bit of effort, we can improve and will probably enjoy it, we will be more likely to give things a go and experience some level of enjoyment. You can see that the way you **think** changes the whole experience.

There are many different ways of thinking that can affect self-esteem, and you may have heard of Cognitive Behaviour Therapy (CBT), which was first introduced by Beck and Ellis in the 1970s. CBT aims to help people understand and challenge the unhelpful ways they have learned to think, which in turn helps them feel better and act in more helpful ways. There are many different ways of thinking that can keep children feeling sad and there are lots of self-help books that go into this in more detail. According to Professor Martin Seligman, there are 3 particular ways of thinking that are especially important in helping children cope with difficulties and develop optimistic ways of thinking. Check out whether your child regularly expresses these kinds of thoughts.

1. Blaming themselves when things go wrong:
"I'm such a loser"

The research suggests that children who feel bad about themselves have a higher tendency to automatically blame themselves, and will usually think a problem is due to something negative about them:

> *E.g. "I'm so stupid – I always mess up everything" or*
>
> *"Things always go wrong for me"*

This kind of thinking makes a difficult situation even more overwhelming and causes feelings of guilt, embarrassment and deep shame, all of which undermine confidence further. This does not mean it is helpful to blame others and not take responsibility for your own part in situations, but helping your child develop a balanced and accurate understanding of their role in a situation is the best way forward.

2. Thinking that nothing will change:
"What's the point, I'll never be able to do it"

This refers to the belief that when something goes wrong, you think it will always be that way and never change for the better.

> *E.g. "I am never going to be any good at maths" or*
>
> *"No one will ever like me"*

This style is unhelpful because it leads children to feel hopeless and stops them problem solving or persevering.

3. Making sweeping statements:
"Everyone always picks on me"

This is when a child tends to make very general statements about things.

> *E.g. "My teacher is mean" rather than sticking to something more accurate and specific like "My teacher shouts sometimes for no reason, but can sometimes be funny"*
>
> *Or: "I hate school" rather than "I don't like maths and science, but I have good friends and PE is okay"*
>
> *Or: " I always mess up" rather than " I didn't do very well in my spellings test"*

Sweeping statements make it hard to see the shades of grey in a situation. It is also sometimes called Black and White thinking. For example, your child might think they are "stupid" if they make a couple of mistakes, rather than recognising that everyone makes mistakes sometimes, or they only made 2 mistakes but got everything else right.

Look out for words like "*always*" and "*never*", and extremes such as "*rubbish*" "*loser*" "*hate*" as these words indicate your child is thinking in very black and white or sweeping terms.

What are your own thinking styles?

While you are thinking about the way your child views the world, don't forget to consider your own thinking styles! You might be surprised to find that your child is learning how to think about things from listening to and watching how you deal with and think about situations. One of the very important things you can do to help your child is to develop your own helpful thinking styles, and become more resilient and optimistic yourself. You are their role model.

How can we apply this to Harry and Belinda?
What thinking styles might be relevant for them?

Harry, aged 9 years.

Remember that Harry wants to give up going to football because he is finding the training hard. He is showing all styles of thinking if you listen carefully to what he says:

"I'm no good at football". In Harry's mind, it is a quality in him (being no good really) that explains why he is struggling at the moment.

He is also demonstrating his belief that it won't get any better – it is an unchangeable fact that he is no good. Finally, Harry is thinking in black and white when he states that the exercises are hard, he can't do any of them. If his mum were to speak to the coach, she may find that Harry continues to perform many tasks with skill and only a few are more difficult for him. Harry needs a way of helping him understand that just because he finds some of the exercises difficult, it doesn't mean he isn't good at football. It means he has some new skills to learn and with determination and perseverance, he can and will get better. He also has to learn that he won't always be the best at everything, but that doesn't mean he is no good.

Instead of saying "I couldn't do anything right", it is more helpful and accurate to say "I struggled when we had to shoot with our left foot, but I did fine when we were practicing tackling".

Harry's thinking styles are a big part of the reason why he has lost his confidence.

Belinda, aged 11 years.

In Belinda's case, her mum writes down the things she says.

"I'm fat and ugly". Being fat and ugly are statements about personal flaws. Being fat and ugly are also permanent statements – they don't give her much hope of change. Belinda's thinking styles are part of the reason why she is feeling so low about herself. "Everyone thinks I'm horrible" and "No one likes me" are generalisations as of course she has some friends and her family love her.

4. Behavioural

As well as considering your child's developmental stage and understanding more about how they think about difficult situations, it is important to consider whether there are well-learned behavioural patterns that your child gets stuck in each time a similar situation occurs. Behaviour refers to anything that someone DOES in response to something else. Remember that confidence is not only based on how you think and feel about problems, but also on your actual experience of DOING things.

Belinda, aged 11 years.

In Belinda's case, her mother notices that she is spending a lot of time fussing and worrying about her clothes and hair before she goes out. Belinda will not leave the house until she looks absolutely perfect. She is spending a lot of her time trying to look her best (behaviour). Belinda then goes out feeling as if she can cope. While this may seem like a solution, take a moment to think about the consequences of doing this. How might this behaviour help or hinder Belinda's self-esteem? In the short-term, it certainly helps her feel better, but she is learning that the only way she can face the world is if she is all dressed up. This means that she is not learning that people will treat her very similarly even if she wore more casual clothes and her hair wasn't so perfect. In the long-term, she will continue to feel underconfident without her "safety net" of looking perfect.

Another behaviour that Belinda does is that she tends to look tense and does not make any eye contact in case someone is looking at her. She is trying to avoid the uncomfortable feeling that she experiences when she thinks someone is thinking something bad of her. However, Belinda's lack of eye contact makes her look nervous and shy, so others may be more likely to judge her negatively.

In both these examples, Belinda's behaviour has the effect of stopping her having fun and getting to know people and maintaining her belief that she isn't popular or pretty enough.

Harry, aged 9 years.

If we think about Harry's behaviour, we can see a similar vicious cycle that keeps him feeling underconfident. Harry does not want to go to football because he is finding it hard to cope with the challenges his new teacher sets. At first his mum tries to convince him to keep going, but Harry is having none of it. He cries and begs mum not to take him. So mum is in a dilemma. She doesn't want Harry to have a difficult time and wants him to be happy. She decides to give him a few weeks off, hoping he will miss it and decide to try again later. This might work, however, there are also some potential problems. When Harry avoids facing his difficulties, he can never learn how to overcome them. Instead, Harry learns that if something is difficult, you don't have to do it. He is also left with the view that his new coach is horrible and that he is not very good at football after all. He cannot develop more confidence in his footballing ability by giving up. Most children do not go back, and if they do, it is likely to be another difficult experience and they certainly won't go back a second time.

Consider how your child's behaviour might keep them stuck and stop them from developing more confidence. You can see that little vicious cycles are easily set up.

When you next encounter the problem you have identified in the **SPELL IT OUT** section, take a moment to write down what your child actually does, how everyone else reacts to this and what happens in the end.

It is often helpful to split this into 4 different parts:

1. What seemed to start the problem?

2. What actually happened in the problem situation?

3. What happened next?

4. What do you think your child might be learning or not learning as a result of his behaviour and what happens in the end?

Once I have some ideas, I find it helpful to draw a simple flow chart or circle that shows what might be happening.

What starts the problem?
Won't go to football because it's too hard

What is the behaviour that you see?
Cries and refuses to join in

How does this help in the short term?
He feels happier because mum says he didn't have to do it

How does this hinder confidence in the larger term?
Doesn't learn that he could get better if he kept trying

This can be a difficult idea to get to grips with. Don't worry about getting an absolute right answer. Use it as a way of reflecting or thinking about the different ways your child's behaviour (and even your own responses) might be stopping your child from gaining confidence in the long-term. Particularly notice things that allow your child to avoid facing struggles either by getting someone else to do them, by avoiding them completely, or by using more subtle methods like Belinda (using safety strategies that mean she doesn't have to experience the struggle or fear directly).

It is also important to keep this in perspective – if, despite considerable efforts to support and keep going, your child is still very unhappy and hates an activity, it is most likely that they are not suited to it. Continuing to force them to take part is probably unhelpful in the longer term. You must use your judgement about how long you persevere and your understanding of why your child doesn't like it to help you decide whether and how to support your child. The main point here is that you a) try and understand and b) consider how your child's behaviour might be maintaining their difficulties.

5. Relationships

Children do not exist in a vacuum. They live in families, go to school, have friends, teachers and coaches that all contribute to and react to a child's behaviour.

If you are trying to understand the reasons why a child might be struggling to feel competent in different areas of their lives, or show resilience in the face of challenges or stay optimistic about the future, we need to consider whether anything about your child's pattern of relationships might be adding to the difficulties. This is often the hardest part for parents, as we are all doing the best we can, and the idea that we might be making the problem worse is hard to imagine. It is certainly worth remembering that it is not usually a parent or teacher's intention to cause more problems, but sometimes things get in the way without us realising.

Consider the Role of your relationship with your children

Researchers and therapists from many different approaches all agree that a fundamental building block for a confident child is the role that we, as parents, play in providing three key experiences at home. Three key ideas from the positive parenting, attachment theory and self-esteem literature include:

a) Feeling loved, accepted and approved of by your family.

This is not the same as giving your children what they want or accepting unacceptable behaviour. Instead it relates to the 3rd basic belief in Dr Lucy Russell's introductory Chapter. It is the strong bond you have with your child, expressed through affection, playful interactions, the time and interest you show in your children that tells them that you love them and they are lovable to you. It is this stable and "safe-base" that provides the foundations for our children to get out into the world and explore it. Without it, children will be overly focussed on their feelings of insecurity in their relationships with you, and will not be able to focus on the challenges of the world outside. They certainly won't be able to develop confidence when they are feeling insecure in their relationships with you.

b) The way you discipline and guide your children.

Research shows that discipline that is consistent, clearly and carefully explained so your child understands your perspective and the reasons why you are disciplining them helps the development of a positive self-esteem and builds positive relationships. On the other hand discipline based on coercion, shame, punishment and control undermines self-esteem and leads to poor relationships. Obviously, your explanations for your parenting guidance and boundaries need to adapt to your child's level of understanding, but the basic principle is that:

Your child should know what they are doing wrong and why you are telling them off or carrying through with a consequence, without being made to feel frightened, confused or humiliated by the consequences.

The reason this has such an impact on confidence is that it makes your child's world predictable and gives them some feelings of control over their lives. They can then choose how to behave knowing the rules. They also know that if they are in trouble, it is not because they are intrinsically "bad" or "naughty" but because they have "behaved" inappropriately. This is something they can choose to change rather than something they can't.

c) How much you involve your child in decisions and value their contributions to the family.

Children benefit hugely from feeling valued and important within your family unit. This helps them develop the belief that what they think and say is worthy of being listened to and that you respect their ideas and views, even if you don't always agree.

The research is clear that the most important thing for happiness and a positive self-belief is not self-love, but good stable relationships with parents or at least one main caregiver.

Involve and value your child's contribution in the family

Consistent, clear and fair discipline

Warmth, affection, acceptance, approval

Secure base

Below are some other things to consider when thinking about how your child's relationships with you and their other significant family members might impact their confidence.

- How secure do you think your child feels in their relationships with their main caregivers and wider family? Maybe there has been a recent family break-up, or a parent has started seeing a new partner. Has there been a bereavement or illness or financial worry recently? These will all affect how secure your child is feeling at the moment.

- What are the main messages you and others give your child about themselves, especially in situations of conflict and challenge? Do they hear fixed statements about their personality (you're lazy, naughty, argumentative, disrespectful, stupid) – we have all sometimes said things to a child in frustration that we are not proud of. Ask yourself in all honesty how often this happens and what the main message your child may have heard about him/herself is.

- When your child wobbles in confidence, what messages do they get about coping? How do you try to help them work through it? Some parents choose to solve the challenge for their child (e.g. if homework is too hard), and others let them avoid doing things they aren't confident to do. Or maybe you get frustrated and an argument ensues with everyone becoming very upset and angry. Do you and your child's other parent agree or disagree about how to deal with situations? Is there avoidance of difficulties, or does it create unresolved conflict and anger?

- Consider how the people close to your child react when they are feeling under-confident, or when something goes wrong, including yourself. Do they/you avoid situations or blame others, or work hard to overcome anxieties? Think about your own levels of confidence in different areas of your life. What is your child seeing and learning from those around him or her?

- Do you as a family solve problems together by discussing things openly, or do you or your partner only ever decide on the solution and then let your child know what they have to do? How much does your child learn about effective problem-solving and how much do you let them get involved in appropriate decisions that affect them? How much choice do you give them about their day to day decisions? How often do you ask their opinion or seek their understanding about a situation?

- How did your parents support you when you felt unsure or wobbly? What is the model that you learned, and how do you think this has helped or hindered your own confidence? What about others that are important to your child?

- How do you celebrate achievement in your family? Do you only recognise exceptional achievement (e.g. top grades) or do you praise for all achievements? Do you praise for effort and perseverance or only for actual achievement?

When you have thought about these issues, think about how they might help or hinder your child's confidence.

How might the issue of Relationships be relevant to Harry and Belinda?

Harry, aged 9 years.

In Harry's case, his dad tended to get angry when things didn't go well and he did the same when he found out Harry wasn't going to football anymore. Dad had really been proud of Harry's talent and he didn't want it to go to waste. He showed this by getting frustrated with Harry for refusing to go anymore, saying "you're just throwing away your opportunity" and "you're being a wimp". Harry's mum would try and protect him, which resulted in his parents arguing. Harry would feel even worse and blame the stupid teacher for everything. He didn't say it, but Harry felt his dad was disappointed that he wasn't as good at football as he had thought he was. Harry felt a failure. His mum continued to tell him he was a great footballer, and that the new teacher's methods were not very good. She would tell Harry that other children also found it hard with the new teacher in order to try and help him feel better. Deep down, Harry didn't really believe mum. He felt dad's disappointment and his own shame too deeply to believe mum's kind words. Harry decided to try and stop thinking about football because it made him feel too upset.

Belinda, aged 11 years.

Belinda had always had a difficult relationship with her mum. She felt that her mother favoured her brother for some reason. Whenever she and mum disagreed, there would always be a big row, which would end with Mum sending Belinda to her room saying things like "Get out of my face – I don't want to see you or hear you. You're driving me insane". When Belinda traded insults back, their row would escalate further and mum had, in her anger, said things like "You're so horrible, no wonder you don't have any friends!"

Although this sounds extreme, in the heat of the moment, it is easy to lose control and say awful things to each other. In Belinda's case, her rather insecure relationship with her mum often led her to feel angry and isolated. Deep down she felt she was not a nice person and she found it hard to believe that anyone would really like her if they knew what she was really like. Belinda's insecurity in her relationships at home was having a bit impact on her ability to cope with situations at school, and her confidence was really suffering.

6. Wider Environment

This section considers how the general and wider environment may be contributing to any difficulties with confidence, and refers to Dr Russell's fundamental principle that "Sometimes it is the environment that needs to change and not the child".

1. Consider whether there are factors in the immediate situation that are affecting your child's general mood and feelings about things.

- Are they feeling tired, hungry or overwhelmed by noise and people in certain environments? This will make them much more negative and less resilient than usual.

- Are they frequently faced with a sibling or friend who they are compared negatively to? Are they often undermined?

- Is the environment predictable and calm enough for them to know what is expected of them, are their efforts noticed and appreciated and not constantly overtaken by unpredictable events?

- Are they feeling safe and secure in their environment? Sometimes activities are poorly run, or beyond a child's developmental stage. If your child does not feel the environment is safe, predictable and manageable, they will hold back, and be reluctant to join in.

- Are they attending activities and events regularly enough to build confidence? Remember that skills building and competence grow from experiences of step-by-step success. If a child misses lessons, or there is an unstructured approach to learning, it will be much more difficult to build confidence since the foundations may not be firm.

- Are they doing too much for their current needs? None of us can function when we feel overloaded with new things to learn. Your child is already spending 6 hours a day in school and probably has homework. If they are also learning a musical instrument, a few sports, computer club, science club etc. they may just be feeling overwhelmed and stressed.

- Sometimes a particular adult or teacher is not right for your child's personality. Consider carefully whether trying a different teacher/club with a different approach might make a difference to your child's confidence. This applies to school and extra-curricular activities.

2. Is your child engaged in activities that nurture their natural interests and strengths?

- Sometimes parents are so keen to help their children learn and develop, they forget to think about what their child enjoys doing. Check your child really enjoys the extra-curricular activities they do, and that some of their spare time is spent doing things of their choosing rather than yours. We thrive when we do things that we love doing. Nurture your child's individual interests and strengths.

- In the same way as doing too much can be overwhelming, doing very little leaves children feeling unconnected and isolated. With the rise of technology and particularly TV, computers and game consoles, it is often easy to let your children stay home and play for hours. If we want our children to develop confidence, remember they have to **do** something. Sitting home most evenings and weekends in technological isolation will not enhance their confidence in themselves.

Children thrive when they feel connected to others, and are developing relationships and interests with like-minded people.

Reflect and Summarise

Now you have had some time to reflect on some of the underlying factors that could be contributing to your child's lack of confidence at the moment. You might find it helpful to fill out the following questionnaire to help you clarify what issues might be most relevant. Answer each question thoughtfully, using the ideas above to help guide you. You may find there is more than one area contributing to the problem, which is completely fine and very typical.

Relevant Issues	Helpful questions to consider	Y/N	what exactly do you see in your child?
Developmental	1. Are you expecting too much? 2. Are there any developmental changes that are normal for their age and stage? 3. Are there normal changes/ transitions coming up or occurring?		
Neurological	4. Does your child struggle more than expected with their concentration, memory or learning in school?		
Cognitive	5. Does your child often blame themselves when things go wrong? 6. Does your child seem to feel helpless or hopeless about changing things? Do they think nothing will ever change? 7. Does your child often make sweeping statements and use words like "Always", "Never", "Hate", "Loser" etc.?		
Behaviour	8. When struggling, does your child: a) avoid difficult situations? b) get you to do everything for them? c) seek a lot of reassurance? d) cry or meltdown? e) hide behind others? f) do unhelpful things that make them feel better? 9. What do you think your child is learning from this? 10. What is your child learning from you and others around him/her?		

Relevant Issues	Helpful questions to consider	Y/N	what exactly do you see in your child?
Relationships	11. Do you think your child feels secure in their relationship with you?		
	12. Do you regularly play with, show interest in and positive affection towards your child? Do you find time to be with and enjoy your child's company?		
	13. Is your discipline clear, predictable, fair and consistent?		
	14. Do you use threats, or guilt or shame to punish your children?		
	15. Do you think your children feel valued and important members of the family (are they often told to shut up, go away, not be so ridiculous etc.)?		
	16. Have there been changes in your family recently (break-ups, bereavements, illness)?		
	17. What messages do you think your child receives about him/herself?		
	18. How do you and any partners/family members respond when your child has a wobble?		
	19. How do you and other family members cope with your own wobbles?		
	20. Do you and your family often work together to solve difficulties?		
	21. When and how do you praise your children? Is it specific, for effort as well as achievement, and is it regular?		

Relevant Issues	Helpful questions to consider	Y/N	what exactly do you see in your child?
Environment	22. Is your child getting enough sleep and a good diet?		
	23. Is your child often with others who undermine them?		
	24. Is your child learning/growing in safe, calm and organised environments?		
	25. Do people notice your child's efforts or do they often get lost in the chaos?		
	26. Do they miss lots of lessons and therefore fall behind their friends?		
	27. Do you encourage them to practice and persevere in between activities?		
	28. Are they doing too much and are overwhelmed?		
	29. Are they doing too little (not engaged in much)?		
	30. Are you recognising and encouraging your child's natural strengths and talents?		
	31. Are your children engaged and connected with others outside the home?		

Consider the answers you gave. Hopefully you will now have some ideas about what might be underlying your child's current wobble in confidence and you may already have thought about some things you can do to support them.

This section should give you more practical ideas about how to help your child build up their confidence. Then you can decide whether your child needs help with building up their feelings of competence, their resilience or their optimism, or maybe a combination of all three. Consider whether working on your relationship with your child might be the priority. Below I have outlined some practical ideas for building your child's confidence under each of these different areas, so you can develop a plan for supporting your child.

How does Confidence (Competence, Resilience and Optimism) grow?

Remember confidence is the belief that you can cope in the world and that with hard work and the right attitude, things will usually work out. It comes from a combination of feeling competent, being resilient in the face of difficulties and having an optimistic thinking style in addition to having strong and secure relationships at home. Although each idea is presented separately, they are in fact all interlinked. As you develop competence, you also develop resilience and optimism. All these ideas feed off each other, so that when you start to think about one area, you should gradually see improvements in the other areas.

You can help your child develop these skills throughout their childhoods.

1. Ideas for developing your child's feelings of competence

Everything your child does has the potential to develop feelings of competence, which is the belief that they can manage a situation and feel that they are **good enough** (not necessarily the best). Give your child a wide range of real-life opportunities to try different activities, including everyday activities like cooking, art, wildlife, climbing, running, reading, talking to others. Try and identify their strengths and natural interests as starting points and then help them widen their horizons by doing new things. Consider the following points when you are trying to encourage your child and allow them to experience some success and mastery when they engage in an activity:

> *Remember, you cannot feel competent if you don't do anything. Prioritise DOING rather than letting your child take the easy route just watching TV or playing computer games.*

a) Help your children experience "FLOW"

The idea of "flow" may sound a little new age, but it is a well-known psychological concept that has been studied by many researchers working in a field called "positive psychology". It is the feeling of total focus and absorption you experience when you are engaged in an activity – that leads to a sense of fulfilment and satisfaction. There seem to be key principles involved when **Flow** takes place. Importantly, if the activity is too easy or too hard, flow won't occur. It is only when an activity is appropriately challenging that we are able to lose ourselves in purposeful, enjoyable and meaningful activity. When we experience flow, we are using our skills to the maximum, gaining competence and feelings of mastery, developing abilities and feeling optimistic. It is really important that we help our children to experience "flow" by providing them with the right level of challenges to their abilities. If you think the challenge is too much, break the task down into more manageable steps, or go back a few steps to an easier task. Children will usually want to move on to something harder when they feel competent.

b) Empathise with their struggles

Empathising means showing your child you understand how they are feeling. Recognising when your child is finding something hard is important. Don't deny their experience by saying "don't be silly" or "you shouldn't feel that way". Instead offer support and encouragement for overcoming it. "I know it's getting really hard and you're tired, but we've only got a little further to go and you'll have done it", or "I know you want to give up and feel like you're never going to get better, but I know you can do it - lets practice some more another day".

c) Support your child to cope when struggling but don't rescue.

It is important that your child perceives you care enough not to let them fail catastrophically – however, it is equally important that your child is presented with challenges that they sometimes need help with. If the task is too difficult for them, your role is to support and help, without taking over. This is hard, as you can of course do it easier, quicker, better than they can. Don't be tempted to do it for them as this will leave them feeling incompetent. Your job is to provide the right amount of support and encouragement so that they can experience some success. Think about teaching your child to ride a bike or swim – you provide just enough support so they don't drown, or crash, letting them do more and more as their competence increases.

d) Let them make some mistakes

It is crucial that you encourage your child to see mistakes as part of the learning process rather than something to be avoided. For example, if they are learning to make their own breakfast, don't fuss when they spill the milk. If your child thinks that making mistakes is not acceptable, they will be frightened to try things in case they get it wrong. If they spill the milk, try not to shout at them or look disapproving. Instead, say something like "Never mind – it is heavy – try and be really careful next time". Encourage them to wipe it up but don't make a big deal out of it. As they get older, you can use mistakes as a way to think with them about what they might do differently next time.

e) Praise effort more than achievement

You want to encourage your children to keep trying and not to give up, so focus more on noticing and valuing the qualities of determination, perseverance and effort. If children are only praised for achievement, they will not believe you if they don't feel they have done well and they will learn to fear failure. Also, if everything they do is praised, regardless of effort or success, they will learn that not much is expected of them and they don't have to try hard at anything. Of course, you also want to recognise when your child has achieved, but there should be more day to day recognition of the effort and determination that has led to the achievement. This will help them make the link between effort and achievement, teaching them that hard work usually pays off.

f) Make sure your praise is specific not general

Praise and encouragement are really important. But it is the way you praise and what for that will help or hinder your child's confidence.

i) Point out the things they are doing well so they hear you strengthening their own experience by saying it out loud. We all remember the kind things people say to us so use it to your child's advantage.

ii) Try and be specific rather than general so that praise is accurate and meaningful (this helps them understand exactly what it is that they are doing well). For example, if you are playing tennis with them, and they are struggling to get the ball over the net, you could say "Your aim is good, you just need to angle the racket to hit it up" (helpful and specific praise and help). or "I am really impressed by your determination - you are going to get it soon if you keep trying like that".

iii) Encourage as much as praise - help them believe they can do it if they keep going/trying.

g) Teach the art of determination and persistence

Many of us will remember learning to ride a bike without stabilisers. It felt like such a daunting task. We wobbled and maybe fell a few times before we got the hang of pedalling and staying upright. It is obvious that we needed to persevere in the face of a number of mini-failures, knowing that if we tried hard enough and practiced enough, we would eventually manage it. But also remember the feeling of exhilaration and pride when you achieved it? You knew you had done something important and taken a big step in the world. The amount of effort and perseverance you experienced will have been related to the amount of pleasure and pride you felt in yourself, and **deservedly so**. If it was easy, it will have felt somehow less of an achievement and you will not have experienced the little boost in self-esteem that comes from overcoming obstacles and persevering in the face of a challenge.

Learning to ride a bike is a good example, because it is a common milestone in most children's lives. We generally expect to fail at first, and every time we do, we know we are one step closer to getting it. Those of us who can ride a bike did not give up but persevered despite a few bumps along the way.

Helping your children to relish a challenge and develop the belief that mistakes or obstacles are not to be feared is a really important step in helping them experience mastery and competence. You cannot get this by skipping the difficult bits. Help your children to expect and enjoy solving problems rather than viewing them as a failure is key. The important idea here is that practice, perseverance and determination will win out. You can talk about times when you struggled and persevered, or use famous athletes or scientists who, despite early failure, achieved huge success as examples.

2. Ideas for developing your child's resilience

Remember that resilience is the ability to bounce back or cope when things go wrong.

a) Help your child develop a "Growth Mindset"

This is a concept proposed by Dr Carol Dweck in the 1990s and has been popularised in her book *Mindset: The New Psychology of Success*. It has become a very helpful way of understanding the way we think about ourselves, and how to help our children cope when facing challenges. Her research has identified that some people have something called a "fixed mindset" (Dweck 2006), which means they have a fixed view of themselves and their abilities. People with a fixed mindset label themselves "sporty", "clever", "shy" or "selfish" for example. This becomes an unchangeable fact about themselves – positive or negative. People with a fixed view of themselves as talented, for example, may think that hard work and effort means that they are not a "natural" and therefore don't value trying hard. If you have a fixed mindset and label yourself sporty, when you lose a game or struggle with a skill, you feel like a failure, because you are supposed to be sporty. This is why Harry was struggling so much. He thought that he was good at football, and when he struggled, this didn't fit with his "fixed" idea of himself.

People with a "growth mindset", on the other hand, are much more open to change and possibilities. They believe that with hard work and effort they can improve and master new skills. They do not see failures as stumbling blocks but as opportunities to learn and better themselves.

Labelling your children with fixed ideas about who they are and focussing only on achievement is therefore unhelpful, even if it is positive. It is much more helpful to encourage and praise children for their efforts, determination and ability to overcome challenges, encouraging them to value these qualities and accept failure as an important step towards success. Teach them that everyone has to work hard to get where they want to be, and teach them to enjoy learning and improving.

b) Teach your children to problem solve, but don't do it for them

When things go wrong, use it as an opportunity to practice problem solving. Teach them that there is always a solution/way forward and help them learn how to break things down into manageable steps.

For example, if your child is struggling with homework, teach them through modelling and practicing, how to focus on one step at a time, or do 15 minutes at a time. If they don't understand, help them to stay calm, and support them to think through what they can do next – how much can they do? Can you help them work it through? Can they tell the teacher they don't understand? If they are having problems with friendships, how can they try and resolve it themselves? Teach them that every problem is a puzzle and nothing is insurmountable.

c) Teach your child to think flexibly

This is an important skill that is often forgotten, and many of us adults are not great at it. It is the ability to adapt to unexpected situations or think creatively in challenging situations. Imagine a situation where you are expecting 2 extra people for dinner, and 4 turn up on the doorstep. In this situation, you need to think flexibly and adapt your plans to include 2 more people. If you can't be flexible, you will find this situation very stressful and upsetting. If you can flexibly problem-solve, you can enjoy your evening and make the most of a good night with friends.

You can help your child practice thinking flexibly in different ways.

Explain to your children that we have flexible brains like plasticine or playdoh – which means we can imagine all kinds of possibilities and creative solutions. If our brains were not flexible, we would only have one solution for every situation and we would not be able to learn or change that response. A good car journey game is to think of a situation or problem and together try and think of as many different ways of solving it as possible. You can make this game silly with ridiculous problems (e.g. if you were a shark and had no teeth, how would you eat? or If you had a superpower, what would it be and how could you use it? If you had only one egg and had to make tea for two, what could you do?). The idea is not to get the answer "right"; it's to have fun with thinking creatively and finding multiple ways round a problem.

Once your children are familiar with the idea of thinking flexibly, you can use it together to think of lots of different solutions in everyday life.

The message is that there is always a solution, and thinking flexibly allows you to open up your mind to find it rather than getting stuck.

d) Teach your child to overcome difficulties rather than avoid them

Help your children understand that avoiding things that worry them or that are difficult does nothing to help their confidence. It is only by overcoming challenges that you grow in confidence and learn that you can cope when things get difficult. This may mean breaking things down into manageable chunks, or trying something a different way, but ultimately, it means ensuring your child faces a difficulty rather than avoids it. You can encourage and support, but you need to be strong and sometimes you need to be the "baddy" as you don't let your child take the easy way out.

e) Develop your child's ability to ask for and seek help

This may seem at odds with the previous sections, but it is an important piece of resilience development. It is really important that if your child is struggling in an area of their life, that they feel **confident they will be supported by the adults that care for them.** Children need to know you have their backs and that they won't be rejected, ridiculed or made to feel ashamed if they need help. The most confident people are not ashamed of struggling and they are not embarrassed or ashamed to ask for help when they need it. Knowing you can rely on others that care for you is crucial for inner-confidence. None of us can solve everything alone. This is not the same as doing everything for them.

3. Ideas for helping your child develop Optimism.

This means teaching your child to think helpfully about the difficulties they experience. The ideas we have explored will all serve to strengthen optimism indirectly, but you can also encourage healthy thinking patterns more directly. These ideas are well known in the fields of positive psychology and cognitive behaviour therapy and there are many books and workbooks, which you may find helpful in the reference section.

a) Help your child recognise their thoughts

The first task is to help your child understand the role that thinking plays in their heads. They need to practice expressing their thoughts and recognising when they are thinking in unhelpful ways. You can help them become aware of their own thoughts in a number of ways. Make "thinking" part of your everyday conversation.

- Talk about your own thoughts - talk out loud to yourself so they can hear your thinking in the moment as well as telling them what you are thinking about particular situations. You might be cooking dinner and notice that your thoughts are turning to what you have to do later, or you are worrying about a conversation you had with a friend. You can edit these so they are appropriate, but try and talk out loud. When your children look at you in a strange way, tell them you are just thinking about things out loud. Regularly explain what you think about things that happen and especially why you think they happened.

- Explain that everyone has thoughts going through their minds and this is normal. Our minds are like busy motorways, with thoughts flashing past – sometimes they go so fast we barely notice them and sometimes they are like police cars with sirens that make us look and pay attention.

- When situations occur in daily life, show interest in what your children are thinking. Ask them what they think and why they think like that. For younger children you can try drawing their face with a "thinks bubble" and help them fill it in. You could also get an interested child to draw a cartoon of a situation, including what people said and might have been thinking using speech bubbles and thinks bubbles.

- When you are reading books or watching films, you can try and guess what the characters are thinking in certain situations.

- Make it playful and see if your children can "catch" their thoughts before they fly away. Try and guess what each other might be thinking about and see if you are right or wrong.

This might sound easy, but it isn't. It takes time and perseverance to be able to notice your own thinking. Don't worry about this, you are laying down the foundations to help your children in the long run. Try and develop a growth mindset for yourself and see it as a skill you are learning.

b) Challenge your child's thinking patterns

Once you and your children are familiar and comfortable with the concept of thinking, you can explain that we all think in helpful or unhelpful ways. Below are some ideas for helping your child learn helpful ways of thinking.

If you have noticed that your child tends to blame themselves when things go wrong for them you can gently help them to challenge this idea.

- **Draw out Responsibility Pies**

   It is rare for only one person to be at fault for a situation. Help them consider what things led to the situation and how other people may have also played a part. Using a **Responsibility Pie** can be helpful for younger children. Draw a circle and help them think about how big a slice of responsibility everyone should take.

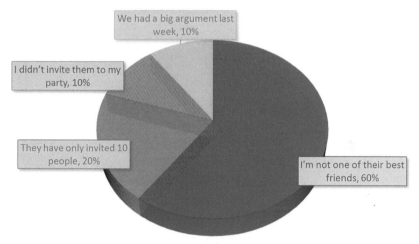

We had a big argument last week, 10%

I didn't invite them to my party, 10%

They have only invited 10 people, 20%

I'm not one of their best friends, 60%

NOT INVITED TO FRIEND'S PARTY: WHY DID IT HAPPEN?'

I am not suggesting that you teach your children to blame others or shirk responsibility, but rather, help them to see the bigger picture and not take more responsibility than is **accurate**. This helps them take some proportionate responsibility and recognise the role that everyone else played as well.

- **Differentiate between behaviour and character**

    It is also really helpful to teach your children the difference between their actions (behaviour) and their character. If they have done something wrong and need to take responsibility for it, help them see that their actions were the problem rather than a personality flaw.

    Think about how you say things, e.g. "You got cross and hit your sister" rather than "You're really spiteful". This is important as it helps them attribute the problem to things they can change. They can choose not to hit. When it feels like it is something awful about themselves, it leads to feelings of hopelessness as this isn't so easy to change.

If you think your children tend to think that when things go wrong they will never get better, challenge this idea:

- **Difficult situations pass – they won't always feel this way**

  Teach your child that difficulties and feelings tend to pass and change – that nothing much stays the same forever. You can explain that being upset and frustrated or disappointed is normal in difficult situations, but that these feelings will pass, and they *will* feel better or differently in an hour or tomorrow. Similarly, you can help them see that that the challenge is temporary – they can overcome it. Teach them to use situations from the past to see how they dealt with it and didn't feel so bad in the end, e.g. "Remember you were really upset when you fell out with Katie, and you thought she'd never speak to you again? Well, she calmed down and you both apologised and then you were friends again". Help them look for evidence that doesn't fit with their belief that a situation will never improve.

For children who have a tendency to generalise and think in black and white, help them challenge this:

- **Be specific, not general**

  Help them gradually to think more specifically. Teach your children to clarify exactly what happened on a particular occasion rather than making sweeping generalisations. E.g. "I think that boy was looking at me in a funny way when we were at the park earlier" rather than "Everyone looks at me weirdly" or "Everyone thinks I'm a weirdo".

- **Look for alternative explanations**

  Notice I have also specified "I think" rather than "I know" as this is more accurate. You can then help your child to consider all the other possible explanations for why someone might have been looking over. The flexible thinking will help here, as they will be familiar with the idea of generating alternative ideas. E.g. Maybe he was curious and interested in what you were doing, or maybe he was absent-mindedly looking in your direction but not thinking much, or maybe you reminded him of someone else? Help your child consider how much they look at other people and what they might be thinking when they do this. You are not trying to convince them of any one argument, but you are generating lots of possibilities that challenge their absolutist and generalised view.

- **Find the shades of grey**

  Finally notice if your child often uses words like "always" and "never" by introducing them to the idea of "continuums"; draw a line between the two extremes (Always------Never) and encourage your child to consider all the shades of grey in between. See the chart below:

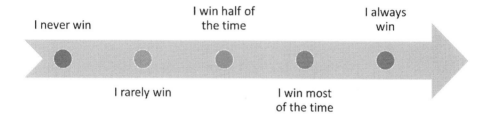

So instead of "I'm a total loser", your child can learn to think "I lost that game, but sometimes I win" which is much more specific, accurate and helpful.

SUMMARY OF IDEAS

Develop Competence	■ Encourage doing ■ Experience flow ■ Understand how your child feels ■ Support but don't rescue ■ Let them make mistakes ■ Learn from mistakes ■ Praise effort and perseverance ■ Make praise specific ■ Teach determination and persistence
Develop Resilience	■ Teach and model growth mindset ■ Teach problem solving ■ Don't do it all for them ■ Teach flexible thinking ■ Face challenges, don't avoid them ■ Encourage your child to ask for help

Develop Optimism	■ Teach awareness of thoughts
	■ Tackle self-blame
	  - Use responsibility pie
	  - Separate behaviour from personality
	■ Tackle the idea that things can't change
	  - Teach feelings are temporary
	  - Remember past successes and challenges
	  - Teach problem solving
	■ Tackle black and white thinking
	  - Teach them to be specific
	  - Separate thoughts and feelings from facts
	  - Teach shades of grey
	  - Use continuums
	  - Teach flexible thinking

So now you have lots of ways to understand why your child might be struggling and lots of ideas for helping them to develop the skills necessary for their confidence to blossom.

It's time to decide which aspects you are going to focus on and begin to put some ideas into practice. Hopefully the previous sections have changed your thinking a little and many of these strategies will start to become obvious – you will naturally begin to demonstrate and model your own resilience, develop your own growth mindset and develop your own competence rather than giving up.

Now, thinking about the problem you spelled out and the possible reasons that might be contributing to it, begin to brainstorm the kinds of things you can do to support your child to continue developing competence, resilience and optimism. If you think your relationship is part of the problem, I would encourage you to prioritise this.

You may have lots of ideas, but take them one at a time and build up slowly. You don't have to change everything at once. Focus on a skill or an idea and think about how you can help your child practice and develop in this way. Maybe you are just going to spend time talking with them about their thoughts and challenging those, or maybe you are going to encourage not giving up and teach them the idea of a growth mindset.

Be specific about what you are going to do. If you are vague and general, it is much less likely to happen. Decide **What** you are going to do and **When** (how often and what days/time?) and **How** (what would someone see you doing – how will you tackle it?).

It can be helpful at this stage to make a note of how bad you think the problem is at the moment. You could rate it 0-10 with 0 being not a problem at all and 10 being a real worry. Try and consider what each number means (a bit like the continuum). E.g. 5 = it's a problem some of the time, but not every day. This will help you review whether your interventions are helping.

Remember it can take time for things to change, so don't expect immediate results. Hold on to the idea that if you want to succeed, just like your child, you need to develop your capacity for patience and perseverance! There are no miracle cures. Developing self-esteem is like slow cooking. It takes all the right ingredients, and then time, followed by occasional checks and tweaks to get the right result.

Let's consider Harry and Belinda to help get energised and put some ideas into practice.

I have filled out a form for Harry and one for Belinda, covering all the points we have discussed so far, and then provided a blank form for you to use for your own child.

HARRY

Harry said he wasn't any good at football and wanted to quit his club.

UNDERSTAND	Y/N	Describe the Issues	PLAN (Brainstorm some ideas for each area of difficulty. Be specific about what, how, where, when you will do them.)
Developmental	✓	New Challenges. Change of teacher.	1. Normalise difficulties and empathise. Encourage growth mindset. Build competence.
Neurological	✗		
Thinking Styles	✓	I'm no good at football. I won't get any better. I didn't do anything well at practice.	Help challenge the idea of "being rubbish" – help Harry explain the difficulties in another way. Encourage Harry to read about other sportsmen who made themselves good, and help him think that working hard and practice will get results. Help Harry think about the skills he has learned already, help him be specific about what skills he is struggling with.
Behavioural	✓	Refuses to go to football anymore.	Encourage sticking with it. Practice skills at home.
Relationships	✓	Dad angry and disappointed.	Dad to try not to get angry, but help Harry learn that with hard work, he could be a good footballer. Dad to encourage practicing and not giving up.
Environment	✗		

Summary of Harry's Plan:

Mum recognised that Harry was struggling to experience competence with new skills. Instead of letting him give up, she explained to Harry that it would take some time to get used to the new coach and that she understands that he is missing his old coach (she showed Harry that she understood why he was feeling that way, which told him that it was a normal feeling). She then agreed that between coaching sessions, they would practice together some of the things he was finding difficult (Develop competence). She explained that, however talented someone is, they have to practice and work hard – no one is born a great footballer (Growth mindset). They found out about successful footballers and found a number of them didn't make the school team or weren't immediately picked up.

Mum then kept to her word, and every night they spent 30 minutes practicing so that Harry began to feel more comfortable with his ability. She explained to Harry that they would keep practicing and he would see that he would get better. She encouraged and supported this practice rather than leaving him to practice alone, but as he got more confident, Harry often went out to practice alone. He was not allowed to give up football for at least a term. Mum said that if he still didn't enjoy it after practicing and giving himself some time to get used to the new coach, they could consider whether to try a new club or give up. Until then, she expected him to give it his best shot. Dad was also supportive and encouraged and praised Harry's determination and the effort he put into practicing, letting him know how proud he was that he was overcoming a difficult experience, and Harry began to experience increased feelings of mastery and competence in this skill. Harry began to learn that difficult situations can be overcome with hard work, and he began to enjoy the challenge of football again (Resilience).

BELINDA

Belinda does not like the way she looks and thinks others are judging her negatively. She will only go out if she has spent hours on her hair and clothes.

UNDERSTAND	Y/N	Describe the Issues	PLAN (Brainstorm some ideas for each area of difficulty. Be specific about what, how, where, when you will do them.)
Developmental	✓	Puberty starting. Feeling chubby. Friends falling out. Moving to secondary school.	Normalise, explain, support and empathise.
Neurological	✗		
Thinking Styles	✓	I'm fat and ugly. No one likes me.	Help Belinda realise that this is a normal stage. Show her photos of yourself at similar ages and reassure her that she won't feel like this forever. Help her consider her other strengths and talents and show her how you value these. Help her consider evidence that people do like her and why. Draw a line between "fat" and "skinny" and also "stunning" and "ugly" and ask her to put all the people she knows, including herself on the line somewhere. Help her see that she is likely to be somewhere in the middle.
Behavioural	✓	Fusses over hair and clothes. Looks down and won't make eye contact.	Encourage her to take small steps and slowly reduce the time she spends on her hair and clothes. Help her to look people in the eye and see what happens.

| Relationships | ✓ | Insecure relationship with mum – lots of arguments. | Spend time together and try and enjoy each other's company. Work at giving compliments and encouragement rather than unhelpful criticising. Problem-solve together how to get on. |
| Environment | ✗ | | |

Summary of Belinda's Plan

Belinda's mum quite rightly prioritised their relationship as the number one area for change. She made a conscious effort to spend time with Belinda and show she enjoyed her company. Belinda loved cooking, and so they made time every week to cook something together. Belinda also showed her mum and her friends how to do their hair. Belinda's mum also shared her thoughts and feelings and showed interest in Belinda's world. She made time to listen rather than always having half her mind on other things. When she was busy, she explained to Belinda that she wanted to make some time to hear her properly, but that she couldn't do it right now. Mum and Belinda also agreed they would try really hard not to shout at each other – it wasn't always easy, but they kept trying and when they messed up, they apologised and made up.

Belinda's mum talked with Belinda about her feelings and helped Belinda to see how many different changes were going on for her. She understood why Belinda was feeling very wobbly and said that many of the girls in her year would be feeling the same even if they didn't show it. She helped Belinda to see that things would get better and that she needed to dig deep and show how strong she could be. Belinda's mum also helped Belinda to see how not looking at people in the eyes might be making the problem worse. She helped Belinda to practice looking at people she felt comfortable with and noticing how it got easier with practice. She helped Belinda notice that people talked with her more when she looked at them and smiled. Gradually, she encouraged Belinda to spend a little less time on her hair each morning (using a timer) and noticing if anyone treated her differently.

Finally, Belinda's mum tried out the continuums. She and Belinda wrote down the words Totally fat and Totally skinny, and another one for

Totally stunning and Totally ugly – and then they thought about all the people they knew and put them on the line. Belinda began to see that perhaps she wasn't the fattest or ugliest person she knew. They problem-solved how they might help Belinda feel fitter and healthier and agreed to stick to a healthier diet and regular exercise.

Below is a blank form that may be helpful to put all your information together and get you started.

Don't forget to jot down:

- Exactly what you are going to do.
- How you are going to do it.
- When you are going to do it.
- How often you are going to do it.

Putting your plan into action

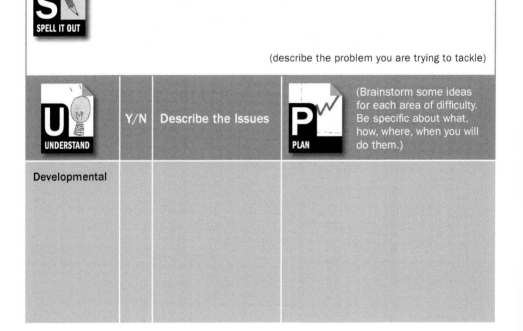

Neurological		
Thinking Styles		
Behavioural		
Relationships		
Environment		

This stage may feel irrelevant, but it is actually a big part of the change cycle.

If you seriously want things to change, you need to spend a bit of time thinking about where you have got to, decide whether anything is changing and whether you need to do anything differently. Otherwise good intentions often slide, and it can seem that the strategies haven't worked. Don't skip this basic stage if you really want to see changes.

Ask yourself the following questions:

- Have you given your ideas enough time to work? There is no magic wand, and change takes time. I would not expect to see small changes in confidence to emerge for a good couple of months.

- Have you stopped implementing the strategies after only a few weeks? This is often a problem, as it is easy to forget or think changes will occur after a very short period of effort. Strategies should not be thought of as quick fixes. I hope this chapter has given you the clear idea that confidence develops slowly with continued support from parents and teachers.

- Have you forgotten how bad the problem used to be? This is a good point to consider and is often overlooked. Unless you have been clear about how to rate the problem at the beginning (being specific about the problem, how often, how severe etc.) it is very difficult to judge changes that happen slowly. Re-rate the current problem using the same criteria as before, and you might find there are some small but definite improvements.

- Are there new difficulties that have arisen in the meantime that you need to address? This happens - it may be that the original ideas you had are not quite so relevant any more. Are there other things you can add to your plan now that your child has made some small first steps?

- You could have a go at Spell it out again and see if you are seeing something different now which may require a slightly different focus.

- Have you been consistent enough in your approach? How well did you really stick to the plan? Sometimes things happen (holidays, illness, work commitments, unforeseen events) that make it hard to stick with a new routine. Don't worry about this; as long as you are prepared to review and "get back on the task", you will be modelling resilience to your child (not giving up because of a small set-back) as well as understanding this is an ongoing process.

Now you have some ways to understand what might be causing your child to feel under-confident, some strategies to try and some ideas for reviewing and keeping on track. I hope you will feel a little more knowledgeable about how to support your children as they face the many challenges of life, and slowly develop into the confident, competent, resilient and optimistic young adults you always hoped they'd become.

References

Beck A.T., Rush A.J., Shaw B.F. and Emery G. (1979), *Cognitive therapy of depression: a treatment manual.* New York: Guilford Press.

Csikzentmihalyi M (1990) *Flow: The Psychology of Optimal Experience.* Harper Collin's: New York.

Dweck C.S. (2006) *Mindset, The New Psychology of Success.* Random House Inc.

Seligman M.E.P. (2007), *The Optimistic Child: A proven program to safeguard children against depression and build lifelong resilience.* Houghton Mifflin.

Further reading

Cartwright-Hatton, S. (2007). *Coping with an Anxious or Depressed Child: A guide for parents and carers.* Oneworld

Dweck C.S. (2006) Mindset, *The New Psychology of Success.* Random House Inc.

Seligman M.E.P. (2007). *The Optimistic Child: A proven program to safeguard children against depression and build lifelong resilience.* Houghton Mifflin.

Willets, L. and Creswell, C. (2007). *Overcoming your child's shyness and social anxiety: A self-help guide to using cognitive behavioural techniques.*

Anger and Frustration
Helping your child to 'tame that temper'

Dr Jennifer Swanston, clinical psychologist

"I just don't know how to stop it from bursting out"

Tommy, aged 7

Managing Anger and Frustration
Anger is Normal – 'but it makes me so mad!'

Anger is a perfectly normal emotion but possibly one which parents find the most difficult to manage. This is because it comes with so many worries for parents – "Will my child grow out of it?", "what will people think", "does this mean they will end up hurting people?" These are some of the many concerns that I hear from parents when dealing with a child who is having difficulty managing frustration and anger. These thoughts are normal, but can often mean that as a parent we are reacting to our own worries, rather than the child's behaviour.

To illustrate this point, we can look at Sharon and Toby (7 years old). Toby was having frequent outbursts where he would shout, throw things and had occasionally hit out. Sharon had the thought that her son Toby would "never be able to control his anger". I asked what would it mean if he never learnt how to control his anger and she replied, "he would never get a job, a partner and would probably end up doing something terrible". Sharon was so worried about the longer-term consequences of Toby's anger that she would often overreact when he had an outburst, sometimes losing her temper and giving him a long lecture about his behaviour. It was key for Sharon to find a consistent approach to dealing with Toby's anger which was in proportion to his behaviour and for her to notice her own thoughts so that they did not influence how she responded.

Master of Frustration or a Learning Curve?

We most commonly associate 'outburst' with toddlerhood when our little ones appear to be one ticking time bomb waiting to burst at the slightest sense of frustration. By school age, it is a common belief by parents that their child should be a master of their frustrations and that outbursts should be a thing of the past. However, this is a myth and the ability to master anger and frustration and react in a way that is assertive is a skill which continues to develop until we are in our early twenties. Even healthy adults can sometimes find these emotions all too much. However, the skill that is needed to manage our emotions is key and something which children often need help with.

As parents, we routinely spend time with our children teaching them to use the toilet, feed themselves, get dressed, tie their shoelaces, read, ride a bike. But the skill of managing and coping with difficult emotions is something which we often believe will come naturally. For some lucky children this is the case. However, as a rule it is not and children need help, patience and guidance to learn these skills from the people they look up to the most.

The Relationship Matters!

We can often get bogged down by all the demands of life and forget to *really* spend time with our children. Most parents (myself included) are guilty of going a whole day where we have said "just one more minute" or "I need to put the washing away first" and before we know it, it is bedtime. I often hear parents tell me how their child is behaving in a certain way for attention. At times like that we have to remind ourselves of how we are all social beings and how we all crave attention in some way. For example, babies will cry to get the attention of their caregiver when they need something (e.g. feeding, changing or a cuddle). Often, we can label bad behaviour as a way of getting attention, whilst forgetting that children *need* attention and if they are not getting it in positive ways, then they may have learnt that the only way to get attention is by acting out.

I will go on to talk about the importance of *really* spending time with your child and engaging in positive play and how this goes a long way to helping reduce negative behaviour. As touched upon in the introduction, nurturing, love, warmth and a strong bond of attachment with at least one adult are so essential to children. Often when a child is displaying difficult behaviour, the relationship between a child and parent or other significant adults can be negatively affected. In this chapter we will touch upon the importance of re-building that bond and relationship as we know this is vital for helping children to move forward and manage their anger.

Our Changing World

Children in the 21st century have access to more and more influences of others. Go back to post-war Britain and children would normally be brought up in a family of two parents, with grandparents close by. As we have moved into the 21st century, there have been significant changes in terms of childcare, with women going back to work earlier and for longer hours. Often children are placed in the care of others, such as childminders, nurseries or nannies. The rise of the internet and media means that children are often exposed to technology from a young age. Both increased working hours and technology mean children often go to bed later and are experiencing sleep deprivation, which can have a massive impact on their functioning during the day.

Other factors such as the rise in childhood obesity and Type 2 diabetes indicate that children's diets are changing. Diet, exercise and activity are factors which play a huge role in regulation of emotions. As a mother of active children, I see a direct link between their activity levels and behaviour. However, in the age of cars, technology and longer working hours, often children have little time outdoors exercising. With all these factors in mind, it is important to recognise that outside influences are likely to play a part in children's behaviour.

Fight! The Primitive Response

The other important thing about anger is that it is often driven by other things (see the primitive 'fight or flight' response mentioned in the Anxiety chapter, chapter 1). When we feel at all threatened, the body's alarm system is activated, and we kick into our primate caveman mode where our two options are to either 'run away' or to 'stand and fight'. Although in this day and age there are no sabre-tooth tigers lurking around the corner, other situations can trigger this primitive response. For example, a crowded classroom with lots of noise and hustle and bustle, could become too much for a child who is hungry and tired. This may cause them to revert to this primitive response, causing them to shout and lash out. We all know that being hungry, tired and stressed can lead us to lose our temper quicker. Children are no different and they have the added drawback of not having a fully developed brain to help them to regulate their emotions.

What is Really Going On?

Children, especially young children find it difficult to put into words how they are feeling when they are worried or anxious. This may mean that their distress is expressed through their behaviour. It is fruitless to punish difficult behaviour, if the cause of the distress is not sorted out. The child may stop the behaviour, but in the end the distress will just come out another way – perhaps through another difficult behaviour. Therefore, we need to look to what is going on in a child's life to get a clue as to whether there is anything else underlying a child's anger.

Some children are sensitive to changes in their surroundings, and a school or house move is enough to raise their stress levels sufficiently to mean that even something small can trigger anger. It is important to put yourself in your child's shoes and consider whether anything has changed for them. This could be obvious, but equally it may not be. For example, it might be they are going through a developmental change. During middle childhood, children go through massive developmental changes, where their physical, social, and mental skills develop at an incredibly fast rate. Friendships become more important and they start to think more about the future. For some children, this can be a frightening time and around this age children can develop fears relating to death and disaster. With friendships becoming more important, children become more susceptible to peer pressure and bullying can become an issue.

There are so many different factors which could raise stress at this time. If we think back to the chapter on worries and the influence of stress on the body, it is no wonder that children will often react by having outbursts when things become too much for them. Understanding what is going on for your child is an important factor in supporting them through their outbursts.

Within this chapter on anger, we will follow **SUPER** and look more closely at anger and how to manage it. Here is a summary of important points to remember:

✓ Anger is a normal emotion.

✓ It is important to have an approach for parents to manage their child's anger so that children learn the vital skills to be able to manage their emotions and impulses.

✓ Anger becomes more of a problem when it leads to consistent loss of control and leads us to do things that we wouldn't do when we have our 'rational' head on.

✓ Anger can often be the result of other emotions such as anxiety.

✓ Situational factors (tiredness, hunger) and the environment (busy, noisy) play an important role in how children cope with anger.

✓ The ability to be able to regulate difficult emotions is difficult and something which a child often needs guidance with. If a child lacks skill in this area then outbursts will be more frequent, longer and more severe.

✓ Children learn by example: If parents respond with frustration and shouting then it is likely that a child is not going to be able to learn how to use skills to calm down and manage their temper.

✓ Parents' thoughts on anger are important. For example, a parent may assign the following meaning if a child gets angry:

✓ Often, we can overreact or make meaning of anger in a way that gets us to respond in a way that is out of proportion (e.g. shouting back, giving consequences out of proportion to the behaviour).

✓ Some children struggle more than others naturally with regulating their emotions. When babies are born, some are placid and seemingly calm, whilst others are constantly on the go, sensitive to their surroundings. Often parents may compare the child who is displaying anger to other children who possibly do not struggle.

✓ Changes in environment and development can be significant for your child.

✓ Exercise and diet are important.

Explain really specifically what is causing a problem.

When dealing with anger it is important to have a full overview of what is going on before, during and after. Therefore I would recommend an ABC approach:

A = Antecedents -- what is going on before the behaviour happens?

B = Behaviour – spelling out what behaviour is occurring

C = Consequences – what happens after

The **ABC** approach is designed not just to look at your child but also those around your child (parents, teachers, grandparents). By asking yourself these questions, you are beginning to build up a detailed picture of the problem and will then be able to move onto the rest of **SUPER**:

A - Antecedents

- What is happening before the behaviour occurs?
- What has your child just been doing?
- When did your child last eat? Are they hungry?
- When did your child last drink? Are they thirsty?
- What has your child just eaten and drunk?
- Are they tired? Are they having enough sleep (around 10-12 hours for school age children)?
- What is their environment like? (e.g. too much noise, lights)
- How have the past few days been?
- Have there been any stressors in the child's life recently?
- Were there any signs that your child was becoming angry (early warning signs)?
- Is your child worried about anything?
- Has your child just come off an electronic device?

B - Behaviour

- What is the behaviour? Describe (e.g. hitting, kicking, shouting)
- Where is it occurring?
- What time of day does it usually occur?
- What is going on at that time (e.g. before mealtimes, in the morning, when demands are placed on them)?
- What do you think about the behaviour?
- How often is this behaviour occurring?

C - Consequence

- How do you respond to the behaviour?
- What happens afterwards?
- How do others respond to the child's behaviour?
- What are the consequences of your child's behaviour?
- Are there any negatives to what happens as a result? (for others and your child)
- Are there any positives to what happens as a result? (for your child and others)

I would highly recommend keeping a diary or record of **ABC** in relation to your child's behaviour. This will help you to notice patterns and trends. Here is an example:

Example of an ABC diary

Date/Time	A	B	C
Tuesday 7th October, 11.30am	Ben was playing football in the garden with his brother, Stuart. It was a hot day. Ben fell over and stubbed his toe. His brother started laughing. Ben had last eaten at breakfast, at 7.30am.	Ben screamed at Stuart and kicked the football full strength at him which hit Stuart on the arm.	Mum came out and yelled at Ben. Took his brother inside and left Ben outside playing football alone.

Look at underlying reasons why the problem developed or continues.

 You have now described your child's behaviour in detail. Now it is time to consider what may be influencing your child's frustration and anger.

In the first chapter we mentioned how there are many factors which affect why a problem, like anger, starts and carries on. Thinking back to all of the factors mentioned at the beginning by looking at the formulation diagram in the introductory chapter, have a look at the case example below and think about what may be influencing Ellie's behaviour and keeping it going.

Ellie, aged 7 years.

Ellie is 7 years old and is having frequent outbursts where she will shout, scream, throw things and has on occasions hit and kicked members of her family. She has a younger brother and an older sister. Ellie's mother, Jane, is expecting a baby and Ellie has just changed schools. Jane has noticed how Ellie's siblings are much calmer than her and Ellie is often the one to lose her temper. Over the years, Ellie's parents have had occasions where they have said to her "why can't you just behave like your brother and sister". Ellie has been noted by teachers to often say "I can't do it" and "I am not as good as others". Jane and Geoff (dad) have noticed how Ellie has outbursts when returning home from school, when she finds something difficult (like homework) and when her siblings have done well at something. When Ellie has an outburst, Ellie's parents will often ask Ellie a number of times to calm down and then can lose their temper themselves and have occasions where they shout back. Jane has admitted that she sometimes just gives into what Ellie wants (e.g. more TV time) just to keep the peace.

Developmental: The upcoming arrival of Ellie's sister is likely to be a big change for her. It can be a time of many worries for children: 'will mum still love me as much?' 'Will daddy still have time to play with me?' They can notice changes in mum, for example morning sickness or tiredness which can add to their worries. Ellie is 7 and around this time, children can develop fears of rejection, failure and getting into trouble at school. These normal fears coupled with changes in Ellie's life may be important.

Neurological *(brain development)*: Ellie is 7 years old. She has not yet fully developed the ability to regulate her emotions and impulses. A part of the brain which is key in this, is called the 'pre-frontal cortex'. The pre-frontal cortex helps us to inhibit our emotional responses and is also involved in planning and organising. Children start to develop these abilities as toddlers, but they continue to develop throughout childhood and adolescence and do not fully develop until our twenties. This is why children have outbursts when experiencing high levels of emotion or stress.

Biological: Temperament can play a big factor. We may have two children living in the same family, where one child is 'laid back' and rarely becomes angry and another child who becomes frustrated much quicker. Often this can lead parents to compare the two children and their behaviour becomes highlighted. We all have different temperaments. What can be changed is the way in which Ellie learns to cope with her emotions and she may need more help than her siblings in doing this.

Cognitive: Ellie is saying things such as "it's not fair" and "I am no good". It may be that she feels things are unjust or she may be experiencing doubts in her own self-worth. Often children who are displaying anger are met with comments from parents, family members and friends such as "why are you like this?" or "you are so naughty". Although these comments often come about due to exhaustion and exasperation, they often lower a child's confidence in themselves and their ability to change the situation. Children can start to believe they are 'bad' or 'naughty'.

Behavioural: What is going on in Ellie's life? Well, she has changes in the family with the upcoming arrival of a sibling as well as starting at a new school. It could be that Ellie is finding these changes stressful and it is coming out in her behaviour. It appears that Ellie is getting much attention (albeit negative) when she has an outburst and there are times when eventually Jane gives into her demands and lets Ellie get her own way. These things may be keeping Ellie's behaviour going (we talk about this in more detail later on).

Environmental: Although this may not appear obvious, Ellie's outbursts often occur when she gets home from school. It may be that the stress of attending a new school and all the demands that go with this (e.g. new teachers, making friends, new environment) are all too much for Ellie. She may be able to hold it together for the day, but as soon as she gets into the safety of her own home, all of this stress 'boils' over. Homework is another trigger and this may need to be looked at further (e.g. does Ellie find the work too difficult, does she need some extra help).

Systemic *(the impact of family and those around Ellie):* Jane and Geoff often compare Ellie to her siblings. We have identified comments like "why can't you behave like your brother and sister?" Although it is understandable that Jane and Geoff are bewildered by Ellie's behaviour, by openly comparing Ellie's behaviour to theirs, they may be unknowingly reducing Ellie's confidence and self-esteem. Children can often internalise comments like this and believe that they are no good or there is something wrong with them. Jane and Geoff also admit that they can lose their temper when Ellie's behaviour gets too much. As parents, we can all have days when things get too much, and we say or do things (e.g. shout) we later regret. However, children follow by example and if they see their parents shouting when upset, then it is likely that they will do the same. If Ellie is to learn how to control her own emotions, it is vital that Jane and Geoff do the same (this will be discussed further below).

> *NB: It is also important to consider whether anger is actually the issue, or whether other areas are more important:*
>
> - Is anxiety the cause of the outbursts? Ellie may be feeling anxious about the arrival of the new baby and her recent change in school.
> - Is self-esteem the issue? Ellie speaks about not being as good as others.
> - If the outbursts are only happening at school then maybe the child is struggling academically or socially? (Read the Academic stress and Friendship chapters, chapters 5 and 2 respectively).
>
> *If you think that other issues may be underlying your child's anger, then I would recommend that you also read the relevant other chapters.*

Okay so now let's explore what may be an issue:

You have spelled out your child's behaviour and considered factors that may be influencing their outbursts. Now it is time to take a quiz on your child. The quiz asks specific questions relating to the different factors touched upon above. It also may highlight other chapters which you might benefit from reading (e.g. anxiety or friendship issues). For each question, make notes on whether this might be important.

Quiz

Quiz below to be in the same format as other chapters

1. **Have there been any changes in yours or your child's life recently? For example, has your child just started a new school/class, have there been any changes in the family like the birth of a new sibling or parental separation?**

   Yes............This could be an issue – jot it down and move on to next question

   No not to my knowledge..........

Sometimes changes in a child's life can lead them to feel overwhelmed emotionally. They have not yet fully mastered the skills to cope with these emotions, then this could result in outbursts. Even small changes can affect children of this age.

2. **Is it possible that your child may be going through some difficulties at school with or without your knowledge (e.g. friendship issues, bullying)?**

   Yes....... This could be an issue – jot it down and move on to next question. You may wish to read the chapter on friendship issues (chapter 2).

   No not to my knowledge.........

This may not be an issue for your child but it is important to keep an eye open. Talk to your child's school or club leader if you have any concerns.

3. **Has your child told you that they have any worries or stress recently?**

   Yes..........This could be an issue - jot it down and consider reading the chapter on anxiety (chapter 1).

   No.......

Sometimes children keep their worries or stress thoughts to themselves, so keep an eye open for these, and consider asking your child whether they feel worried or stressed about anything.

4. **Personality and temperament - Would you describe your child as having always been easily frustrated and sensitive?**

   Yes.....This could be an issue - jot it down.

   No......

5. **Does your child often struggle and become easily frustrated when they find things challenging (e.g. puzzles, Lego models)?**

   Yes.....This could be an issue - jot it down.

   No.....

6. **Does your child ever become frustrated when with other children (for example in relation to turn taking, sharing, games)?**

   Yes..... This could be an issue – jot it down. You may consider reading Chapter 2 on friendship issues.

   No....

Children of school age have to navigate many difficult social situations and learn vital skills. Often peer or sibling interactions can trigger outbursts as children have not yet mastered the ability to effectively handle these interactions.

7. **Behaviour – Are there ever times when your child may get an unintended reward for their behaviour (e.g. attention from others, being given the toy they wanted)?**

Yes…...This could be an issue - jot it down.

No……..

It can be all too easy if we are out and about or have other demands to deal with to take the option of giving in and avoiding an outburst. It may be that grandparents or family members will take it upon themselves to comment on or discuss your child's behaviour when it occurs. Keep an eye open for any unintended rewards that your child may be getting for their behaviour.

8. **Can your child manage to contain their frustration or calm down quicker by being distracted, walking away?**

   Yes…...Good job!

   No…...This could be an issue - jot it down.

9. **Are there things in your child's environment that affect their behaviour? For example, do noises, distractions, temperature affect how your child deals with their frustration?**

   Yes…...This could be an issue - jot it down.

   No…...

Some children are more sensitive to external stimulation than others. Keep an eye out for when the outbursts occur and whether there are any factors in their environment which may be significant.

10. **Does your child not get enough sleep and or eat a healthy diet? Do you notice that they find it more difficult to cope when tired and hungry?**

    Yes…...This could be an issue - jot it down.

    No…...

We all know that tiredness and hunger can make us much grumpier. Children are even more sensitive to the effects of tiredness and hunger as they find it more difficult to rationalise why they feel this way. Keep an eye out for when the outbursts occur and whether hunger and tiredness may be a factor.

11. Do you as parents expect your child to be in control of their frustration?

Yes....... This may be important - jot it down.

No......

It is important to remember that children do not fully develop the ability to regulate their emotions until they reach their twenties. Some children struggle more than others with this.

12. Does your child's teacher have higher expectations of your child's behaviour then you do or vice versa? (e.g. expect them to be well behaved all of the time)

Yes....... This may be important - jot it down.

No.....

13. Do you or others close to your child often lose your temper when your child is frustrated?

Yes......This may be important - jot it down.

No......

Keep an eye out over the next few weeks to see if there are any quiz questions that could have been answered 'yes' rather than 'no', and hopefully things should settle down.

What are we going to tackle first?

What practical ideas are on offer and which are we going to choose? How are we going to tailor it to this particular child?

When tackling anger and outbursts, there is no quick fix solution. It takes time, consistency, perseverance and a lot of patience. Within this section, I will describe a layer of approaches which together will go a long way to helping your child manage their anger and frustration. I use the analogy of a sandwich when thinking about the layer of approaches to tackle anger. Each part on its own is a bit bland and ineffective, but when put together (for example, ham, cheese, mayonnaise, pepper and bread) it makes for a fantastic combination!

Layer of Approaches:

Traffic light system - how to manage behaviour

Emotion regulation skills

Environment and triggers

Building up relationships

With all layered approaches, we start from the bottom and move our way up. If you were building a house, the first thing you would need to consider is the foundations. It forms the solid ground from which all the building can then take place and without it the house would fall down. We start with the building of relationships between parents and their children.

1. Building up relationships

Often when anger is a problem, relationships between children and parents can suffer. This is for a number of reasons. Parents often blame either themselves or their child (or both) for the behaviour. This blame leads to guilt and guilt is a tricky emotion which means we can act in ways we would not otherwise. Parents can sometimes hold onto negative feelings regarding their child's outburst, meaning that when they do something well, it goes unnoticed. Parents can become exhausted and less likely to spend quality time with their child. I have seen this may times in my clinical work, where parents come to see me at breaking point, exhausted and overwhelmed. When I ask what do you enjoy doing with your child, often this has become a thing of the past and parents struggle to find an answer.

We all know when we have had 'one of those days' with our children, we can't wait to get home and get them to bed so we can relax. If 'one of those days' is happening most of the time, it is understandable that as parents, you are doing all you can to get through and sitting down with your child (who has just shouted, kicked, punched) may not be high on the agenda.

Anger does not just affect relationships between parents and their children, it also affects relationships that children have with other people in their lives (e.g. peers, teachers, family members). I use the example of Jonny who is 6 years old. When I met Jonny, he had been having frequent outbursts for the past six months and they were mainly happening when Jonny was at family gatherings or outside of the house. Jonny's mother, Karen, was at her wits' end. She told me how even before Jonny has an outburst, his grandparents will start mentioning his behaviour and that it has become the topic of conversation at family events. She said that friends had stopped inviting Jonny round to their houses for playdates. Karen told me that she has had many family members and friends offer their advice on what may be 'wrong' with Jonny. She told me that she felt blamed, guilty and had started to think that there must be something wrong with Jonny. She had started to avoid going to anything social with Jonny.

In this example, Jonny's relationship with not only his parents had been affected, but with most of the adults in his life. Children pick up on much more than we give them credit for and it is highly likely that Jonny has heard his family talking about his behaviour and how there must be something "wrong". The behaviours which anger often causes can lead parents and others around the child to feel overwhelmed, resentful and stressed. Karen felt constantly on edge, waiting for an outburst to happen.

I have met many parents who understandably avoid doing things with their child just in case they have an outburst. The problem with this is that the parent and child end up having very little positive and precious moments together.

I refer back to Lucy's introductory chapter which talked about how love, warmth, love, nurturing and a strong bond of attachment with one adult is so important for children. When our children are babies and toddlers we will often invest much time playing with them. Play is doing something for fun, enjoyment and recreation, which is something that children do best! Children play in a multitude of ways and often relish in it. As parents, many of us will pretend to drink countless cups of imaginary tea with our 2 or 3-year olds. However, by school age there is often a common belief that we should not need to play with our children and that it is not necessary. However, it is quite the opposite.

PLAY IS....

- **Letting your child lead without direction**
- **Focused on enjoyment and not achievement**
- **Being interested in what your child is going**
- **Fun!**
- **Allowing your child to explore the world around them**

Children, even older children gain so much through play. It builds relationships, helps children to learn vital social skills, try out new concepts, fail, persevere and then succeed. The value of play with children is widely recognised, and many parenting programmes highlight the importance of play between parent and child (e.g. Webster Stratton, 2005). Play with children can often be a platform from which a relationship can be strengthened. However, it is not just play that is important, but the overall building and re-connecting of relationships. Another key feature is the language and words we use with our children. Providing children with approval, praise and encouragement is also extremely important and helps them to build self-esteem, and encourages desired behaviour by providing lots of attention for the behaviour which you want to see more of.

Identify your own feelings and thoughts regarding your child's behaviour. Are these affecting the way you relate to your child? Try to gain some perspective and see things from your child's perspective by putting yourself in their shoes. Can you remember how it felt to be their age?

Are there other children out there experiencing similar difficulties with anger (the answer is yes)? Empathising and understanding how your child is feeling can be the key to helping them to feel better.

The vital elements of re-building relationships (a recipe):

✓ Identify and challenge your own feelings and thoughts about your child's behaviour. Many factors can contribute to the development of anger (as mentioned above) and it is important to move forward from any blame or bad feeling before implementing this plan. Can you talk to a friend whose child has gone through something similar but come out the other side? Remember that anger is normal and does not mean that your fears will be realised.

✓ Make sure that any bad feeling or worries are put to one side after your child has calmed down and you have dealt with the behaviour. It is vitally important to 'move on' and not hold onto ill feeling. Children can become confused, scared and frightened if faced with a parent who holds onto ill feelings. Obviously it is understandable to feel cross, upset and worried about the behaviour. But it is important to park these feelings following the event in order to start re-building the relationship with your child.

✓ Play each day: Make time to play each day with your child (or at least as much as you can). This doesn't need to be for hours. This time is about quality rather than quantity. Try to dedicate between 15-30 minutes per day.

✓ This play needs to be child-led. Let your child lead the way and show you what they want to do. Often as adults we want things that our children do to have a means to an end (e.g. read this book to improve your reading skills). But play should not be achievement focussed or geared at teaching a particular skill. It is what it is – Play.

✓ Make sure that this play time happens when your child is at their best (e.g. they are not hungry or especially tired). If you notice signs of frustration then it might be good to cut the play time short or to move it to another time.

✓ Let your child know that this is their special time together and give them at least two warnings within five minutes before the play time is finished. This will help to avoid any potential issues with ending the special time together.

☑ Try to make play time individual. It can be difficult to juggle this when you have other children. However, it may be beneficial for all your children to have this special time, although you may need to think about how to juggle your life to fit this in. Both parents should ideally take it in turns to have this special time and if there are other significant people in your child's life (e.g. grandparents) then they can be involved too. This may help to lighten the load.

☑ Find out more about your child's interests and become involved in these. This shouldn't involve money. It doesn't mean taking them out and buying them things or ferrying them around to different clubs. It means really connecting with what they like and getting them to *show you*. For example, if your child likes trains, then they can show you their train collection. Ask your child lots of age appropriate questions about their interests. Sit down together and talk about trains or look them up on the internet (if this is something your child wishes to do). Any questions should be curious and have no pressure attached.

☑ Make the playtime enjoyable for you and your child and let your child know that you value spending time with them. For example, saying 'I have really enjoyed our time together' or 'I really like spending time with you'. This will go a long way to helping build your child's confidence.

☑ It is really important to encourage your child and praise them for their genuine effort. The self-esteem chapter (chapter 3) gives a very nice account of how we can help children to work through their struggles and develop competence and resilience and how to give the 'right' kind of praise. I recommend reading this particularly as children who struggle to manage anger can often view themselves or believe others view them in a negative way.

☑ Sit down at the end of the day and consider whether you have had any positive experiences with your child. If the answer is no, then seek for tomorrow to be different. Find opportunities for spending quality time with your child, getting the best out of them.

☑ Record these positive times with your child. Build up a positive store of memories. Take pictures together, make a scrapbook or put pictures in a photo frame. This store of positive experiences and memories will help you to get through and stay strong during the hard times.

2. Environment and Triggers

The next layer is to look long and hard at what is going on for your child in general and before they become angry. The quiz should have gone a way towards pinpointing some important issues for your child. These can be wider issues which are going on in your child's environment (e.g. stresses at school or home, changes in routine or family structure) and immediate issues that trigger your child's behaviour (e.g. lots of noise, busy family gatherings, hunger, tiredness). Below in Table 2 is a quick rundown of potential issues to consider:

Table 2: Examples of things that can set anger off

Environment	Triggers
Change in schools	Noise
House move	Crowded
New sibling (pregnancy or birth)	Hunger
Parental separation	Tiredness
Parental issues (arguments)	Temperature (hot/cold)
Changes in financial situation	Demands
Change in class at school	Long periods of inactivity
Bullying or peer issues	Disagreements
Death of pet	Homework
Death of family member/friend	
Illness	

Identify the Triggers

If we go back to the first chapter – a few of those fundamental beliefs very much comes into play here. Namely: Small changes make a BIG difference and often it is the environment that needs to change and not the child. Sometimes, it is as simple as knowing what triggers your child's behaviour and reducing or removing their exposure to these triggers. Obviously for some situations this is easier said than done, but you may find that it is simpler than you had expected.

So, the next step is to consider all of things that may be influencing your child's behaviour and work out a plan to tackle this. Below I have considered some of the factors mentioned and ways to tackle this. There may be many other factors playing a part so get creative and think about other ways you could remove or tackle one of these triggers. Enlisting the help of friends and family can also produce some creative ideas.

☑ Busy/noisy environments: For example, is the TV always on at home or do you often attend very noisy parties or gatherings? Consider alternative, less stimulating experiences for your child. You child may just not be able to cope with going to really busy, stimulating experiences. That does not mean that this will not change in the future. But it may be that for the time being, you need to consider going to a quiet park, instead of crowded busy play areas.

☑ Outbursts happen at a certain time of day: Consider different timings for doing things and shifting around the day. For example, playdates in the mornings instead of afternoons and afternoons considering some relaxing time together when your child gets back from school. Getting home from school is a common trigger time for outbursts and one which can be managed by a bit of juggling or shifting in routine.

☑ Exercise: If your child is not getting enough exercise or activity, consider things you can do after school or at the weekends to work off some of that unwanted energy. Exercise does not need to be expensive or elaborate. Playing football in the garden or running around the park or walking the dog together are all great ways of getting some exercise.

☑ Hunger and diet: Consider mealtimes and snacks and whether your child is getting enough of the right foods. There are many resources and guides out there for healthy snacks and what children should/should not be eating. The rule of thumb is that if you do not want your child to eat it, then you should not keep it in the house. Children live what they learn. I learnt this very early on with my son, who every time he saw me eating crisps or cake, wanted some. In the end I had to resign myself to the fact that unless I wanted to see him turn into a giant Quaver, I was not going to be able to eat crisps myself or keep them in the house. I switched Quavers for oat cakes and whenever I had one, I gave him one too. Obviously not nearly as tasty but it was much better for him and me!

☑ Sleep: If you have noticed that tiredness plays a part in your child's outbursts then you may wish to consider bedtime. Can you bring this earlier? Parents often set far too late bedtimes for their children. This only serves to make parents and children more tired. By gradually bringing bedtime earlier (5 minutes each night), it will help your child to adjust to the new routine.

Environmental Issues

The environmental issues are likely harder to tackle as they are often outside of our control. However, they are equally if not more important to try and consider. I often use the analogy of a cup when talking about stress. We all have our own cup which fills up with different stressors. Most people's cup is about 1/3 full of 'normal life stressors' (e.g. work, school, cooking, washing, finances etc.). However, life events can lead to our cup filling up and up. For some children their cup can fill up much quicker than others. Now if we think about everyday stresses for children like doing homework, having squabbles with siblings, getting dressed. If your child's cup is nearly full, what is likely to happen if another everyday stress is poured in? That's right.... The cup will overflow. Now, by overflow I am referring to what happens when a child has an outburst. I am sure as adults we can all relate to when our cup has 'overflowed' and we have overreacted to a situation which we would have dealt with much more calmly had we been in a better frame of mind.

Children may need overall strategies to tackle and manage their stress. I would recommend reading the chapter on anxiety (chapter 1). I would recommend taking time to talk to your child about what is going on in their life. Having 'feeling time' each day where a child is encouraged to express themselves through drawing or talking can be a good way of finding out whether there is anything that is bothering them. There may be things that can be done. For example, if your child is being bullied at school, it is vital that you speak with the school to consider ways of managing this. If someone in the family has passed away, your child may have a number of fears or questions. By creating this space for them to talk about what is on their mind, you will have the opportunity to address any fears, promote problem solving or consider more practical ways of helping your child. Other chapters may be more relevant here. For example, if you suspect that bullying is an issue, please read the chapter on friendships (chapter 2).

3. Emotion regulation skills

A common misconception is that children *should* automatically master anger and frustration. However, as I have already mentioned this is a skill which continues to develop until we are in our early twenties and children often need support in doing this. As parents we are best placed to help our child learn these skills but they require perseverance, patience and practice! Some fundamental principles of teaching children to calm down:

- [✓] Like any skill, we need to help our children to practice this outside of times when they are angry. It is like riding a bike. You wouldn't expect your child to suddenly get on a bike and ride it in the Tour de France. The same is true of emotion regulation skills. We need to practice them to become skilled enough to use them when we need them the most – when we are angry.

- [✓] Let your child know why you are practicing these skills.

- [✓] Make it as creative and fun as possible.

- [✓] Use age appropriate examples of how you deal with anger and skills that you use. Make sure to use these when you do actually feel angry to model to your child what to do when they feel angry.

- [✓] Have a range of tools for your child to use and practice. The more there are the greater their chances of success.

- [✓] Introduce them at the first signs of anger and not when your child has hit boiling point. It will be much harder to use them when they are very angry, then when they are a bit frustrated.

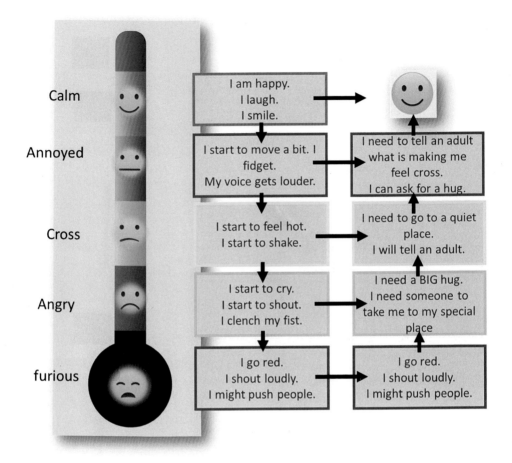

These are ideas of creative ways of helping your child to calm down and are not too demanding. If your child becomes interested in a certain one then encourage them to pick a few to practice. Having a physical box which your child decorates and puts coping skills in (e.g. pencils and a pad, stress ball) can be a nice way of involving them in the process.

Here are some creative ideas for a coping with anger to add to your child's toolbox:

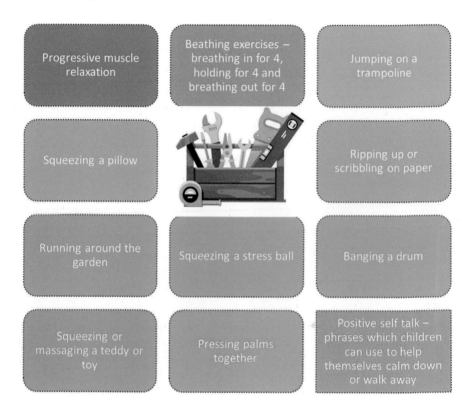

Progressive muscle relaxation

Beathing exercises – breathing in for 4, holding for 4 and breathing out for 4

Jumping on a trampoline

Squeezing a pillow

Ripping up or scribbling on paper

Running around the garden

Squeezing a stress ball

Banging a drum

Squeezing or massaging a teddy or toy

Pressing palms together

Positive self talk – phrases which children can use to help themselves calm down or walk away

It is also important to teach children to recognise their emotions at each stage of the process. I often use a thermometer and ask children to describe what happens (in their bodies, to their behaviour) at each stage of the anger thermometer. The skills in your child's toolbox are going to be much easier to use when they are a bit frustrated rather than extremely angry. It is also important to encourage your child to use these skills when they start to calm down from an outburst to help them to calm quicker and to give them the experience of practicing these skills. Children are unlikely to be able to use skills effectively when they are 'out of control' as the rational part of our brain ceases to function. At these times, it is your job as a parent to 'ride out the storm' in a calm way. It is important to give your child space and time to calm down. These emotions are scary for children and it is important that you stay as calm as possible while the anger subsides.

4. Managing Behaviour

There are many different parenting systems/approaches out there, some of which you may have already tried with some or little success. Often there are reasons why systems fall down and there are some common pitfalls which will be talked about in the R part of **SUPER**. The system that I routinely recommend to parents in dealing with their child's behaviour and outbursts is a **'Traffic Light System'**.

This is a clear and simple structured reward/consequence system which can help children to feel contained and promote structure, and it is highly indicated for children with who are having difficulty managing their emotions. The traffic light system is clear and can be easily understood by everyone, younger and older children. Where possible I would very much urge that you include older and younger siblings in this system so that it appears fair for all and promotes desired behaviour in all family members.

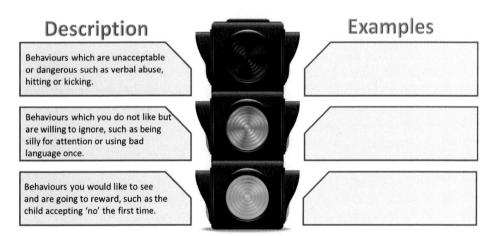

Description

Behaviours which are unacceptable or dangerous such as verbal abuse, hitting or kicking.

Behaviours which you do not like but are willing to ignore, such as being silly for attention or using bad language once.

Behaviours you would like to see and are going to reward, such as the child accepting 'no' the first time.

Examples

Green

The most important thing to remember about the traffic light system is that rather than focussing on punishment, this system puts emphasis on paying attention to behaviour you would like to see and heavily rewarding it with praise, affection and/or instant material reward (e.g. stickers). The way I often encourage parents to identify green behaviours, is to 'flip' the unwanted behaviours around. For example, if you wanted your child to stop answering back and hitting, we would then flip these to work out what you wanted to see:

- Stop answering back and not doing as told → Accepting no the first time and doing as told

- Stop hitting and shouting → Staying calm and being gentle

The greens should always be positive and should not include 'not doing something'. We want to outline what we *want* to see as parents rather than what we do not want to see.

It is important for the rewards to be meaningful for your child and this is something which needs to be closely explored with them. If the reward is not something which means something or motivates your child, then the system is unlikely to work. Rewards do not need to be expensive and can be as simple as a sticker every time a green behaviour is displayed. It is important to set a future target and slightly bigger reward (e.g. 20 stickers = going to the park with dad on a Saturday). As your child gets older, you can work towards rewards that delay their gratification. For example, your child earning a certain number of tokens which equate to a new football. This also helps children to persevere and see how hard work and effort can pay off.

I am often asked whether it is okay to reward behaviour which their child *should* be using (e.g. doing as they are told). As adults, we expect other adults to behave in a certain way. For example, if our boss at work asks us to do something which is in our job role, we are likely to follow this instruction. However, for children of this age, they are struggling with an internal battle to carry on with the things they are doing which are enjoyable (e.g. playing a game) or follow an instruction given which is not so enjoyable (e.g. tidy up their room). It is important for children to learn the benefit of following instructions and for this to happen it needs to be something which is a positive experience for your child. I often find this is harder for parents where one of their children will follow every instruction without a fuss. As we have already discussed, we are all very different and some children struggle with this more than others. Just like some babies will be born and have very little trouble sleeping whereas others fight this at every corner.

Amber

This is often the hardest part for parents to consider and implement. The amber behaviours are not dangerous or unacceptable, but are annoying and undesirable. For example, being silly or using some silly language and teasing. Often parents talk about how they do not want these types of behaviours to go unpunished or unnoticed. The problem with this, is that it may mean we are spending the majority of our day telling our child off or focussing on this negative behaviour. Instead the system proposes that we pay as little attention to this behaviour as possible and seek to re-direct our child's attention elsewhere. If we do this then children will often realise that there are better more positive ways of get our attention. Here are some top tips for ignoring amber behaviours:

- ☑ Like riding your bike up a hill, be prepared for the behaviour to ramp up a notch before it settles. Your child may soon realise that they are not getting the desired reaction and try a more drastic tactic. But like riding a bike up a hill, if you can keep going with your resolve, then the behaviour will reduce and you can lift your feet up and let the bike do the rest of the work on the other side!

- ☑ Ignoring means ignoring. Which means do not engage in discussion or rhetoric about the amber behaviour. Consider where you are looking, what your body language is saying. Ignoring is not just about not saying anything, it is also about ignoring with your body too.

- ☑ Try to divert and distract. If you can distract your child onto something more positive then you have just avoided both silly behaviour and a potential outburst – well done. Have a few tricks up your sleeve to do this. For example, you could say, do you want to help mummy cook or shall we go out in the garden and play catch?

Red

In terms of consequences, I recommend 'time out' as a strategy to deal with red behaviours. 'Time out' is a technique where children are taught to calm down by themselves, essentially promoting emotion regulation. It was invented by Arthur Staats (1962) and has since taken many forms. You may have seen different TV shows which use time out or the 'naughty step'. As psychologists, we believe the use of 'time out' should not to be seen as a punishment, but rather as a break for the child to have some space to calm down free from distractions and learn that essential skill of regulating their emotions. It is not a time to leave a child to cry but rather a time when a child can practice skills to calm down.

Children are not born with the ability to control their impulses and emotions; this is a vital skill which they develop and learn as their brain develops and their experiences widen. As a parent, it is important that you help your child to use these skills as they are calming down. However, whatever the child does in time out should not be rewarding. As a rule of thumb, it is often suggested that children are given a minute per year of age for time out (e.g. 7 years old = 7 minutes). It is also extremely important to give your child praise immediately after your child has calmed down after an 'outburst' and completed the time allocated in time out.

Time out is only to be used if your child has lost control. It is to promote emotion regulation. If a child has engaged in aggressive behaviour while calm (e.g. hitting a sibling) then it is important that a logical consequence would follow (e.g. loss of a privilege) rather than time out. Logical consequences teach children that there are consequences which will ultimately follow when they engage in certain behaviour. This is an invaluable life skill and one which children take into adulthood. For example, if your child was to break their sibling's toy, then a logical consequence may be that their pocket money is deducted to pay for a new one.

Removing privileges should only be used as a last resort and it is recommended that this is discussed when your child is calm. It needs to be in proportion to the behaviour. I often see parents who have threatened removal of something (normally an iPad) for a long period of time when a child has an outburst. However, this is often not sustainable and parents inevitably give in and give the iPad back after a few days. Also, children of this age are unlikely to really understand the implications of a month and the consequence can sometimes become meaningless. Instead, having a consequence of removal of any screen time for a day is something children can connect with and relate to.

Jump into action and carry out the plan.

 So, we have worked through the layer of approaches to try to tackle your child's anger and outbursts.

By now, you should have worked out the factors influencing your child's behaviour and also put together a plan of what to do. Obviously, there are a few things to consider before Energising into action and carrying out the plan:

1. Firstly, is this the right time? If you have a big project on at work or are ill then it may be better to wait a few weeks when you have more time and strength.

2. Secondly, are all those caring and looking after your child aware or your plan? It is important to include all those who are important in your child's life in this plan. Otherwise it will fall down. Consistency is key and if your partner is not on board then the plan will likely crumble. Make sure that everyone has had a say and that they know what to do.

3. Thirdly, do you have support in place to help you carry this plan through? We all need time to rest and recoup. It may be that if you are tackling the behaviour all week, that you schedule in a rest on Saturday morning where a family member/childminder takes the children whilst you have a well-earned break. How can you and your partner seek to support each other and know when the other is getting burnt out? I often recommend a 'tag' team approach whereby if a parent is starting to lose their temper that they walk away and let the other parent deal with the behaviour. Obviously, this is not always possible but can go a long way to keeping your cool, keeping things consistent and persevering to success.

In this section, I will discuss a few case examples and the plan for tackling behaviour. This may help to cement some of your planning and motivate you to putting the plan into action.

Jonny, aged 6 years.

Do you remember Karen and Jonny? When I met Jonny and his mum, Karen, Jonny had been having frequent outbursts for the past six months and they were mainly happen when Jonny was at family gatherings or outside of the house. Karen told me that she has had many family members and friends offer their advice on what may be 'wrong' with Jonny. She told me that she felt blamed, guilty and had started to think that there must be something wrong with Jonny.

After meeting Jonny and speaking with Karen, it became clear that Jonny felt extremely overwhelmed when he went to large family gatherings and when on playdates. The family events were noisy, chaotic and very much adult focussed. Jonny often had to wait longer than he would normally for his dinner and ate and drank things that he wouldn't normally (e.g. crisps, chocolate and cola).

When we explored the playdates that Jonny's outbursts tended to happen on, it became apparent that it was particularly when he played with other boys who had lots of energy. After a while, their play would turn from being boisterous to rough and then an outburst would occur.

Karen kept an ABC record of Jonny's outbursts and was able to learn much of the information above which she shared with me. Also Karen acknowledged that she often became carried away with talking to her friends and would notice that Jonny had missed a snack or his dinner time was due. Karen and I formed a plan with her partner, Dennis to tackle Jonny's behaviour.

Karen and Jonny's plan:

Building up relationships

Karen decided to spend 20 minutes each day either playing with Jonny or doing something he enjoyed. She ensured this was led by him. Karen kept a record of this and how she felt afterwards. She told me that she started to re-connect with her little boy and was really enjoying spending time together.

Environment and Triggers

For Karen this was a particularly important part of the puzzle. She decided to reduce Jonny's exposure to triggers. For example she tried out taking him for shorter periods of time to family gatherings and making sure he was well-fed and was not at a point of the day when he was most tired. Karen initially set out things for Jonny to do when at family gatherings. For example, build a Lego tower with his older cousin, which she initially supervised. These small changes started to significantly improve Jonny's behaviour and made going out much more enjoyable.

CONTINUED ON PAGE 221

Emotion Regulation Skills

Karen downloaded a breathing exercise app on her phone and spent time each afternoon with Jonny practicing this together. Karen shared with Jonny how she often counts to 10 when she feels angry to give herself some space.

Jonny designed his own superhero box in which he put some vital tools for calming down. When Jonny was faced with the anger villain, he would look to his superhero toolbox to beat anger and put it back in its place. Jonny found that bouncing on the trampoline and squeezing his favourite teddy helped him to calm down when frustrated.

Managing Behaviour

Karen designed the traffic light system specifically for Jonny. She outlined behaviours that she wanted to see (greens) and what would happen if Jonny displayed those behaviours (e.g. sticker). Karen was clear with Jonny about behaviour that was not acceptable and what would happen if he displayed this behaviour. She showed him where 'time out' was and they practiced what he could do in time out. Karen also discussed with Jonny what would happen if he did not go to time out – he would not watch his favourite programme that day.

Karen put the traffic light system into action when she had a week annual leave so she could concentrate on it fully. She enlisted the help of her husband in carrying this through and taking over from her when she felt herself getting frustrated. Other family members who they saw regularly were told about the system and asked to ignore any unwanted behaviour.

JONNY, *CONTINUED.*

By using this plan, Jonny's behaviour began to significantly improve. Karen kept a record of outbursts and rewards earned and noticed that the more rewards she gave, the better Jonny's behaviour became and the less he had outbursts. Jonny still had the occasional outburst, but Karen was able to notice when he was starting to show signs of frustration and get in there quicker, distracting him and helping him to calm down. Others also started to notice and comment on how well behaved Jonny was being, which gave him a boost and his confidence started to grow.

Description

Behaviours which are unacceptable or dangerous such as verbal abuse, hitting or kicking.

Behaviours which you do not like but are willing to ignore, such as being silly for attention or using bad language once.

Behaviours you would like to see and are going to reward, such as the child accepting 'no' the first time.

Jonny

Hitting, shouting, throwing objects and mean or hurtful language

Using silly words and teasing

Accepting no the first time and doing what has been asked

Now it is your turn. Below is a blank plan for you to look at and consider what you can do in each area to help your child manage their anger:

Your plan:

Building up relationships:

Environment and Triggers

Emotion Regulation Skills

Managing Behaviour

Description

Behaviours which are unacceptable or dangerous such as verbal abuse, hitting or kicking.

Behaviours which you do not like but are willing to ignore, such as being silly for attention or using bad language once.

Behaviours you would like to see and are going to reward, such as the child accepting 'no' the first time.

Examples

So, you have implemented the plan and jumped into action. The next step is to sit down and take a good long look at what you have done and what worked well, what could be improved and what could be done next.

I often recommend that parents and anyone else involved in this system sit down together to do this so that any issues can be ironed out as a team. As discussed above, it is important to keep a record of the system so that you can use this to look back on when you review:

Table 4-3: Example record of progress

	Monday	Tuesday	Wednesday	Thursday	Friday	Saturday	Sunday
Number of stress or anxiety outbursts (0-10)							
Number of rewards earned (0-10)							
Overall stress level (parents) 1 = very stressed, 5 = no stress							
Overall stress level (Child) 1 = very stressed, 5 = no stress							
Child happiness (parent rating). 1 = terrible, 5 = great							

Here are some useful questions to ask yourself:

- ✓ What went well?
- ✓ Why do you think this went well? What were the key factors to success?
- ✓ What did not go so well?

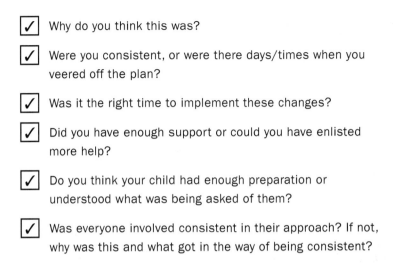

✓ Why do you think this was?

✓ Were you consistent, or were there days/times when you veered off the plan?

✓ Was it the right time to implement these changes?

✓ Did you have enough support or could you have enlisted more help?

✓ Do you think your child had enough preparation or understood what was being asked of them?

✓ Was everyone involved consistent in their approach? If not, why was this and what got in the way of being consistent?

Once you have answered and considered these questions, it is important to get back to the planning stage and consider upgrading the plan to give you the best chance of success. If consistency was lacking, then it would be important to think with others involved what got in the way of this and troubleshoot it further. If it wasn't the right time or you didn't have enough support, then how could you get more support or when would be the right time.

I am also going to take a look at common problems I often encounter with parents and ways in which we have dealt with them.

Troubleshooting:

"I don't have time!"

This is a common problem amongst parents these days. There are so many demands and often parents work long hours, have mountains of chores to do and barely keep up a semblance of social life. However, it is important to ask yourself the question of how important is your relationship with your child, how important is it that they learn the ability to manage their emotions? If these things are important, then something else has to give.

Is there a way of reducing work or getting someone else to help around the house? Even small changes can make a big difference. For example, one of the parents I worked with, Julie, realised she spent more time worrying about the appearance of the house and getting the washing done then spending time playing with her children. She said the demands of life had just taken over. I am sure we can all relate to this and how easy it is to fall into the trap. However, this realisation prompted Julie to gig things around and take a step back. She said she took a big deep breath and left all the mess until it was time to tidy up. She enlisted the children in 'tidy up' time which earned a reward to help her with some of the mess, and she also decided to get a cleaner to come once a fortnight to ensure that certain jobs were kept on top of. Julie found that by leaving things and letting more go, she actually felt less stressed and her relationship with her children blossomed.

"My child ruins our special time or has a tantrum!"

This can be a common worry for parents. If your child is 'ruining' the special time then it is important to look at whether this is actually child-led. Is the time led by your child and something which interests them? It should not be governed by any expectation and demand. Are you letting yourself go and being curious? Often parents can find it really difficult to 'let go' and just let their child lead the way.

For example, Alexander likes playing with trains. His father, Richard, spent special time with Alexander playing with his trains. Alexander likes just to talk to them and ride them around the living room, driving them through imaginary tunnels. Richard had grander plans and would try and steer Alexander towards building the train set and playing in a structured way with the trains. This would often lead to special time becoming not so special. Richard was able to take a step back and just go with the flow. He remained curious and asked Alexander to tell him about where the tunnels were and what was his favourite train. The special time was soon back on track.

"My child does not care about getting the rewards"

If this is the case then the rewards are not meaningful for your child. Ask yourself how were they selected? If you selected them yourself then this could be part of the problem. Involving your child in what the rewards could be and focussing these on their interests is key. They do not need to be material rewards but could be doing something together. It may be that these types of rewards are more meaningful. Is it that your child does not like stickers? Could you use marbles or coloured gems in a jar instead? Get creative!

"We just seem to be constantly sending our child to time out"

If you are finding that the traffic light system is weighted too heavily on consequence, then something has gone wrong. The system should be ideally weighted at 90% reward and 10% consequence. It may be that you need to set more achievable green behaviours and really seek to find these. I often advise parents at the beginning to give stickers/rewards to their children for even glimmers of green behaviour – this starts the ball rolling in the right direction. Also, can more behaviour be ignored, or could we avert an outburst with distraction?

"My child does not go to time out"

If your child refuses time out then it is important to outline what will happen. It is important to give a warning so that your child can have the opportunity to go. It is also important for them to be really clear on what time out is, where it is and have practiced this when calm. I recommend that if there is continued refusal, then there should be removal of privileges at this point. However, as mentioned above this needs to be in proportion to the behaviour and time limited.

It is also important that this has <u>absolutely no connection</u> with the rewards your child is earning. This is a common mistake parents make - to take away stickers or rewards when there is bad behaviour. Unfortunately, this completely undermines the system and often is the cause of it breaking down. Rewards and consequences should be completely separate, and your child should not lose their stickers or rewards if they display red behaviour. That said, the consequence needs to be deterring enough that your child will be more inclined to go to time out the next time they are asked. I often recommend using withdrawal of technology for a stated time period (e.g. 1 day) as a removal or privileges. However, if this is used, then technology should be in no way associated with the rewards.

NB: Each one of the strategies outlined in the PLAN section could have a book written about it in its own right and therefore it is important to remember that the suggestions in this chapter are the tip of the iceberg and can be expanded upon if that is needed once you have identified your own plan. It is also important to recognise and understand when is the time to seek further support. Obviously, we are talking about normal childhood problems in this book, but there can be times when anger does escalate and becomes something which needs to be worked on with a professional. Therefore, if in doubt do not hesitate to seek support and guidance from your GP and consider whether any additional support would be helpful.

References

Denham, S.A., Mitchell-Copeland, J., Strandberg, K., Auerbach, S. & Blair, K. (1997). Parental Contributions to Preschoolers' Emotional Competence: Direct and Indirect Effects. *Motivation and Emotion, 21*, 65-86.

Paluska S. A. & Schwenk, T. L. (2000). Physical activity and mental health: current concepts. *Sports Med 29*: 167-180.

Richardson, A. (2006). *They Are What You Feed Them.* Harper Thorsons.

Staats, AW; Staats, CK; Schutz, RE; Wolf, M (1962). "The conditioning of textual responses using "extrinsic" reinforcers". J Exp Anal Behav. 5: 33–40

Further Reading

Collins-Donnelly, K. (2014). *Starving the anger gremlin for children aged 5-9.* Jessica Kingsley: London.

Siegel, D. J. & Bryson, T. P. (2012) *The Whole-Bran Child. 12 proven strategies to nurture your child's developing mind.* Robinson: London.

Webster Stratton (2005). *The Incredible Years: A trouble shooting guide for parents of children aged 2-8.* Incredible Years: Seattle.

Whitehouse, E. & Pudney, W. (1998). *A Volcano in My Tummy.* Peace Foundation

School related Stress

"Maths is Impossible!"

Dr Katherine Hodson, clinical psychologist

As parents it is natural to want your child to feel happy and relaxed about their school life and academic work. Not surprisingly, children feel the same way.

The NSPCC recently did a study with school aged children, and found that their biggest cause of stress was 'academic worries' – affecting nearly 50% of the children surveyed.

It is not unusual for children to have times when they find schoolwork more difficult. This may be when a child finds it tricky to manage the day to day challenges of learning, such as making mistakes with work, finding the work too hard or putting too much pressure on themselves to succeed.

Or because of a specific reason, like before an important assessment or because they've been off school with an illness or injury and have to get 'back into school mode' again. Sometimes these stresses can last longer than you would expect, and may upset your child more than you would like them to. Therefore, we will be looking at school related stress within this chapter, to see what can be done.

Day to day school work

If you are worried about your child's school related stress, the first challenge is to work out how big a deal it actually is for them. Some children are more than happy to chat about work being too difficult; however, this is not always the case -- and not surprisingly, the younger the child, the harder they can find it to open up. Therefore, it can be good to keep an eye out for different signs of academic stress.

Signs of academic stress

Unwilling to complete homework (particularly when they've been keen on doing so in the past)

Worried they will 'do it wrong'

Stalling / delaying tactics

Over-dependent on your involvement, finding it hard to complete homework on their own

Complaining about finding the work too hard

Over working – doing more than what you or school would expect

Sleep problems in the week and in term time, that may improve at weekends/ holidays

Becoming irritated or cross more easily

Becoming anxious or tearful about going to school or completing school work

Withdrawing in school

Worrying about being told off or getting in to trouble at school

Becoming overly upset if they get an answer wrong

It is worth noting that children can show the above signs of stress for all sorts of other reasons too. For example, children can become anxious about leaving you, and at such times they may start to cry before school, and find it hard to sleep on a school night. Children can also become cross and irritated if they are feeling a bit poorly so don't have their normal level of resilience to stick with a tricky homework task. Therefore, you may need to be a bit of a detective, and keep an eye on your child for a few weeks, to see if their stress is sticking around.

If your child seems to have been having difficulties for a little while, it can be helpful to try and work out in a sentence or two what their exact problems are.

For example, "my child gets cross when they make a mistake" and "they refuse to do their maths homework - especially on a Monday night".

Be as specific as you possibly can, below.

My child...

_____

_____

_____

_____

_____

_____

_____

_____

_____

_____

_____

If you've worked out your child is feeling stressed about their day to day school work, and the problem has been around for a while, then it is important to have a clear idea about what is causing it.

This will help you know what the most effective solutions are going to be. Let's take our 'understand' quiz, and find out what might be important.

Understand Quiz

Read each question on the quiz, and if it seems like it could be a problem, put a tick next to that question in the table on page 237. This table shows you the page numbers for the relevant information about that question.

Developmental / Stage of life

Q1) *Has your child just started a new class?*

- Yes............Go to Q2

- No.... move on to Q3

Q2) *Does the work seem to be harder than what they were doing before?*

- Yes.........This could be an issue - jot it down, and move on to Q3

- No.......move on to Q3

Q3) *My child seems to be showing signs of a growth spurt (e.g. eating and sleeping more), or is young for their school year.*

- Yes.........This could be an issue - jot it down and move on to Q4

- No.........move on to Q4

Q4) *My child is starting to show signs of puberty (e.g. body odour, and increased body hair).*

- Yes.........This could be an issue - jot it down and move on to Q5

- No.........move on to Q5

Neurological (brain development)

Q5) *My child appears to quickly become overly emotional when finding work difficult, rather than slowly becoming more upset.*

- Yes........ This could be a problem - jot it down, and move on to Q6

- No.........move on to Q6

Q6) *My child seems to have difficulties concentrating on their work for long, and they've always found concentrating hard.*

- Yes........This could be a problem - jot it down and move on to Q7

- No.........move on to Q7

Q7) *Are there specific areas of work that your child always finds difficult? For example, numeracy work or reading?*

- Yes....... This could be a problem - jot it down, and move on to Q8

- No........Move on to Q8

Q8) *Has your child's teacher ever commented that your child tends to find a specific area of work hard (e.g. numeracy)?*

- Yes........ This could be an issue - jot it down and move on to Q9

- No.........move on to Q9

Q9) *Does anyone in your family also struggle with particular areas of academic work -- such as having dyslexia?*

- Yes......This could be an issue - jot it down and move on to Q10

- No...... move on to Q10

Thoughts

Q10) *Has your child told you that they have any worries or stress about the schoolwork? e.g. 'this is too hard for me' or 'I hate making mistakes'?*

- Yes......... This could be an issue - jot it down, and move on to Q11

- No....... move on to Q11

Q11) *Does your child ever talk to themselves in a negative way, whilst attempting their schoolwork? For example, "I'm hopeless at maths" or "why am I so stupid?"*

- Yes........ This could be an issue - jot it down, and move on to Q12

- No......... Sometimes children keep their worries or stress thoughts to themselves, so keep an eye open for these, and consider asking your child what they're stressed about when they next seem concerned with their school work. Move on to Q12

Personality

Q12) *Would you describe your child as a bit of a perfectionist with school work?*

- Yes..... This could be an issue - jot it down and move on to Q13

- No...... move on to Q13

Q13) *Does your child often struggle or appear stressed when they find things difficult (e.g. puzzles, lego models, writing tasks)?*

- Yes..... This could be an issue - jot it down and move on to Q14

- No..... move on to Q14

Behaviour

Q14) *Are there times when you let your child stop doing the work because they're finding it too stressful, and they don't end up finishing it off later?*

- Yes...... This could be an issue - jot it down, and move on to Q15

- No....... move on to Q15

Q15) *Can your child manage to 'stick with' tricky schoolwork with your encouragement and support?*

- Yes...... Good job! Move on to Q16

- No...... This could be an issue – jot it down, and move on to Q16

Environment

Q16) *Does the amount of noise or distractions in the room change how your child gets on with the work?*

- Yes...... This could be an issue, jot it down, and move on to Q17

- No..... move on to Q17

Q17) *Has your family or child experienced a very difficult event over the last few months, such as a bereavement or a serious accident?*

- Yes........This could be an issue, jot it down and move on to Q18

- No........ move on to Q18

Expectations

Q18 *Be honest with this one! Do you as parents have higher expectations of your child's grades than they can sometimes achieve?*

- Yes....... This may be important, jot it down, and move on to Q19

- No.......move on to Q19

Q19) *Does your child's teacher have higher expectations of your child's grades than they can sometimes achieve?*

- Yes...... This may be important, jot it down and then you've finished the quiz

- No...... you've finished the quiz

Q20 *Does your child's teacher seem to have low expectations of your child's performance compared to what they can achieve at home?*

- Yes...... This may be important, jot it down and then you've finished the quiz

- No...... you've finished the quiz

If you've answered no to all the quiz questions, but you are worried about your child's academic stress, then do chat to their teacher and see if they are worried. Keep an eye out over the next few weeks to see if there are any quiz questions that could have been answered 'yes' rather than 'no', and hopefully things should settle down.

If you've answered yes to some of the quiz questions, then it is worth exploring these in a bit more detail. I will now discuss each one in turn.

Quiz Question	Tick if it could be a problem	Page number of the explanation of the issue	Page number for the possible strategies to help this issue
Development / stage of life		237	250
Neurological (brain development)		241	253
Thoughts		242	257
Personality		243	259
Behaviour		247	264
Environment		248	267
Expectations		249	270

1. Development / Stage of life

There are a great many changes in the expectations and set-up of a classroom, depending on which year your child is in. All school years bring their own challenges, given the increasingly difficult work and higher expectations of teachers. However, certain school transitions can be particularly difficult for children, as outlined below.

Starting reception:

The start of schooling is a huge transition for any child. Your child has to......

- learn all the new rules and expectations of their classroom
- get a sense of their teacher
- learn new names and get a feel for the other pupils in their class
- work out how to get around the school

- when they are allowed to eat and drink
- be independent in managing their belongings, along with getting dressed for PE etc. all by themselves, and so on......!

If you think about how exhausted you can feel when starting a new job, it will give a little insight into the experience of your child... and they may even be doing it for the first time. Whilst the work itself is not always too demanding, they may be having to cope with reading regularly and completing a certain level of homework - often when exhausted due to them having to cope with the longer school days. Being young for the academic year can also contribute to children finding the demands of the school day more difficult, as they adjust to five long days a week when only just 4 years old.

Year 1:

Children can feel very excited about moving up to Year 1, as they will be aware that this means they are no longer the 'babies' of the school. The increased structure of Year 1 can help some children, and decrease their levels of stress. For other children the change in teaching style from play based, free flow to more structured, directed learning can be tough to manage.

Year 2:

Often brings the challenge of SATs examinations, which are usually the first testing scenario your child has had to deal with. This process can result in stress for some children - particularly when they feel pressure to do well. Such pressure can come from their school, their family or even from their own self-expectations; and the SATS themselves can be very tiring for youngsters to manage.

Year 3:

This can be a difficult transition, given that the children are starting Key Stage 2, and the demands of the schoolwork can shift to a higher level. Schools often increase the length of the school day for Year 3 students too – or remove break times to ensure greater time within the classroom. Therefore, your child has to adjust to potentially greater fatigue alongside the academic demands. Research shows that children in year 3 go through an emotional shift where they focus attention on which social group they belong to. Children may feel pressure and have times when they feel excluded from certain groups. These feelings may then transfer from the playground into the classroom and can block learning.

Year 5:

Depending on where you live or the kind of school your child attends, your child may be involved with tutoring for the 11-plus examination or the common entrance exam throughout Year 5, and across the summer holidays into Year 6. This can be stressful for some children - particularly the ones who feel they may struggle to pass the examination or understand the work. It can also contribute towards children's fatigue, given their increased workload during a year when they often have more school homework too.

Year 6:

Year 6 can be an exciting year for many children, as they have made it to the 'top of the school'. However, Year 6 students are also having to prepare for their transition up to secondary school, which can be difficult for those who are less confident about moving schools, and for those students who find it hard shifting to taking more responsibility for organising their own workload, school bag and even journey to school. There are also the KS2 SATS examinations to manage in Year 6, which can cause further stress.

General Transition Issues

There is often a certain amount of 'playground' talk between the students in anticipation of a change in class - which is completely normal and understandable. (Doesn't everyone enjoy a good gossip from time to time?!!) For example, children have often been told by the older pupils in the school, and also from some of the teachers themselves, that the work in a new class will be 'more difficult', or that their next teacher is 'very strict' which can lead to natural anxiety about what is coming next. Therefore, if your child is expressing such views early on in the autumn term, their talk may well just reflect a normal process, and doesn't need a great deal of intervention.

Once your child has been in the class for a few weeks, they may start to adjust to the higher academic demands, and get a better sense of their teacher's teaching style and requirements of work, leading to their stress levels starting to fall. This tends to follow the same pattern as the 'anxiety curve', described in chapter 1, where everyone's anxiety shoots up when initially experiencing a difficult event, but then gradually comes down over time, as they become desensitised to the worrying events, and become used to the demands on them.

Growth spurts

Other 'life factors' can also impact upon how a child is coping with their school work. Children often seem to have endless appetites when going through a growth spurt – and tend to need more sleep as well. The everyday demands of school and life can become exhausting for a child who is doing some major growing. However, they should return to their normal energy levels once the growth spurt has finished. Growth spurts can also accompany the start of puberty, typically occurring earlier in girls (around 10 to 14 years) than boys (around 12 to 16 years), and sometimes even earlier than this, in the case of 'precocious puberty'. Given the significant increase of hormones, children can start to display mood swings, and may become more focussed on the changes to their body and their friendships than the academic work they need to be completing.

If your child appears consistently stressed about the work demands over a few weeks, it can be good to chat to a teacher about how they think your child is settling into the new class - to take their view as to whether they have any concerns or not. It may also be worth introducing a few of the strategies outlined in the 'Plan' section below.

2. Neurological (Brain Development)

Everyone's brain is wired differently, and individual differences can sometimes cause problems for children at school, including certain neurological differences.

3 to 5% of children are diagnosed with Attention Deficit Hyperactivity Disorder (ADHD), a neurological condition that makes it difficult for children to manage certain 'executive function' tasks (Bartley, 2000). Executive functioning is the term given to a group of processes that are often controlled in the front of the brain (the frontal lobes), that allow an individual to manage the tasks and goals they are trying to do - such as focussing, organising themselves, managing time and so on. Therefore, if your child has ADHD, it will be more difficult for them to concentrate on different tasks (particularly those that are less interesting for your child), sit still for extended periods of time, and act thoughtfully and in an organised manner rather than impulsively. As you can imagine, such symptoms can make school life very difficult for children with ADHD. For example, it can be difficult for them to sit still during carpet time or assembly, focus on schoolwork and homework, and organise themselves in a timely manner to undertake school projects etc. For more detail on the impact of this condition, I would recommend looking at the ADDISS website, or Christopher Green's book *Understanding ADHD: a parent's guide to attention deficit hyperactivity disorder in children* (details are at the end of the chapter).

All children vary in terms of how physically able they are, how in tune they are emotionally, and also how cognitively able they are. Cognitive ability refers to a child's ability to solve complex verbal, visual and practical problems and is commonly known as intelligence or IQ. For children who fall below average intelligence, or have been diagnosed with a specific learning difficulty (e.g. dyslexia), learning can prove challenging. Therefore, it can be helpful to have a specific plan as to how best to support them at school (as outlined below).

Finally, it is worth noting the potential impact of anxiety on the ability of a child to complete schoolwork. When our brains identify a potential 'danger', they release a particular hormone (adrenocorticotrophic hormone or ACTH) that then causes the adrenal glands in the kidneys to release adrenalin throughout the body. As discussed in chapter 1, this is our body's "fight or flight" response. For some children who find schoolwork stressful for whatever reason (e.g. generally finding the work hard or aiming for perfection in every piece of work), adrenalin may then be released in their bodies, resulting in them demonstrating anger or anxiety about the homework / school project in hand, or causing the child to try and avoid doing it in order to 'save face'. This hormonal reaction may also reduce the child's ability to focus attention on their work - increasing the likelihood that they will struggle to understand or remember it. This can unfortunately cause the child more anxiety when next having to complete a similar homework task, or having to revisit the work topic they found difficult.

ACTH can also cause the stress hormone cortisol to be released, which can make it tricky for some children to fall asleep - making them more tired, and thus finding it harder to concentrate or manage their school work. Too much cortisol can also affect learning directly, by reducing a child's ability to remember information, increasing their stress levels even further, and creating a vicious circle.

3. Thoughts

Our thoughts can be incredibly powerful in changing how we view the world. As we have already seen in this book, our unhelpful thoughts can fall into particular groups, often called Thinking Traps, which can cause children problems when coping with schoolwork.

For example:

Thinking Trap	Example
Negative glasses	I will never understand this work I'm hopeless at fractions
Fortune telling	I'm going to fail the 11-plus exam I won't get any spellings right on the Friday test
Positive doesn't count	I only got these sums right by luck
Overgeneralising	I don't get long division so I'm rubbish at maths
Putting yourself down	I'm so stupid I'm an idiot
Black and white thinking	I should have got 8/8 answers correct, 7/8 isn't good enough
Catastrophising	I'm never going to be able to get punctuation. So I'll do badly in all my tests and won't ever get a job.

4. Personality

We are all born with different personality traits (e.g. sociability), with some of us at one end of the trait, some at the other end, and most in between. I wonder how you would rate yourself now in terms of these four personality traits?

With social **confidence**, you may be:

Very outgoing and love being the centre of attention...VS... Prefer being out of the limelight and feel shy in new situations.

Our level of **competitiveness** can vary greatly too between:

Wanting to 'win' or 'excel' above anything... VS... Preferring to celebrate others' victories.

Our **perfectionism** may fall somewhere along a continuum between being:

Very easy going...VS... Being a total perfectionist.

And even our tendency to **worry** can vary from:

Being a total worrier...VS... Being laid back about everything in life.

Would you say you are the same as how you remember being as a child? Sometimes our personalities can be quite 'rigid', and stay the same throughout our lives, whereas for other people, things can change quite a bit - often depending on the different experiences you have.

Our children often inherit personality traits from us - both the good and the bad! These can have an impact on their experience at school, and with schoolwork. For example, children who lack social confidence may struggle to put their hands up in class, to answer questions, or to manage the performance elements of the curriculum such as speaking in front of classmates or in assembly. Other very competitive children may focus more on finishing a work task as quickly as possible, than finishing it more thoughtfully, with more accuracy.

I will now focus on a couple of personality traits in a little more detail.

Perfectionism

A certain amount of perfectionism can be motivating for people, as it can help spur them on with tasks, make them work hard with their schoolwork and result in them making great achievements when it is channelled in the right way. Therefore, it is certainly not a personality trait we would want to reduce too much, as this would cause a whole new set of difficulties!

However, being a perfectionist can unfortunately result in people experiencing greater stress at times. If you feel your child is quite a perfectionist, it is worth thinking about whether it impacts on their learning.

DO THEY:

- spend too long on homework? ('burn out')
- avoid doing work because they are worried they might do it wrong?
- criticise what they have done?
- struggle to cope when they make mistakes?
- seem overly sensitive to criticism?
- need you to micro-manage their school work?
- find it hard to work independently? (need you to sit with them)

Once you know how perfectionism is causing problems, you have a clearer goal to work on, which should help your child channel it more helpfully.

Resilience

Our children's resilience can make a great difference to their ability to cope with difficult schoolwork. I'm sure you can remember a time when you found a particular piece of schoolwork difficult, and all of the different feelings you experienced whilst trying to make sense of it - perhaps frustration, anger, worry or even feeling upset? As discussed in chapter 3 on self-esteem, children can also vary in their ability to cope with the difficult feelings they experience when starting to find work difficult. When a child starts to struggle with something they are doing, or makes a few mistakes on a piece of work, their resilience will determine whether they give up, or keep on trying. Resilience can also help children take criticism constructively rather than personally, and realise that if they find one topic tricky (e.g. punctuation), it doesn't mean that they will find all of that subject area difficult.

Learning styles

As outlined in chapter 4, a child's academic mindset will be important in understanding their school related stress.

To recap, Carol Dweck first described two mindsets:

A FIXED MINDSET:

Children with fixed mindsets believe that they are fundamentally a certain level of intelligence, which can't change however much work or effort they put into learning. Therefore, rather than enjoying being challenged by difficult work, these children may actually be quite fearful of getting things wrong, and may end up avoiding such challenges.

A GROWTH MINDSET:

Children with a growth mindset do not see their intelligence or ability as an immovable quantity, but instead believe that they can develop their own talent by working hard and learning from any mistakes.

Gardening!

Ravi, 10 years old (with a growth mindset) vs Andrew, 10 years old (with a fixed mindset)

Ravi and Andrew were friends at school, and were both keen gardeners. They decided to try their luck growing vegetables after their parents let them have small patches in their gardens. Neither had tried this before, but both were feeling confident and enthusiastic about giving it a go after learning about plants at school.

Ravi borrowed a gardening book from the library and Andrew chatted to his dad about getting started. Neither of them were sure what to do, but went for it anyway.

Ravi planted his seeds a bit too close together. Andrew planted half of his seeds too deep. Therefore when their plants started to grow, Ravi's did not thrive, and many of Andrews didn't survive.

Ravi thought to himself: 'Whoops - I need to plant them further apart. At least I know to check the spacing between the plants now'. So he had another go with some spare seeds, and changed his approach.

Andrew thought: 'Oh no, I can't do this. I don't seem to be able to grow vegetables'. He felt a bit put out, but decided to try again with a few more seeds.

This time Ravi planted his seeds too deep, and Andrew planted his seeds too close together. So Ravi's didn't grow at all, and Andrew's did not get very big or mature to produce a crop.

Ravi thought: 'Ah, I've done something wrong here. Let's try again!' He had another go, learning from his mistakes again.

Andrew thought: 'I knew it, I just can't do this. None of my plants are growing properly. This is pointless!' He didn't bother planting any more seeds, and let his veggie patch grow over.

On the third attempt Ravi got it right. He felt happy that he had learnt how to grow vegetables, and kept going for the rest of the season, despite the occasional odd shaped carrot!

As you can see, children with fixed mindsets are much more vulnerable to feeling stressed when they do not meet expectations. They find it more difficult to tolerate the feelings associated with learning something new, feeling challenged or coping with mistakes.

However, is a mindset necessarily permanent? Luckily, no. I have outlined various strategies to help children shift to a growth mindset in the Plan section below.

5. Behaviour

Children can be clever at learning how to avoid less enjoyable tasks if they can help it. This can start from a very young age, and we then fall into patterns of behaviour with our children, that keep them acting the same way too.

For example, young children will often 'play a game' of dropping a toy out of their pushchair, or off the table. As parents, we tend to pick the toy up for our children, to help them out and ensure they have all their toys close by to play with. This pattern can then often continue, where parents find themselves picking up all sorts of toys, pens, pencils, books, cups, coats and so on and so on, to save the child from doing so. Over time, the child learns that if they act in a certain way (e.g. pointing at a fallen pencil, making a particular noise or appearing upset) then their parents will respond in the usual manner, and pick up the fallen object to save them the hassle or upset of doing it. This can keep extending - for example a child might find it hard to put their shoes on, and they have learnt that if they show their usual behaviour (e.g. a cry or demand) then their parents will again assist and save them the job.

Does this sound familiar?

When faced with difficult homework, children can commonly fall into the same pattern of behaviour. They may make the same gestures or expressions that indicate to you as the parent that they are finding it very difficult or do not want to undertake the piece of work. If they are allowed to avoid doing it - either by not completing the homework, or by 'roping you in' to complete most of it for them, then they have managed to 'escape' their unpleasant stressed feelings quickly, and will be more likely to do the same again, when faced with a tricky task.

Whilst this can feel a relief to the child in the short-term, they are being prevented from learning how to 'sit with' uncomfortable feelings, in order to stay focussed and finish the work. They may also attribute any academic success with your input rather than their effort. This may reinforce the idea that they are not clever enough to work independently and reinforce a dependent approach to learning.

6. Environment

In our children's clinic, we often see children who experience different sensory difficulties:

> **Easily overstimulated**, and bothered by too much information bombarding their senses:

- Sounds - noise from siblings, television or music
- Sights - television picture, siblings playing
- Touch - clothes, the feel of work materials, or room temperature
- Smells - cooking smells

> **Feel their senses are under stimulated**, and thus want to seek out sensations (e.g. sitting upside down to watch television, punching a wall or bouncing or fidgeting)

Or they fall somewhere in between.

As you can imagine, sensory differences can cause problems at school. For example, an easily over-stimulated child may find it difficult to concentrate on what they are doing in a busy classroom or home environment.

Research shows that 1 in 6 children aged between 7 and 11 years find it hard to process sensory information (hearing/touch), affecting their ability to focus on what they are doing.

Children may also struggle to manage their emotions, or have attention and concentration difficulties if they are overly hungry, are having disturbed sleep, or suffer from a food intolerance or allergy. This may be a direct cause, for example the hyperactivity displayed by some children who have certain artificial colourings, e.g. sunset yellow (E110), tartrazine (E102) and allura red (E129). Or difficulties could be more indirect, such as a child struggling to focus on school work because of suffering tummy aches and cramps, given a physical condition such as Crohn's disease.

Tough Life Events

Another issue that can understandably impact upon children is experiencing a significant life event, such as bereavement, loss of contact with a loved one through separation or divorce or other trauma. Depending on the child's personality (e.g. their resilience and ability to communicate openly about their feelings) they may vary on how they cope with the difficult experience, and how they manage to deal with any additional pressure from school. For example, children who are having to process difficult emotions around a tricky life event may not be sleeping as well, and may struggle to have the capacity to cope with the additional stressors from school including the schoolwork. Their progress may stagnate and they are at risk of underachieving in relation to their learning potential.

However other children who are learning to adjust to a difficult life event may throw all their energy into their schoolwork, and actually excel to a greater extent. Therefore, if your child has unfortunately suffered from a difficult life event, keep an eye on how they are coping with their work over a few weeks, chat to their teacher about how they seem within the classroom and talk to them about how they are doing when the time is right.

7. Expectations

It is natural for a parent to strive to support their child to do their best and reach their learning potential. It is also not surprising, that sometimes we as parents can hope our children may achieve something in their life that perhaps we did not. Therefore, over the course of a child's life, they will be receiving messages about what we think their ability is, and how well they could be achieving, in all areas of life.

As parents we may also see our children as being very similar to us at times, and thus if we struggled with an area in life, we may expect our children to as well. Conversely, if we found something easy or boring, we may be more likely to wonder whether our children feel the same.

This is often true with academic work, and children frequently have a sense of how clever they are based on the messages we give to them, which may or may not reflect reality.

Teachers will also have an impression of how able the children in their class are, as calculated by the student's ongoing school work and even formal assessments. These tend to reflect children's ability fairly well, however there can be some exceptions. For example, a child with speech and language difficulties may present as less able academically, given that their literacy levels are below the expectations for most children their age and they have difficulties expressing what they are thinking.

That same child may actually be intellectually able, they just need teaching staff to make the curriculum more accessible by making it more visual and practical, so they can show everyone what they can do.

Teachers may also gain an impression of a student based on the child's previous performance at school, and a 'narrative' about their ability can be passed down from teacher to teacher. Whilst this is a helpful guide to a child's ability, it is not always a fair measure - as sometimes children respond better to one teacher's style than another, or may have been suffering other issues (e.g. a bereavement in the family) that affect their academic performance.

A child who has negative expectations of themselves, viewing themselves as less clever than classmates, and criticising themselves (e.g. 'I'm rubbish at maths'), is likely to feel anxious when approaching learning tasks.

 I will now go through each of the areas listed in the 'understand' section above, and discuss some ways to address each one.

1. Development / Stage of life

Schools are aware of the times in a child's school life where they transition (move from one stage to another - reception, year 3 and year 6) and usually have a careful transition plan in place. If your child is having to adjust to the demands of a new class, it is always worth chatting to their teacher about how they are getting along. Their teacher will typically have experience in how young people your child's age cope with the transition into the new academic year, and the issues they commonly face, which may help give you some reassurance and strategies to try.

If your child is in reception and is not yet 5 years old, it can be worth chatting with the teacher or Special Educational Needs Coordinator (SENCo) in the school about whether your child could be allowed to attend a certain number of half days initially, until they adjust to the longer school day.

We all know the restorative impact of sleep; however, the children who present in our clinic are often finding it difficult to have a good night's sleep, due to overtiredness or having 'busy brains' at bedtime. It is always important to support your child in maintaining good sleep habits. Tips to remember include:

- Avoid caffeine – this can be found in cola or other energy drinks, chocolate as well as hot drinks like tea and coffee. At the very least save these for the morning or early afternoon

- Put away electronic devices away at least one hour before bedtime too, as the blue light they emit can disrupt the brain into knowing it is 'sleep time'

- Have the same or similar routine every night, such as a shower, story and bed

- Keep the bedroom calm and clutter free. Beds should be places where they just sleep or 'wind down' so when your child climbs into bed, they always associate it with sleep time

- Bring their bedtime forward a little if they are getting overtired

Sleep can be particularly important when your child is going through a growth spurt and is just as important as food. When having a period of growth, you may want to consider increasing the size of their breakfast, and packing extra snacks for your child to take to school during the day, plus increasing the size of their after-school snack as well.

However, always balance the number of snacks you give them with the quantity of dinner they are subsequently having, as you want to ensure they are having a sufficient amount of a well-balanced meal rather than allowing them to 'fill up on' snacks.

It is always important to maintain your patience and understanding, and avoid putting any extra pressure on your child. Therefore, consider the number of extracurricular activities they are undertaking, and the amount and frequency of out of school work you are encouraging them to do. As the demands of the work increase (e.g. extra spelling tests and longer pieces of homework) it may be worth chatting through with your child about how best you can support them. For example, whether they need help to break down larger pieces of work, and whether they want you to help them revise for tests or whether they would rather do it on their own.

If your child appears anxious about moving into a new school or new year, find out if there is a transition plan in place. Transition plans involve a meeting with your child and their new teacher to discover what their teacher is like and what the expectations will be of them. Teaching staff may take photos of the new classroom which you can look at during the summer holidays to remind your child of what to expect when they return to school. This supports your child to be prepared for the new academic year and transition more confidently.

It can be helpful working out a 'hook' for them to stay engaged with more challenging work - such as a reward for them having a go at the more difficult work. Every child is different with the sorts of rewards that work for them, but ideas can include:

- Sweets or treat food
- Bonus time on games consoles
- Watching an extra television programme
- Additional time playing with yourselves
- Points that can be traded in for different items, like pocket money or a toy

Hormonal changes can understandably impact upon your child's ability to focus at school. It may be useful to give your child gentle reminders to keep focussed on their school work, and remember all your parenting strategies that have worked in the past, to cope with any hormonal outbursts or upsets your child may demonstrate. They may also appreciate you offering time to chat about the changes that are occurring in their body if helpful - to make sense of it all, and learn that puberty is normal and happens to everyone. This may then help them shift back into 'work mode' when needed, and allow you the chance to discuss how they want you to support them in school work at this particular time in their life.

A final strategy is ensuring there is 'listening time' incorporated into family life every day to give your child space to share any new difficulties they are having at school. This could be during their after-school snack, in the car on the journey home or to out of school clubs, over dinner or at a time convenient for your family. The more your family is able to keep up an open channel of communication, the quicker and easier it will be to manage any problems that come up.

2. Neurological (Brain Development)

All children have strengths and difficulties across the different areas of the curriculum. Rather than over focussing on your child's trickier areas, identify their abilities as well. You can chat to their class teacher to get some further ideas about their learning strengths too. This can be anything: for example, a core subject such as science or maths, a more creative subject, such as drama, music or art, or even a skill they might bring to the classroom, such as being a thoughtful or organised child. Giving them opportunities to shine by paying attention to their strengths helps to strengthen your child's self-esteem. This has the knock-on effect of supporting them to feel more open and resilient to work on their weaker areas.

If the ADHD description in the Understand section above seems to match your experience of your child, do chat to their GP about whether it would be worth taking them for an ADHD assessment. It can also be helpful to try these strategies to support your child:

✓ Remember sleep!

There have been some interesting studies that indicate that sleep deprived children can falsely appear to have ADHD. Therefore, think through your child's bedtime routine, and other aspects of improving their sleep patterns, as outlined in the above section of this chapter.

✓ **Don't forget diet**

Perhaps keep a food diary and check whether there is any pattern in what your child eats compared to how they behave. Do they regularly have foods with the known 'trigger E numbers' outlined above? You could think about experimenting with changing their diet, to see if this has any positive effect. Always take advice from a dietician or doctor if significantly changing your child's diet, to ensure they are keeping to a well-balanced diet.

✓ **Break school tasks down**

into smaller, more manageable chunks. Ideally ones that last the length of their attention span.

✓ **Give your child 'movement breaks'**

Structure in breaks between chunks of work, for example play 'Simon says' if your child is younger, or get them to pick out a card at random that has a different physical activity on it (e.g. do 10 star jumps). It could also be less structured, such as suggesting that they go and kick a football in the garden for 15 minutes, or put on some music and dance around the living room.

✓ **Allow your child to fidget if they need to**

Some children need to move to concentrate on their work. Having something to twiddle, or squeeze in their hands helps them to focus better.

✓ **Praise and reward your child for concentrating**

You may need to start small (concentrating for a few minutes), and then gradually increase the length of time they are concentrating for.

✓ **Measure how much time your child has focussed attention**

Sand timers are a good way to measure how much time your child has sustained attention – these can be ordered from school resource sites such as LDA (Learning Development Aids).

✓ **Coach your child to develop organisational skills**

Initially organise your child's school bag, academic work etc. for them, if needed. You can then take one item at a time, and coach them to manage the organisation themselves. Prompts like lists can give them extra support to start with.

✓ Use visual prompts

Visual prompts are a good way to remind children what they need to remember – stick them in useful places – like the back of their bedroom door or front door.

Noel, aged 10 years.

Noel found it very difficult to sort out his school bag, and he was often in trouble for forgetting various belongings, such as his sun hat, reading book and any homework. His mum took over packing his bag for him, but would always do it at breakfast time when Noel was around, so he could listen to her descriptions of what was going into his bag. She then started putting a post-it note on his cereal bowl, that reminded him to pack his reading book into his school bag, but she packed all the other bits for him. Noel sometimes forgot to do this, so his mum would remind him before leaving for school.

Once he had got into the habit of packing the reading book at breakfast time, she then moved on to his sun hat, and continued with this strategy until he had taken over control of packing his bag. After holidays his mum tended to leave him post-it notes with the lists of what might need to go into his bag to refresh his memory, but he generally found it much easier to remember everything.

Give your child short, clear instructions, always making sure that you have their attention by getting eye contact first. It can sometimes be helpful to support what you are saying with visual prompts -- such as pictures or key points written down.

Keep the environment as distraction free as possible - see the 'Environment - sensory overload' section for ideas.

If you think that your child may have a specific learning difficulty, or generally finds the learning tricky, then it is very important to meet with their classroom teacher, and the school SENCo if needed, to work out a plan to best support them. The school SENCo may carry out some assessments to work out exactly where the difficulties lie. She will discuss these assessments with you and may if you agree, make a request for the involvement of an educational psychologist, or other professional.

The educational psychologist will meet with you, observe your child in their classroom, consult with their teacher and work with your child directly. They may recommend if the involvement of other professionals would be helpful and recommend a referral to another professional such as a speech and language therapist, an occupational therapist or paediatrician.

Following assessment, an individual plan is agreed with you on how to best meet your child's needs taking into consideration advice from professionals. Specific strategies and interventions are agreed for your child to be delivered at school and at home. These may include their working environment, such as positioning your child in the best place for them within the classroom, and managing distractions and noise. Strategies may also involve the way in which your child is taught new information, such as breaking tasks down into 'bite sized pieces', using visual information to back up any verbal instructions, ensuring instructions are short in length and easily understandable and giving your child more processing time before responding to questions.

If your child is given a 'label', it can be very helpful to spend time with your child chatting about the meaning of their difficulty. It may be useful for your child to know that lots of other young people also have similar issues, and that they shouldn't stop them from having a successful and happy life.

Anxiety

Finally, if you think your child is struggling to cope with school work because of suffering from an anxiety related 'fight or flight' response, it can be really important to support them in getting control back over this feeling. Techniques to think about include relaxation exercises and ways that your child can distract themselves away from their anxiety. Chapter 1 has some lovely examples about how best to do this work.

It may also be helpful to use some of the ideas in the 'Thoughts' section below, to coach your child into facing up to their anxious thoughts, and finding more realistic and helpful ways of thinking.

If you feel your child is not making enough progress after trying the anxiety management techniques suggested in this book, then talk to their teacher and SENCO. Schools have resources to support children emotionally, including specialist teaching staff that can work with your child individually or in small groups to develop their emotional literacy (self-awareness and ability to regulate their feelings, develop empathy with others and stay motivated when learning). Some schools fund their own school counsellor or therapist to work directly with children who are struggling to manage their feelings. Following this intervention, you may think it is necessary to involve a more specialist service such as the local Child and Adolescent Mental Health Team (CAMHS). These referrals are usually through the GP but the school SENCO can also make this referral after consulting with you as parents.

3. Thoughts

The 'Coach'

If your child has started telling you things that indicate they are having anxious or stressed thoughts about their school work, then it may be helpful to think about helping them find a more positive viewpoint that better reflects reality. It is important that this viewpoint is not 'black or white' - e.g. 'perfect or a failure', but instead falls somewhere in the middle 'shade of grey'.

One way to do this is to think about what a good coach would be like to your child. This could be a sports coach, dance teacher, swim teacher or anyone that matches your child's interests. Chat together about how that coach would be with them, for example:

OTT coach ('white')	Good coach ('shade of grey')	Critical coach ('black')
You're amazing!	You're doing well! (e.g. encouraging)	You're hopeless!
You're the best!	Well done! (e.g. kind language)	You're stupid!
You always get it right	There will be a way to work this out (e.g. optimistic)	This will never work
You're so clever, it's easy	You may find this hard (e.g. honest but fair)	You'll never get this
You can do this completely on your own	Stick with it! (e.g. motivating)	You'll never get this

You can then work through all of the 'good coach statements', and collect them together.

THIS MIGHT BE:

- In a special box or book
- A visual reminder on their phone
- On their homework diary
- Recorded in their voice on a tablet or phone
- Any other helpful place!

You can then read through or listen to these statements together or let your child do so on their own before they undertake a difficult homework task. You may also review them if they start to struggle midway through a project. You are aiming for them to grow a 'good coach' mindset to support them through, rather than allowing the negative and stressed thoughts to take over.

It can be very helpful chatting to your child about any worries they might be having about school. However, children do not always find it easy to answer direct questions about their feelings, and you may need to be creative in how you talk about them. For example, drawing a picture together about school, and using this to explore what is good and bad about their school day.

Alternatively, you might want to use a story or a television programme that has characters in who are feeling similar emotions to your child, to base your discussions on. Younger children often respond to 'acting out' their feelings with toys – so you might want to use one of their toys / teddies to represent them, and use other ones as different people in their lives (e.g. their teacher and parents), to get a sense of their feelings and worries.

If you are able to spot any of the 'thinking traps' discussed above, it can then be helpful to support them in finding more helpful ways of thinking.

The following case example shows how this can work:

Lucy, aged 8 years.

Lucy had started to become anxious about math. She says "I just don't get maths…I'm never going to be able to do it".

She had found maths okay when in key stage 1, but when starting Year 3, the increased demands of the curriculum made it much harder for her to understand. Lucy and her dad worked through the following headings, to discover whether her anxious thought was a reality or not, as outlined below:

Signs her worry is true:

Lucy couldn't think of anything

Signs her worry is not true:

Lucy's mum was very good at maths, and had told Lucy that she could help her if she needed it. Lucy's teacher was confident Lucy would understand the work, and had told Lucy that lots of children found Year 3 maths hard to begin with, but got the hang of it after a few weeks.

Conclusion

Lucy realised that she had learned to understand tricky schoolwork in the past, after putting in some effort and checking areas of confusion with her parents and teachers. Therefore, this was likely to happen with the Year 3 maths too.

Working through the above example gave Lucy the confidence to 'stick with' the work, and feel better about not understanding it all straight away.

4. Personality

As I'm sure you are aware, we can't completely change our personalities, or our children's personalities, and we wouldn't want to either. However, it can be useful to identify if areas of their personality are causing them unhelpful stress, and to try and bring in more balance to their lives.

Perfectionism

Let's have a look at the list of issues that perfectionism can cause, and think through strategies that might help reduce them:

Possible issues	Strategies
Spending too long on homework	- Chat to your child's teacher about how long they should be spending on homework. You can also ask for them to offer clear guidance on what they are expecting from schoolwork tasks, so your child knows what is expected of them. - Ask your child's teacher to give an example of a completed piece of work – it helps to have a framework to refer to - Ensure your child has a drink and snack before. undertaking homework, to make sure their concentration is not being reduced by dehydration or hunger.
Avoiding doing work for fear of doing it wrong	- Encourage your child to produce a 'draft' piece of work that they can then hand in to their teacher for feedback and comments. They can then use this as a foundation for their 'final' piece of work. You will need to chat to their teacher about this plan beforehand. - Sit down with your child and think about the positives and negatives of not doing work, for fear of getting it wrong. Use this conversation to help them see that it is better to try something and get some mark, than get no mark at all for the work. - You may need to sit with your child during homework tasks, and offer them encouragement and praise for having a go at the work. - Consider giving your child a reward for handing some work into the teacher - before they even get a grade back.
Being self-critical	- Use the 'good coach' idea from above, to help your child see that they need to be kind to themselves about their work, rather than being too hard on themselves. - Provide genuine, specific and positive feedback. - Whenever you see your child doing something well, let them know. This can be non-school work areas as well as academic work – whether playing computer games, playing a sport, being a kind friend or being helpful around the house.
Struggling to accept that they make mistakes	- Be open about when you make mistakes in your day to day life, and describe how it is okay, because of what you have learnt from them. - Don't be tempted to correct your child's mistakes for them, as this may give strength to the idea that it is not okay for them to make mistakes. - Give your child lots of attention and praise for correcting their own mistakes in school work, ideally as calmly as possible.

	- When your child makes mistakes in non-school work areas (e.g. making an inaccurate pass in football, or forgetting some dance steps), chat about how good they were about getting it wrong, and all the great things they have learnt about that activity from making the mistakes (e.g. you will be less likely to forget those dance steps now, as you've gone over the tricky bit and got it clear in your head).
Being overly sensitive to criticism	- Think about the words you are using with your child, when trying to let them know they've done something wrong. It may be that gentler words help them to hear your message, or starting off by praising the work they have done well.
	- You could use a tool that schools sometimes use, asking your child: WWW. ..What Worked Well..... EBI... Even Better If.
	- When people give you criticism, chat out loud about how it was helpful to hear that you hadn't done something quite right, and that you will try to change what you are doing.
	- Remind your child to 'stay calm' whilst doing homework – you may need to prompt them a few times if you need to correct their work or give criticism; then praise your child for staying calm.
	- It may be useful to practice some relaxation techniques described in chapter 1 before starting the homework.
	- Some schools play calming music to soothe children when they work.
	- Check that you are calm – for example your tone of voice and body language.
Needing you to sit with them and check every piece of work	- Encourage your child to 'have a go' at something very small - e.g. the first couple of letters of spelling a word, or the first sum on a page of maths work. Give them a lot of praise and attention for their efforts, even if they get the answer wrong. Gradually build up the amount you ask them to try.
	- 'Busy yourself' during periods when your child is working – for example pop to the bathroom, unpack the dishwasher, or check your phone (there are nearly always jobs to do!). Come back to your child and 'check in' with them, and then repeat this if possible. Praise them for the work they manage to do whilst you are away, and chat about how grown up they are when they work on their own.

It is always worth trying to make homework times as enjoyable and 'fun' as possible.

One example might be looking on a laptop to watch videos about the Antarctic, after your child has had to draw a picture, or write some information about Antarctic wildlife.

Another example might be playing a round of 'top trumps' with your child after they've finished each section of maths homework.

Can the learning be done practically? For example, through cooking in the kitchen? Or outside in the garden? Or even whilst shopping? These strategies can take a bit of adult time, but they can often pay off later, as your child starts to relax into completing school work, and becomes more independent of you.

Fixed vs. Growth Mindset and Resilience

As outlined in chapter 4, if you believe your child may have a fixed mindset, this does not have to remain the case for life. A few pointers on how to help this process include:

- ✓ Avoid labelling your child 'clever' or 'good at a subject'
- ✓ Give them lots of praise for sticking with work
- ✓ Praise them for not giving up with tasks
- ✓ Give them rewards when they attempt work that they find tricky
- ✓ Focus on effort grades in school reports rather than over focussing on academic grades

The Pit

James Nottingham has made famous the idea of "The Pit", to help describe how someone with a growth mindset might approach learning a new idea or topic that they don't fully understand.

1. Initially, a child learns about a <u>concept</u> - this will be potentially new to them – such as understanding fractions.

2. The child then goes through a <u>conflict</u>, where they try to learn some new information, but may not fully understand or make sense of everything. This can feel uncomfortable for the child, and feel frustrating and confusing.

3. After sticking with their confusion and learning for a while, the child may have a 'lightbulb' moment, where they start to <u>construct</u> a new understanding of the work, and gain clarity about this new area.

4. Ideally the child can then <u>consider</u> what they have learnt, which will help them in similar situations in the future.

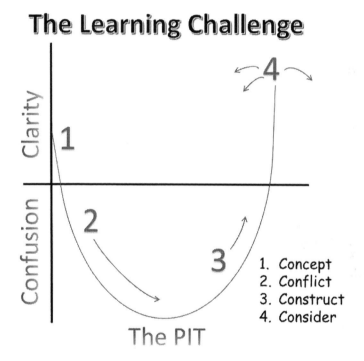

The Learning Challenge

1. Concept
2. Conflict
3. Construct
4. Consider

The PIT

It can be extremely helpful to show your child a copy of the diagram above and talk to your child about 'The Pit'. Let them know that they are likely to go into The Pit when they are learning something new and tricky - and this is okay. You might want to discuss the feelings that YOU get, when YOU are in The Pit too (e.g. frustration inside, or butterflies and worry). Talk through how they can get out of The Pit... For example, they could:

✓ Stick with the work for a little longer, to see if they can work it out themselves

✓ Chat to a friend about the work – commonly used in schools ("talking partners")

✓ Ask a teacher or Teaching Assistant for help

✓ Ask you for your support after school.

Many teachers are knowledgeable about 'The Pit', and may have used it in their classroom too. It can be very useful to chat to your child's teacher about how to use this idea both in school and back at home, so everyone is "singing to the same song sheet" to support your child in building up their resilience in sticking with tricky work.

Teachers are also using a variety of methods these days, to help children receive feedback about their work. If your child finds it difficult to take constructive criticism from a teacher, it might be that their teacher can alter the method of feedback at times. For example, getting your child to evaluate their own work, or to respond to their teacher's marking (e.g. by writing or discussing key points). They could even earn a reward for 'taking criticism well', and work at practicing this skill when out of school too. For example, taking feedback well on the football pitch or in a dance class.

5. Behaviour

We've explored in the section above, how we as parents sometimes get drawn into certain patterns of behaviour by our child, often without realising it. If you've noticed this with your child, it is worth working out exactly what the 'function' of their behaviour is (e.g. what are they trying to achieve from their behaviour).

If you are not sure of the answer to this question, it can be really helpful to jot down a few examples over a week or so, and then sit back and look for any patterns. The sorts of things you might see are:

Trying to get your attention and / or affection, e.g.:

Time / date	What they did	What I (parent) did
15th July 3.40pm	Said they couldn't do their project work, got upset and needed comfort	I stopped preparing their lunchboxes for tomorrow, and gave them a big cuddle. Sat them on my knee to finish the work.

Trying to avoid the work, e.g.:

Time / date	What they did	What I (parent) did
24th Nov. 5.45pm	Had an angry outburst and refused to finish their fractions	I told them all the answers, to have a quieter evening (even though I know they could work out the answers with time).

Delaying tactics, e.g.:

Time / date	What they did	What I (parent) did
4th Dec 4.20pm	Pleaded to play on the Xbox before doing the work, then asked to do it after dinner too	I told them they had to do it straight away. They ignored me, but I was too busy with their sister's homework to follow through with my threats.

Once you have a good idea of the function of their behaviour, you will then need to change how you respond to your child. Think about:

Reason for behaviour	Strategies
Attention / affection	- Give your child plenty of positive attention at non-homework times. For example, having juice and snack together after school, and before they start their homework. - Change the time they complete their homework to a slot when you are available. Over time you might want to gradually reduce the intensity of your attention: for example, moving them from your lap to a seat next to you; and shifting from giving them 100% of your time to occasionally 'popping off' to finish a quick job, and so on until it is at a level you are happy with. - Consider how much one to one time you have with your child away from clubs and the school day. For example, in evenings or weekends.
Avoiding work	- Don't let them avoid their work! Therefore, resist the temptation to either complete some / all of your child's homework for them, or allow them to not hand anything in - Consider breaking down their homework tasks into smaller chunks for them, and encourage them to finish one section at a time, so they don't feel overwhelmed by the work, and can have a sense of getting through it. - Use a timer to record how long they have stayed on task – children usually enjoy using a timer. - Think about rewarding your child for sitting down and 'having a go' even if what they produce isn't perfect.

Delaying tactics	
	- Decide upon rules around homework, such as when and where it takes place, for all your children.
	- Stick to these rules consistently (for everyone!).
	- It may help to introduce a small consequence for your child 'breaking these rules'. For example, losing 15 minutes of TV later on in the day, or having less social media / gaming time.
General pointers	
	- Have clear expectations as to what you want your child to do with schoolwork. It can help to show these visually (e.g. a poster on the fridge) close to where your child does their revision / work.
	- These expectations need to be realistic. For example, some children may be too tired to complete their homework as soon as they get home from school, so giving them a snack and short playtime might reduce the amount of 'battles' you then have.
	- Always give specific, genuine and positive feedback.
	- Consider incentives for behaviour change or sticking with a new rule.
	- **You** may also need a reward for staying patient and positive, such as having a relaxing bath or reading a favourite book after your child's bedtime to reward yourself for changing the patterns at home.
	- Talk to your child's teacher about any struggles you are having. It may be that the teacher can help. For example, working with your child to break down overwhelming projects into 'bite sized pieces', and clarifying their expectations of your child with schoolwork.
	- Find out if your school has a homework club so that your child can be supported to complete homework within the school day.

6. Environment

Sensory overload

Look through the below table for ideas on how to manage your child's potential sensory difficulties when they are attempting to complete school work.

Sensitive to this sense	Ideas
Noise	- Think about where your child does their homework - is this the right place?
	- Would it be better in their bedroom, a study, on the kitchen table or anywhere else that best suits their needs?
	- If you have younger children, it can be worth trying to occupy them with quieter activities, e.g. colouring in, drawing, looking at books or reading stories with you, their own homework, a quieter imaginative game, helping you with household jobs. Tablets and other electronic devices can be useful, as long as they are quiet (headphones are helpful if necessary!), and don't distract your older child.
	- Turn off the television, radio and any unnecessary background noise.
	- Use ear defenders (big ear phones) if your child is noise sensitive this may improve their concentration.
Sights	- Turn off the television, computer and other visual devices.
	- It can be worth having a 'rule' around mobiles during homework. It is worth your child handing these to you or putting them well out of sight to avoid temptation.
	- Check that their place of work is not a busy area of the house.
Smells	- If cooking smells are off-putting, then set up your child's work station away from the kitchen.
	- Hunger may also cause greater distractibility with cooking smells, so you may want to offer your child a drink and snack before starting their homework.
Touch	- Some children feel more comfortable getting changed out of their school uniform to do homework. Chat to them about which clothes are most relaxing for them.

	- Watch your child undertaking projects, to see whether there are any issues with the feel of work materials. For example, would your child feel more comfortable with a pen or a pencil? How relaxed does their pencil grip appear? If they seem to be having difficulties holding a pencil or pen, it may be that they need their grip assessed, to check whether any additional supports would be helpful. If this is the case, do chat to your child's teacher. - Assess the temperature of your child's place of work - does this suit their needs, or could it be changed to help them? - Is your child's sitting position comfortable? Can they use a desk? Remember: good sitting supports concentration.
Tiredness	- School can often be exhausting for children, given the demands on their day. Therefore think about when the best time for homework / school work is. It may be best straight after school, or after they've had a period of 'down time' to play or relax. A weekend morning may suit them better than waiting until the afternoon. If you can get your child to agree on the best time, they are also more likely to stick to it, helping avoid all of those 'time to do your homework' arguments. - Is your child having their sleep disturbed? Or are there any other factors that are reducing the amount of sleep they are having? For example, your child is a 'bookworm' and they are staying up late into the evening, reading their favourite books in private. Try to change any issue causing your child reduced sleep, such as removing books, mobile phones, games consoles and other 'distractors', and shifting a sibling's bedtime to a different time to this child, if the sibling is somehow causing a disturbance. - Work through the tips from earlier in this chapter on having a good sleep routine.
Food reactions	- If you think your child might be having a reaction to a particular food group, then experiment with cutting it out of their diet. You will probably need to do this for 4-6 weeks, to ensure it has fully left your child's system. Then add the food back into their diet on a day when there is no new or unusual event planned, and see if their behaviour changes. It can be worth keeping a diary of your child's behaviour to track if there is really a change or not. - Do have a chat with your doctor if you have any particular concerns about more serious food intolerances, e.g. Crohn's disease. - It is also always worth chatting to your doctor or a dietician to gain advice if making big changes to your child's diet.

Trauma or Bereavement

A trauma could be any kind of significant event such as a divorce, friendship breakup or a house move. A trauma or bereavement can greatly impact upon your child's capacity to focus on and achieve well with school work. If this has unfortunately happened to your child, it is worth considering the following areas:

- Check that your child is having a good night's sleep, and if not, introduce the tips outlined above.

- Chat to your child's teacher about how they are managing at school. Has their teacher seen any changes in your child's emotional state, behaviour or academic work? It can be worth making a plan with their teacher about how your child can be best supported in school - which will be very individual to them.

- If your child is struggling to complete work, their teacher may be able to make certain allowances for your child, and help prioritise what work needs to be done over and above the rest. If your child has been overworking to block out their difficult emotions, it might be that the teacher needs to be clear in asking your child to do LESS work than before.

- It might be that your child is keen to have a designated person to turn to if they are feeling overwhelmed by their emotions. However, your child may instead want to keep school as 'normal as possible' and an escape from their difficult emotions. Therefore, planning for their daily school life to be as routine as possible, with minimal talk about the trauma or loss would be more helpful.

- Decide which members of the staff team should know about their trauma or bereavement, and agree a way of regularly communicating how they are doing.

- If you feel your child's teacher is struggling to understand the impact of loss and grief, it might be worth referring them to a local specialist service, or a national service, such as Child Bereavement UK.

- Most schools have staff trained in emotional health. You could find out if there are any support staff at your child's school that could offer individual support.

- Consider asking your GP to refer your child to the local CAMHS services or other relevant child services for trauma or grief work.

7. Expectations

Note it

It can be helpful to try and notice how often you talk about school work, or your child's ability / cleverness throughout each day. Things that could be worth including are shown in the example table below:

Date	Time	What I said	How I said it	How my child reacted
13.05.16	3pm	You're so smart at maths	Pride	Smiled and kept working
13.05.16	3.10pm	You know the answer - you're always good at fractions	Slightly annoyed	Looked stressed and cross too

Look for patterns

See if there are patterns in what you say, that might seem helpful to your child on some occasions, or less helpful on other occasions. Things you may see that can be less helpful include:

- Commenting on your child's ability a lot in a short space of time
- Saying a direct, negative comment; e.g. 'you just don't seem to get percentages'
- Saying a direct comment about how well your child needs to do; e.g. 'you must get all your spellings right this week'

Change it up

This is the hard bit, as your comments and statements will nearly always be motivated by you wanting your child to succeed to the best of their ability. Therefore, in order to 'hold the comments in', you will need to keep reminding yourself of the reasons to do so: i.e. that if you can keep your child as relaxed as possible with schoolwork, and enjoying the process of studying, then they are much more likely to be in the right mindset to understand and learn the work at hand, and will also gain that 'love of learning' that will propel them forward for the rest of their education.

This is easier said than done!!!

Your diary / notes will tell you which times are the risky ones for your comments about your child's ability / work approach. At these times, try to be mindful of what you are saying, and each time you are tempted to comment on your expectations of your child, catch yourself and work out if this is a good time to say it or not. This will take a lot of practice, but can be worth the battle!

If you are feeling brave enough, it can also be helpful to ask a family member or a close friend if they think you ever put too much pressure onto your child, and how they think your child responds to that pressure. They may also be able to feedback the areas where you help your child the most, so you know what is good to keep going with.

Teacher expectations

If you are worried your teacher has the wrong expectations of your child, it could be worth exploring this further with them.

If you think the teacher has overly high expectations of your child: chat to the teacher about the reasons behind their view of your child. Perhaps your child has shown some skill in class that you have not seen, which would reassure you about the teacher's view? Or maybe your child is appearing to understand a topic well in class, but is confiding in you that they are actually copying their friend's work, or getting help from their neighbour, which the teacher is unaware of. It may be that your child is more able than they realise in an area, so you are hearing all their worries, but actually their skill in the topic is very good. These types of issues should come out of your discussion with the teacher, and you can then work as a 'team', so you are giving your child the most helpful messages at home to support them when back in the classroom.

If you think the teacher has overly low expectations of your child: it will again be worth chatting to the teacher about your difference in opinion on the basis of what they have seen. This may help to resolve your worries. However, if you are concerned your child may have a specific issue with learning that has not been picked up (e.g. dyslexia or a poorer memory than you would expect), it could be worth consulting with an

From the "Plan" section above, choose which areas are relevant to your child. Write it in one of the empty boxes, and write in the strategies you have selected. For example:

You do not need to fill all 5 boxes, for example if you feel there are only 3 underlying causes.

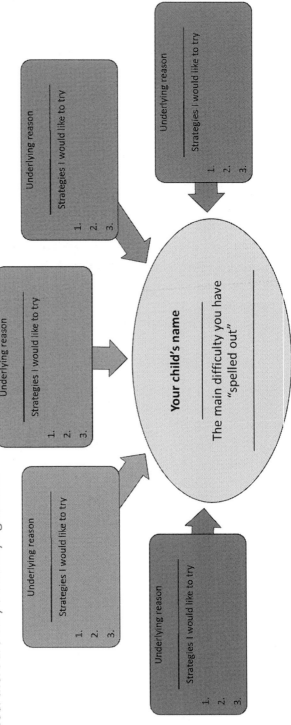

Underlying reason
Perfectionist
Strategies I would like to try
1. Change the words I use
2. Try the "good coach" idea
3. Try not to correct all his mistakes

Underlying reason

Strategies I would like to try
1.
2.
3.

Underlying reason

Strategies I would like to try
1.
2.
3.

Underlying reason

Strategies I would like to try
1.
2.
3.

Underlying reason

Strategies I would like to try
1.
2.
3.

Underlying reason

Strategies I would like to try
1.
2.
3.

Your child's name

The main difficulty you have "spelled out"

educational psychologist. Educational psychologists can explore a child's ability profile, and identify if they have any underlying issues with their learning. There is an educational psychologist attached to every local authority school, however, some are limited in the amount of time they can offer to a school. Therefore, if it is not an option to use the school's educational psychologist, you can seek the advice from an independent educational psychologist (check the 'find a psychologist' page on the British Psychological Society website for more details).

 If you feel your child has an issue with more than one of the above areas, then it may be worth prioritising the ones you have most control over first. For example, it may be quicker to change the environment where your child studies compared to helping them channel their perfectionism differently.

Using my planner on page 272, the area I have decided to tackle first is:

The main strategies I am going to try are:

1. ....

2. ....

3. ....

These are the problems I might come up against (e.g. negativity from others, challenging behaviour from my child):

1. ....

2. ....

3. ....

These are the things I am going to do to try to prevent or manage these problems and stay motivated (e.g. try to stay calm, try to keep going no matter what, share what I am doing with my child's teacher and try to get them "on board"):

1. ....

2. ....

3. ....

 Keep an eye on how the strategies are working - what are the signs that things are improving?

Write them below:

1. ....

2. ....

3. ....

If things are getting better, celebrate and be proud of what you and your child have achieved. Keep going!

Remember: it can sometimes get worse before it gets better. If your child is used to you completing their work for them, then they may try every trick in the book to get you to still do this. Be ready for an increase in their outbursts and upset moments, but after a little while (any time between a couple of days to a couple of weeks -- depending on the nature of your child), this should then improve and stop being an issue.

Once you are happy with an area, then look back to your results on the 'understand' quiz, and check if there were any other potential stressors for your child. If there were, and these still feel an issue, then take one as your next goal, and start trying out the strategies listed above.

Was your plan too ambitious?	• Return to your plan. • Take a step back. • Simplify your plan or try to make it more achievable.
Did you try too many things at once?	• Return to your plan. • Take a step back. • Which area are you going to focus on first?
Have you allowed enough time?	• Being persistent is so important. • If you have only been trying for 1 or 2 weeks, keep going!
Is someone working against the plan, either deliberately or accidentally (a teacher, your partner or a grandparent?)	• Speak to that person openly and honestly about what you are trying to achieve. • Show them this book if it will help.
Is the timing right?	• If you are trying to make a change but life is too busy for the child or for you, for example if your child is busy with Christmas school productions and celebrations, take a deep breath and plan to start again at a better time.

References

Barkley, R.A. (2000). *Taking Charge of ADHD: The Complete, Authoritative Guide for Parents*. Guilford Press

Ben-Sasson, A, Carter, AS, Briggs-Gowan, MJ (2009). *Sensory over-responsivity in elementary school: prevalence and social-emotional correlates*. Journal of Abnormal Child Psychology 37 (5), 705-716.

Dweck, C. S. (1997). *The New Psychology of Success*. Ballatine Books.

Green, C. & Chee, K. (1997). *Understanding ADHD. A Parent's Guide to Attention Deficit Hyperactivity Disorder in Children*. Vintage / Ebury.

Pitt, J. (2010). *Challenging Learning*. JN Publishing Ltd.

Further Reading

Balter, L. & Zembar, M.J. (2006). *Middle Childhood to Middle Adolescence: Development from Ages 8 to 18*. Pearson.

Child Bereavement UK: www.childbereavementuk.org/

Committee on Toxicity of Chemicals in Food, Consumer Products and the Environment (2000). *Adverse Reactions to Food and Food Ingredients*, London: Food Standards Agency.

NSPCC study. http://www.dailymail.co.uk/health/article-145732/Is-child-suffering-stress.html

The National Attention Deficit Hyperactivity Disorder Information Support Service www.addiss.co.uk

6

Concentration and motivation

Attention, listening and concentration

Dr Lucy Russell, clinical psychologist

"I've said it three times and I'm not going to say it again!"

Introduction

Let's face it, all children struggle to listen, attend and concentrate sometimes. Often this is because they simply have different priorities to us adults. Putting a coat on might be the most important thing if you are a parent or teacher, but if you are a child, finishing your Lego might be your priority. However, attention, listening and concentration skills are hugely important for learning, and in the modern world of technology and constant distraction, I worry they are skills that have been lost by some children.

As parents, it is so difficult to know what is "normal". What age should my child be able to follow instructions first time round, and concentrate on a given piece of work at school without support or reminders? How long should my child be expected to concentrate at any age?

Then we have ADHD: Attention deficit hyperactivity disorder. Children with ADHD show a persistent pattern of these of symptoms:

- Difficulty paying attention (inattention)
- Being overactive (hyperactivity)
- Acting without thinking (impulsivity)

Its lesser-known partner is ADD: Attention deficit disorder. Some children struggle with their listening and concentration so much that they are given this label. In the "R" of our "**SUPER**" model – at the end of this chapter – I discuss what to do if you think your child may have ADD or ADHD. Even if they do, many of the strategies in this chapter may be helpful to you.

Though undoubtedly the condition exists, many professionals, like me, worry that ADHD is over-diagnosed, and that for some children problems with lifestyle could be partly to blame. Should there be so much focus on young children sitting still and on academic learning, rather than play? Is our home-based culture at fault, with too much time spent on sitting-based activities such as computer games and TV? How are changes in lifestyle, such as reduction in the amount of exercise children do in the last few decades, contributing to problems with attention and concentration?

Whilst some of these questions do not have clear answers, this chapter aims to help you feel more confident in understanding how to support your child, if this is something they appear to be struggling with.

One thing is for sure: If a child can listen well, and can concentrate on a task, they can end up feeling really good about themselves. It can help them build all sorts of skills, and set them off on positive paths that they may not otherwise have been able to take. Let me explain.

My daughter is lucky enough to have strong listening skills. When she was about 5 years old, I noticed that this helped her hugely when learning to swim, even though she is not necessarily naturally talented at swimming. In a class of 6 to 8 children, the teacher would call out an instruction, and would expect the children to follow the instruction first time. It might be something like: "grab a float, and swim to the other side on your back, just using your feet to paddle". I noticed that repeatedly, she was the only child listening and attending to the instruction. She would follow the instruction straight away, whereas others would stand mystified, or try to copy her, or need a second (rather stern or cross) reminder of what they were supposed to do. Over time, this meant that my daughter had a very positive experience of swimming lessons, and made faster progress than some of her peers, even though many of them had higher natural swimming ability than her. Her fast progress made her feel good about herself.

Children with difficulties attending and listening may end up:

- Being told off more, and therefore developing a view of themselves as "a problem".

- Becoming disillusioned at school or during sport/hobbies, believing them to be boring or too hard.

- Giving up on tasks because they believe they can't complete the task, even though it is listening and following the instruction, rather than completing a task (such as swimming a width with a float) that they struggled with.

- Giving up a whole activity (e.g. swimming lessons) that they may otherwise have gone on to succeed in, and would have led to a positive sense of well-being.

Attention, listening and concentration are all connected, yet slightly separate things. Let's think about what each of them involves.

In order for a child to **attend** to something that is important, they need to have the skills to:

- Be alert for something to attend to (for example, in the swimming class they need to stand ready and waiting for the next instruction, rather than playing or being caught in a daydream).

- Be able to stop one task, if they are being asked to do another which takes priority ("stop playing Minecraft, and go and brush your teeth").

- Recognise which things are important to attend to, and which are not. For example, in class as a rule of thumb it is important to attend to what the teacher is saying, but not the other students. On a page of written information, they would need to be able to scan the page with their eyes and quickly figure out where to start (e.g. they may notice that the instructions are written in bold.)

- Be able to tune out or filter out what is not important, such as background chatter.

Listening involves the following:

- Taking in/understanding verbal information.

- Processing this information. For example, dividing it into steps to make use of it. ("First I need to get a float from the side of the pool. Then I need to find a space. Then hold the float to my tummy. Finally, I need to use my feet to kick off and swim to the other side.")

- Sometimes, it involves providing a written or verbal response rather than an action. The child needs to be able to decide which course of action is most appropriate.

Concentrating involves staying on a task until it is complete. This might involve:

- Motivating themselves to get started.

- Tuning out distractions.

- Moving from one step to another without losing concentration ("okay, I've got the float, what do I need to do next?").

- Knowing how to deal with obstacles. For example, some children might give up if they get stuck. This results in a loss of concentration. Another child might decide: "I'm stuck on that question but I will move on to the next one, then come back". This requires a kind of mental flexibility, and also resilience (the ability to "bounce back" from problems).

Motivation

Some children seem able to concentrate very well on certain activities, such as computer games, yet cannot pay attention or concentrate adequately in class. This is because the level of motivation to try hard to concentrate or attend to something, depends on how much "reward" the brain is getting. The reward centre of the brain is called the nucleus accumbens. This sends out pleasure signals to the prefrontal cortex (the thinking part of the brain), providing the necessary drive or motivation to focus. Therefore, if it seems that your child is "selective" about what he can (or will) concentrate on, it is not entirely within his control. He may not always lack the ability to pay attention or concentrate, but find it hard to do this consistently or on command.

Giving your brain the "best chance"

Your child may have mastered the many skills required for successful attention, concentration and listening. He may have acquired the mental maturity to prioritise what is required, over what he wants to do. Yet still, his performance may vary considerably, depending on how well his brain is functioning and his state of mind. Things which can affect how well a child's brain is functioning at any given time include: how regularly he is eating; if he is eating enough of the nutrients required for brain and body functioning; how much sleep he has had; how much exercise he has done; how many demands he is already coping with (for example, if a child already completed 3 tests today, fatigue may contribute to a poor performance in the 4th test); other demands a child may be facing in life (e.g. illness, family life events). I will look at each of these further in the "Understand" section below. State of mind, however, is also crucial.

A psychologist called Professor Paul Gilbert, who is famous for developing a form of therapy called Compassion Focused Therapy, first presented an idea which I find very helpful, as follows:

- He proposes that we regulate ourselves through a 3-part system, each associated with different chemicals in the brain. People are either in a state of "threat" (red), "soothing" (feeling safe and content - green), or "drive" (blue) (motivated towards achievement or competition).

- To live successful and happy lives, children need to develop the ability to move between these three states of mind.

- The most appropriate state of mind for learning may be the "drive" state. In order to hear and follow instructions, a child could be in "drive" or "soothing" states, but if in a "threat" state, the brain may not be able to follow instructions or concentrate, listen or attend, because the brain senses threat or danger, and is focussing on survival.

- A child needs to spend adequate time in the soothing state, in order to recover from mental and physical fatigue. Therefore he needs to have the ability and opportunity to *be soothed* and eventually learn to *self-soothe*. Parents play a crucial role here, and teachers are also important. They need to be able to help a child recognise the signs that they are tired or overwhelmed, help them move into the soothing state to take a break and recover, then move back to drive state to be ready to learn again. Eventually, the child will learn to do this for himself.

- For example: "I can't concentrate on writing this story. Maybe it's because I've completed so much work already this morning. I will take a break."

You may notice that the example above requires a child to be kind and compassionate to himself. Self-compassion is central to Professor Gilbert's therapeutic approach. When it comes to attention and concentration, I fear that many children are likely to take a harsher approach to themselves ("I should be able to do it"/"I'm no good"). Unfortunately, this can take them into the threat state, because they feel they are not capable of what is required of them, which makes them feel vulnerable. Once in the threat state, a child's advanced thinking skills are impaired, and he will struggle to concentrate or pay attention. This is because the brain has decided that survival is at risk, so it focuses on "fight or flight" (getting to safety). It temporarily shuts down the prefrontal cortex, the part of the brain which is responsible for rational, clear thinking (as well as planning, organisation etc.), as this might get in the way of survival.

As well as harsh or critical thoughts (which are explored further in the "Understand" section), many other things can put a child in "threat" state, where the brain will be focussing on looking out for threats and or getting to safety, so attending, and concentrating on tasks will be low down on its list of priorities. See the Understand section, where we will explore this further.

As you may know already if you have read the previous chapters, in order to help a child, we must be really specific about what they find difficult.

We must spell it out. It is not helpful to say, "my child is no good at listening". Instead, it may be helpful to think about which situations your child struggles to listen, and what may help or hinder their listening. For example, "my child struggles to listen to the teacher in the classroom when there is a lot of background noise, and especially in the afternoons. He can sometimes follow simple instructions, but can't manage if the teacher asks three things in a row."

Think about: What do they struggle with? Is it attention, listening, concentration, or maybe all three? If you look at the separate elements of these three abilities described above, can you see any particular areas that your child struggles with? Are the struggles both at home and at school? What about other settings, such as clubs and hobbies? Are there times when your child can listen, attend or concentrate better, for example at the beginning of a school term, in the mornings or after they have eaten?

Let's meet two children whose struggles with listening and concentration are having an impact on their lives.

Bobby, aged 6 years.

Bobby is an energetic, full-of-life little boy. He settled into school well in his reception year. By year 1, teachers started to remark to his parents, Jackie and Simon, that he wasn't learning as effectively as most of the other children. When sitting down he fidgeted constantly, and struggled to stay in one place. He couldn't follow instructions very easily, especially at the end of the day. He was starting to fall behind academically. Bobby would often get up and run around when he was supposed to be sitting down practising his writing or his maths. He needed frequent reminders from staff to stay on task. His behaviour began to distract the other children, and he began to get a reputation as a naughty child. This was having an impact on friendships. As he was such a ball of energy, some children found him overwhelming and began to avoid him. By year 2, Bobby disliked school. Jackie and Simon had to physically lift him into the car each day. Bobby would say: "I'm useless at learning, I don't want to go." At home, Jackie and Simon found that they had to repeat instructions many times before Bobby "heard". Bedtime was a nightly battle. By this time, Bobby was exhausted, and seemed to find it harder to carry out basic instructions such as "brush your teeth". Bedtime was often later than ideal because of this, and Bobby would wake up tired. Jackie and Simon felt at their wits' end.

Ellen, aged 11 years.

Ellen is a sensitive girl who has always been a worrier. She is doing well in certain subjects like maths, but finds open-ended tasks such as creative writing very difficult. Ellen feels she doesn't know where to start, and gets overwhelmed by the task. She then gets easily distracted. She finds homework particularly distressing. Often, she will sit for half an hour or more doing her homework, but when her mum Vanessa checks her progress, she has not started the task. She has lost her concentration and has been doodling in her notebook instead. If Vanessa tries to help Ellen, she becomes very distressed and angry. Teachers find that some days, Ellen is very quiet and seems to have the worries of the world on her shoulders. On such days she finds it harder to follow instructions and get on with her work, and sometimes gets upset.

A questionnaire to help you "Spell it Out"

My child...	Yes/No
Tends to be fidgety and constantly moving	
Normally notices when an instruction is given or something important is said, rather than being distracted or in a daydream	
Has the ability to stop one task, in order to switch to another which takes priority	
Can normally pay attention to the most important voices or tasks while "filtering out" other noise or putting other tasks aside temporarily (for example, can listen to a teacher's instructions if other pupils are talking).	
Can normally "filter out" what is not important, such as background chatter	
Normally has the maturity to be able to prioritise what is required of them, versus what they would choose to do	
Can normally understand verbal information	
Can "process" verbal information – think it through and work out what action (if any) is required	
Can motivate her/himself to get started on a task	
Can tune out distractions while working	
Can move from one step to another successfully during a task (e.g. write a paragraph about volcanoes, then draw a picture of a volcano)	
Can deal with obstacles without losing concentration (e.g. moving on to a different question if they get stuck, then returning to the more difficult question at the end) – this is called mental flexibility and resilience	

Once you have thought about your Child's particular situation, write down exactly what he or she struggles with in the space below, giving as many specific details as you can:

Spell it out: **Bobby**, aged 6 years.

Bobby struggles to stay still and fidgets when he is asked to sit in one place.

Bobby cannot follow instructions given by the teacher or his parents, especially at the end of the day, without extra prompts and reminders from adults. His teacher thinks he can understand instructions, but when tired he does not "hear" (attend to) them in the first place.

Spell it out: **Ellen**, aged 11 years.

Ellen finds it hard to get started with open-ended tasks such as creative writing.

Ellen finds it hard to complete her homework; to persist enough to get the task done before she loses concentration.

Ellen is easily distracted when doing open-ended pieces of work.

Now we have spelled out the problem, we need to figure out why it has developed, and what may be keeping it going. We need to understand, so that we can decide on the most appropriate courses of action.

Let's consider things from the different perspectives I outlined in the opening chapter: Attachment and developmental stage, cognitive (thinking), brain development, behaviour (including how the environment your child is in might be affecting their behaviour) and "whole family" perspective.

1. Attachment and developmental stage

This chapter will focus on children who already have a healthy attachment ("secure-base") with at least one adult. (If this is not the case, this is a priority, and you may find that reading the introductory chapter and chapter 3 will be more beneficial for you right now.) Therefore, let us move on and consider developmental stages.

A child may not yet have enough mental control to attend, listen and concentrate on a task. Children need to develop the ability to realise the importance of cooperation, and be able to ignore their own desires in favour of following an instruction or request. Young children may simply not choose to prioritise this, preferring to play and follow their own agenda. This is perfectly normal behaviour. It also takes mental control to be able to sit still. But to apply this mental control, a child first has to realise that this is important. Your child, especially if they are around six years old or under, may well not have reached these stages yet. In the UK, children start school much earlier than in many other countries in the world, and expectations of them to sit still, complete tasks, and so on, are very high. This is especially the case for those who are younger in the year group. In my view it is very important that children at this age are not labelled with a diagnosis or condition, when in fact they just need time to develop the skills and mental control required.

Many of the skills required for successful attention, listening or concentration – for example, the ability to scan a document with one's eyes and pick out the important bits – require practise and experience, and therefore tend to improve with age. Does a child lack skills because they are too young to have perfected them yet, or do they need specific support with a skill?

Have expectations changed recently? For example, if your child has recently moved from reception to year 1, or from year 1 to year 2, the curriculum may have become more formal and less play-based. In year 2, children often have to cope with SATs testing. Your child's development may not match up with this sudden hike in expectations.

Physically, your child may be experiencing changes that are impacting his/her ability to attend and concentrate. A surge in physical growth can make a child more tired, and need to eat more. If more rest and food are not provided, the child's body may struggle to cope with demands. Similarly, if they are fighting infection or have been unwell, the body will prioritise healing, and the brain might not be functioning at its best.

Does your child need more time to develop the following skills:

- Understanding the importance of cooperating and listening?
- Mental control to inhibit their own desires in favour of following an instruction?
- Mental control to keep their body still?
- Scanning a document with their eyes to work out what is important?
- Listening to a set of words and picking out the important parts?

Are you expecting too much? Is your child's teacher expecting too much?

Have expectations of your child changed recently?

Are there physical changes going on, such as a growth spurt or recent illness?

Is your child one of the younger ones in their school year group? Were they a premature baby?

2. Cognitive (Thinking style and state of mind)

Unless this is a very new problem, the chances are your child has developed some thoughts and ideas about his/her difficulty. It is useful to understand whether these are helping or hindering. For example, beliefs that may get in the way of overcoming the difficulty include:

- "There is something wrong with me. I will never change." (As mentioned in chapter 3 on self-esteem, this is unhelpful because it is a belief about permanence. The child believes things will never change.)

- "I can't do listening/concentrating/paying attention, so I must be stupid." (This belief is problematic because it is an *overgeneralisation*. Although listening and concentrating skills can affect the ability to learn, difficulties with these do not mean a child doesn't have the ability to learn.)

- "I can't do it (e.g. concentrate), so there's no point trying. I'm no good."

Unfortunately, teachers and parents can sometimes unwittingly strengthen these beliefs and they can become very difficult to change. For example, if a child is struggling to complete a task at school because concentration has wandered, rather than teaching persistence the teacher might instead give them an easier task, reinforcing the view that the child "can't do it".

A child may then start to see academic tasks or instructions as threatening, as the harsh thoughts put the child into the "threat" state of mind. The child may become disillusioned, angry or fearful when faced with such tasks.

If a child is struggling with their well-being (for example if he is feeling generally anxious or depressed), concentration may be affected. Low mood affects a child's ability to motivate themselves to get started on a task and to keep going, persevering through any obstacles. If a child is feeling anxious, then their body is likely to have higher levels of the chemicals cortisol and adrenaline in the bloodstream. This means they are more likely to be in the "threat" state; the brain is constantly on the alert for danger. A child is therefore less likely to be able to pay attention to instructions, or concentrate on a piece of work, because the brain is looking out for dangers at the same time and attention is therefore easily pulled away.

Does your child feel low in mood, or tend to get anxious? Has your child developed unhelpful thoughts or beliefs about the difficulties, which could be making the difficulties worse or keeping them going? If so, list them below:

3. Behaviour (including how changes in their environment may be causing changes in behaviour)

Expectations: I remember when a teacher referred a 4-year-old boy to our clinic, telling us that he did not seem to be able to attend and concentrate well enough in lessons or complete tasks by himself. She wondered if there was something wrong with him. However, a child's ability to attend and concentrate generally increases with age. In formal, non-play-based learning (for example, having a teacher describe a new topic, then asking a child to complete a piece of work about this), a 4-year-old would not have the ability to concentrate for more than a few minutes. There will be variability between children; those who are older in the year group may have developed better attention and concentration skills. Those who have had more practise in this area may also have developed stronger skills. It is important for adults (parents and teachers) to regularly take a step back and think "are my expectations reasonable?"

What is your child used to?: If a child has not yet learned the skills of listening, paying attention and concentrating, it will take a while for them to practise these new skills. For example, at home if a child is regularly asked to perform small tasks (e.g. put your plate in the dishwasher, hang up your school clothes) the brain will have had more practise at spotting when they need to listen, and having sufficient attention and concentration to get the task done. If a child has very few demands made of them, they may not have experienced the need for listening, attending and concentrating. Another way to help your child learn these skills at home is through play. For example, if you do a jigsaw with your child, in a quiet environment with no distractions such as TV, he will be able to practise in a fun way listening and paying attention to your suggestions, and concentrating for a few minutes to build up the puzzle.

Is there a problem with listening, attention or concentration, or is the problem one of cooperation?: Being able to listen to instructions, pay attention to written or verbal material and concentrate on a task, require the ability to cooperate. That is, the ability to think "it is important to listen/pay attention/concentrate on this task". It is possible that a child has the skills to do these things, but does not have the skills to cooperate. They have not yet learned that cooperation tends to bring rewards, but these rewards are not always immediate. For instance, "Continuing to mess about with my friends might be more fun than working. But if I finish my story, I might get a gold star from the teacher. Which should I choose?" Many children, even towards the older primary school years, would choose the short-term reward. In other words, they haven't learned to delay gratification, to get a bigger or better reward.

Do the expectations of your child to listen, pay attention and concentrate, match up with her/his age and developmental stage? Is your child used to listening, paying attention and concentrating? For example, do they do small chores at home, play games which require listening or attend clubs/hobbies outside of school where they get plenty of practise? Has your child learned the importance of cooperation? Has your child learned the importance of delayed gratification (good things come to those who wait)?

Environment Your child's environment includes many different areas and I will try to cover the ones I believe are most significant.

Home set-up and routine: At home, there needs to be enough calm and quiet spaces, so a child can feel calm whenever they need to. There are two reasons for this. Firstly, if a child is bombarded with noise, bright lights and other sensory experiences constantly, he will become overloaded – the brain will not be able to cope with any more. Thinking back to Paul Gilbert's three states, the body needs to get into its soothing state as often as possible at home. Home should be a haven where the brain and body can rest and recover from the demands of the outside world. Secondly, a calm and quiet environment, with few distractions, provides the best opportunity for a child to practise listening, paying attention, and concentrating successfully. It can be very difficult to create a calm atmosphere, especially in a busy household or a large family. Even if your child cannot have his own bedroom as a place of calm to retreat to, it is worth spending some time thinking about what could be done: A quiet corner? A play-tent? A den?

Another important factor is for home life to be predictable. As much as possible, children feel safer and more ready to learn if they know what is expected of them and they know what is going to happen. Therefore, sticking to roughly the same daily routine, having some house rules, and regular routines (such as bedtime) are really important. Again, these provide your child with the best chance of success in listening, paying attention and concentrating. If they know that bath time always follows dinner time, they will be more ready to listen for the instructions to go and get ready for bath time, and will be able to prepare to concentrate on the tasks required, such as getting undressed.

Does your child have a calm/quiet space at home? Does s/he use it? Is her/his daily life generally predictable?

_____

Classroom set-up and routine: Following exactly the same rules as home life, a classroom should be set up to support calm learning (or regular periods of calm) with few distractions. It should be as predictable as possible with a clear daily routine. Attention should be paid to how much noise there is at each point in the day, and if there is too much sensory input of other kinds (for example, too many shiny or bright things to look at around the room which can overwhelm or distract). Also, is there enough opportunity to rest and recover after a sustained period of concentration? Is there a quiet corner inside or outside of the classroom, where students can go if they need to? Are there winding down activities (such as colouring, stories) scheduled after more demanding tasks?

One particularly important area to think about is the level of movement opportunity provided for children at school. At playtime, is there a good selection of options for play which can get children running around and releasing any pent-up stress? For example, play equipment (hula hoops, skipping ropes) and staff-led games such as football? Are children encouraged to go out, whatever the weather?

Is your child's classroom calm? Is there a predictable daily routine? Do the seating arrangements provide the best chance for listening and attention – for example, can your child see and hear the teacher clearly?

Outdoor time:

One of the reasons for poor attention can be mental fatigue. It has been shown that time spent in nature helps to restore mental energy, improving attention and memory

Though all outdoor time may be beneficial, it is time in a natural environment which really seems to matter. One study looked at concentration in children with ADHD. It found that children concentrate significantly better after just 20 minutes spent in a park, but the same thing did not happen when they spent 20 minutes walking in a town or a suburban area.

Does your child spend time in nature several times per week?

Diet:

An astoundingly undervalued area when it comes to children's well-being, as well as their abilities to listen, pay attention and concentrate, children's brains will only function correctly if they are provided with enough of the right "fuel" – nutritious food. There are certain foods that a "standard" diet in the UK is widely believed by nutritionists to provide too much of – such as sugar and artificial additives. Also, there are many nutrients we are not getting enough of. According to nutritionists these include:

OMEGA-3

Much of the brain is made up of fats, and the brain needs a good supply of omega-3 fatty acids to pay attention, listen and concentrate.

In one recent study by Dr Alex Richardson and colleagues, children given omega-3 showed improved attention and memory and less disruptive behaviour, as well as faster reading and spelling progress, compared with their peers over a three-month period.

Foods high in omega-3 include walnuts, flaxseeds, sardines, salmon, and soya beans. It is important that omega-3 is eaten in the right proportion to omega-6 (a nutrient very few of us are deficient in), and if you are interested in learning more about this you may wish to read *They Are What You Feed Them* by Dr Alex Richardson.

MAGNESIUM

Magnesium is an essential mineral for many bodily processes, but especially for a healthy nervous system. If the nervous system is not functioning well, children may be less able to calm and soothe themselves, and therefore learn effectively (if the brain is focussing on threats or survival, it prioritises these over learning).

Many children in the UK do not get enough magnesium, and it is even more common than calcium deficiency. Also, if they have significant amounts of sugar, they may also be magnesium deficient; researchers have found sugar (and the insulin it triggers) increase the amount of magnesium that comes out in urine.

In one study, 18% of children with ADHD were found to lack magnesium. Giving children magnesium supplements improved their cognitive performance.

Foods high in magnesium include spinach, potato with skin, soya products, peas, lentils, brazil nuts, sunflower seeds, almonds, pine nuts and cashew nuts. Another way of helping children to get adequate magnesium is to add some Epsom salts to their baths, something I try to do twice a week with my children.

SUGAR

Sugary drinks and cheap snacks make it very easy to consume sugar without realising it. Some shop-bought bottles and cans of drink contain more than a child's whole day's recommended sugar intake. Too much sugar can contribute to a range of health problems such as tooth decay and diabetes, but surprisingly research suggests it does not generally make attention and concentration worse. Some children, it is thought, may be "sugar sensitive", and may become hyperactive after eating refined sugar, but this is not the norm. The best way to find out of your child is one of these is to keep a food and behaviour diary for about a week, and consult a nutritional therapist or dietician if you are not sure what to do next. There are no reported benefits at all of eating added sugars, so it is worthwhile trying to reduce the number of foods with added sugars your child eats, in any case.

ADDITIVES

Some research indicates that a proportion of children react with hyperactivity (including impulsiveness, problems with paying attention and concentrating) to artificial sweeteners, preservatives, colourings and dyes as well as foods high in natural salicylates (these are commonly found in most stone fruit, berries, some vegetables and other foods). Some children have also reacted to milk, chocolate, soy, eggs, wheat, corn and legumes. However, the evidence is limited. Some children with ADHD have shown significant symptom improvement when consuming a diet free of artificial colours. If you suspect that your child might have food sensitivities, it is important to seek the help of a nutritional therapist or dietician.

EATING REGULAR MEALS

Eating regular meals is, without a doubt, important for attention and concentration. In particular, many studies have shown that breakfast is important for general "cognitive performance" including attention and concentration. It is also important that meals (especially at breakfast time) help children to release energy slowly and feel fuller for longer. These types of foods include oats and whole grains, and protein-rich foods. If the food eaten releases energy too quickly, such as some sugary cereals, the body will run out of fuel and blood sugar will dip. If this happens, the body (which hasn't changed much since we were cavemen and food was scarce) can go into survival mode, where it prioritises finding food over anything else. When it is in this state the brain will not be able to focus on "non-essential" tasks such as concentrating on school work. Eating regular meals is therefore essential to keep the brain ready for paying attention and concentrating. There are certain foods which are thought to enhance attention and concentration. These include blueberries, beetroot and dark chocolate.

DRINKING ENOUGH WATER

If the brain is even slightly dehydrated, attention and concentration suffer. Just a 2.1% (of bodyweight) level of dehydration impairs performance in tasks that require attention and memory skills.

In general, does your child eat healthily? Do they eat breakfast? Do they eat regularly enough? Do they have protein/complex carbs regularly enough? Do they eat too much sugar? Do they eat lots of foods with additives? Do they get enough of essential nutrients such as omega-3 and magnesium?

Exercise:

The human body was built for movement. As hunter-gatherers, early humans spent a great deal of time on the move. If we sit still for too long, especially in one position, the body starts to initiate movement. Fidgeting is the body's way of telling us to move around. Most would agree that children spend more time sitting than previous generations, and less time moving and exercising.

There is a strong relationship between movement and attention in the brain. They share overlapping pathways. This may be one reason why martial arts (and other forms of exercise which require complex movement) have been shown to benefit children with ADHD; they have to pay attention while learning new movements, which engages and trains both systems. The attention pathways in the brain are regulated by two chemicals, dopamine and noradrenaline. Exercise increases the amount of these, with immediate effect. Furthermore, regular exercise increases the baseline levels of dopamine and noradrenaline, by spurring the growth of new receptors in some brain areas.

Does your child exercise every day (walking, running around, sports etc.)? Does your child do any form of complex movement exercise such as martial arts, gymnastics, dance? How much exercise does your child have each day?

Sleep:

A sleep-deprived child will not be able to pay attention, listen or concentrate to their best ability. Vatsal Thakkar, an American psychiatrist, has suggested that chronic lack of sleep can in fact explain many cases of so-called ADHD, rather than it being ADHD itself.

One study found that sleep quality was related to a child's academic performance in the morning, whereas afternoon performance was related to overall tiredness. Furthermore, a full night of sleep has been shown to make us three times more likely to be able to find creative solutions to complex problems (a task requiring significant attention and concentration skills). It has been shown that important synaptic connections (connections between brain cells) are linked and strengthened overnight, whereas those that are less important fade away – something called "synaptic pruning".

Sleep is also a crucial time for the processing of information. Studies have shown that when new learning takes place, it is strengthened by sleep. In other words, if a child learned a new skill, then had a good night's sleep, they would be better able to remember that skill and perform it again in the future. Though this is not directly related to attention, listening or concentration, it is important to know.

Quality of sleep is just as important as quantity. If a child has a disturbed night or wakes up frequently, for example, they may not experience the full cycle of sleep regularly enough (a sleep cycle lasts approximately 90 minutes in primary school aged children). The sleep cycle consists of five stages of sleep, the final of which is Rapid Eye Movement (REM) sleep. REM sleep is thought to be particularly restorative, enabling the brain to be working well the next day. During REM sleep, the information a child absorbed during the day is processed. The brain forms neural connections that strengthen the memory. Neurotransmitters (like feel-good chemicals serotonin and dopamine) are replenished. Lack of REM sleep can negatively affect concentration, motor skills and memory.

How much sleep does a child need?

Age	Hours
4 years	11.5
5 years	11
6 years	10.5-11
7 years	10.5
8 years	10-10.5
9 years	10
10 years	9.5-10
11 years	9.5

(Source: They Are What You Feed Them)

Does your child get enough sleep on average? Is their sleep interrupted or disturbed (e.g. regularly wetting the bed, coming in to your room for comfort, waking up with nightmares or bad dreams)?

SENSORY CONSIDERATIONS:

There is massive variation in how much information an individual child can successfully:

- take in ("hear"),

- filter (decide what is important and prioritise) and

- process (decide what to do with the information).

Our senses are in action all the time. We must deal with sounds, sights, smells, tastes and touch, as well as keeping a sense of where we are in the space we fill and how our body is moving/balancing in it (proprioception and vestibular processing). Some children are more sensitive to certain sensory information. For example, they may have a very keen sense of hearing. This may mean that they hear every little sound, and therefore are more likely to become distracted.

Others may be touch-sensitive or sensitive to certain textures. For example, labels or scratchy items of school uniform may be more noticeable for them, making it harder for them to concentrate on a task or instruction.

Other children may be "sensory-seeking". In other words, instead of being sensitive to certain sensory information, the body requires more stimulation from that sense than other children. For example, they may feel driven to explore things through touch. This can distract them from the task at hand. Another example of sensory-seeking behaviour is movement-seeking (vestibular). A child experiencing this may move around and fidget a lot, hang upside down or roll on the floor.

Occupational therapists (OTs) are experts in sensory difficulties. We discuss the possible role of an OT for your child, in the R (Review) section.

Does your child come home exhausted and overwhelmed after school (a possible sign of sensory overload)? Does your child show distress at certain sounds e.g. sudden noises, hand dryers? Does your child have difficulty concentrating if there is a lot of background noise? Does your child struggle with other senses, for example sensitive to certain textures? Does your child "seek out" sensory input, for example touching things, putting things in their mouth a lot, or always fidgeting and moving?

WINDING DOWN TIME:

If a child has had a long period of learning, whether that is a morning session at school, or a whole day at school, the brain has taken in a great deal of information. The child may be tired and feel that they are reaching capacity in terms of taking in any more information or sensory information. If we think about Paul Gilbert's "three states", a child may have been in "drive" state, but is at high risk of moving into "threat" state – if the brain could talk it might be saying: "Please, I'm exhausted, give me a break!" Instead, a child needs to be helped to have a period of soothing/rest ("soothing" state), to allow brain and body to recuperate. We will discuss this further in our Plan section.

Does your child have a place to wind down at home? Is your child given time to wind down each day after school, without any questions or demands? Does your child know how to wind down?

SCREEN TIME:

TVs, computers and other devices could be viewed as a constant stream of distractions. Often, they run in the background – some children have devices or TV on while they do homework or while they eat. This presents the brain with a new challenge which early humans did not face, yet our brains have not changed very much. Brains get easily overwhelmed by information, and brains get tired. We (both adults and children) are becoming increasingly used to this way of the world – constantly being pulled in a different direction by distractions (a new post on Facebook, an alien popping up on screen trying to shoot you in a computer game). We get less practise at sustaining our attention for long periods of time. In addition to this, our brains become quickly accustomed to regular "buzzes". Computer games (and many forms of social media and messaging, which may not be relevant to younger children) encourage us to seek short-term rewards: buzzes (e.g. collecting gold coins, shooting a zombie), which is not reflected in everyday life. Each time we achieve this we get a "hit" of dopamine, a chemical which makes us feel good, and is addictive. Before long, we are seeking the next high. The more our brains get used to such frequent highs, the more we seek them. Therefore, academic learning, which requires sustained attention and concentration, and provides far less frequent "highs", may start to be experienced as boring. Children will then find it hard to attend and concentrate because the brain is not getting the highs it is used to.

Screens, especially when held close to the face, also produce blue light which mimics sunlight. This can easily confuse the brain if a device is used in the evening, and the body's "circadian rhythms" can be affected. Guided mostly by light, the brain sends signals to the body to be wakeful and alert during the day, and more relaxed and sleepy in the evenings. If it gets the wrong signals the brain is likely to be too alert in the evenings and may not be able to "switch off", contributing to sleep problems, stress, fatigue, and difficulties with concentration and attention.

Television brings some of the problems described above, especially if it is on in the background and can be a constant distraction, preventing a child from being able to pay attention or concentrate on other tasks. However, compared with devices such as tablets or computer screens, it is likely to be less problematic. One reason is that children do not tend to sit so close to television screens, so they receive a less intensive dose of blue light. Even so, it is not recommended that children have any screens in their bedrooms.

Does your child have more than one hour of screen time each day (not including TV)?

4. Family and relationships

PEERS:

It matters how other children are getting on with the skills of listening, paying attention and concentration. Their attitude to these important skills also matter. My son, who is nearly 9, mixes with 2 groups of boys. One of these is quite a boisterous and fun lot, with whom he plays football. The other group of children are 3 boys he was lucky enough to be placed next to early on at school; boys who have excellent attention and concentration skills and like to do well at school. Mixing with these boys makes my son, ever competitive, want to do equally well, so he places a high value on listening to the teacher's instructions, and concentrating hard to get the job done speedily. However, when he is at football or gymnastics club, he can be a bit silly and doesn't always listen well.

Is your child spending time with other children who have good listening, attention and concentration skills? Do other children around him/her think these skills are important?

TEACHERS:

A teacher who understands that individual children will be at different stages of development and emotional maturity, that some children require more calm and predictability than others, will get the best out of your child. A teacher also needs to understand that listening, concentration and attention are all skills, which must be taught and practised. All children, even those with ADHD or ADD, have the potential to improve these skills.

Does your teacher understand your child's individual needs? Is your child's teacher encouraging your child to work on his/her listening, attention and concentration skills in a positive and constructive way?

HOME:

Children need a family who gently support and encourage these crucial life skills. For example, spending time playing games with your child which put an emphasis on practising the skills. Most board games and card games will be beneficial. It is also necessary to have firm boundaries about things which will harm concentration, such as using devices too much (or too late in the evening), not getting enough sleep, or not eating breakfast. If you know that things could be improved in this area, don't be hard on yourself, but aim to make small and gradual changes.

Are you and the other members of your family encouraging your child to work on their listening, attention and concentration skills in a positive and constructive way?

5. Brain development

The prefrontal cortex, the brain's area of higher thinking skills, is needed in order to inhibit impulses and therefore to sustain attention. For example, it is involved in the decision to stay focussed on the teacher, rather than flick your ruler on your friend's head. In childhood, the prefrontal cortex is underdeveloped. During puberty, it has a surge in development – the synapses (connections between neurons) are "pruned" and strengthened. Our prefrontal cortex does not reach full maturity until at least the age of 25, and possibly as late as 40. One of the reasons why I explain this is so that, if your child has problems with attention or concentration (sustaining attention), you can feel hopeful that this is likely to improve gradually, starting when they reach adolescence.

Let's catch up with Bobby and Ellen, and understand a little more about their difficulties.

Understand – **Bobby**, aged 6 years.

Bobby's parents, Jackie and Simon, noticed that other children were able to sit and concentrate for longer periods of time. *Developmentally*, Bobby was at a different stage. He was born in July, and had been six weeks premature, so this could partly explain why he was behind some of his classmates.

Jackie and Simon also realised that Bobby wasn't getting as much sleep as he needed. As it was so difficult to get him to wind down, Bobby was going to sleep at around 9pm, and waking in the mornings at around 6am. Nine hours' sleep is too little for a 6-year-old.

Jackie and Simon then looked at Bobby's lifestyle including diet and exercise. Although Bobby ate a healthy diet without too much sugar or processed food, they realised he was getting hungry, and this was affecting his ability to pay attention and concentrate. He ate cereal for breakfast, and took a packed lunch to school: sandwich, fruit and yoghurt. By the end of the school day, when his concentration was at its worst, Bobby was very hungry. They realised he needed to eat more, particularly protein and complex carbohydrates, and that he needed to eat immediately at the end of the school day, to help regulate his blood sugar. Jackie and Simon realised Bobby wasn't doing any "formal" sport or exercise, other than running around a lot in the playground and doing PE. He was a child who perhaps needed more exercise than others.

When Jackie and Simon spoke to Bobby's teacher, they also found out that noise easily distracted him, even though he makes a lot of noise himself. He showed signs of being stressed and overwhelmed. He struggled to calm down, to get into "soothing" state, so by the end of the school day his body and brain were exhausted. Bobby was still in this state when he got home, so when demands were placed on him (for example, he was asked to do something) his brain took him into the red, "threat" state and he became angry, feeling overloaded and exhausted.

Understand – **Ellen**, aged 11 years.

Ellen's anxiety was causing her serious problems with attention and concentration. Her mum Vanessa realised that she was anxious for much of the time at school, because her teacher was strict, and she worried about being told off. She was also anxious about going to secondary school. Her anxiety meant she was in "threat" mode, on the lookout for danger, and therefore her brain was not prioritising paying attention to instructions or concentrating on a task.

Ellen's anxiety was also causing sleep problems, which were creating a vicious cycle. She struggled to wind down at night because her brain was still in threat state. She used her iPad to relax, watching YouTube videos. Vanessa realised that the blue light from this may have been making things worse. Ellen got on average 9 hours of sleep but frequently woke in the night, often having bad dreams. She would wake tired, which affected her attention and concentration skills further.

Ellen liked to play cricket in the summer for her village team, but didn't do any exercise apart from PE in the winter. She ate well but didn't like the hot dinners at school, so only had a little bit to eat at lunch time. Vanessa thought hunger and lack of exercise might both have been affecting her ability to pay attention and to concentrate.

We will now look at some of the underlying problems, discussed in the Understand section, and what you can do to support your child with these. Use the answers you have recorded in the boxes.

1. Developmental stage

Read this section if you think your child's level of development may be important in considering why he is struggling with listening, paying attention or concentrating.

Just because other children in your child's year group are better at these skills, it doesn't necessarily mean there is a problem. Children develop at different rates, and they may catch up. Consider the following strategies.

Strategy 1: Watch and wait. In other words, do nothing. Assume there is nothing "wrong" with your child that time and maturity will not solve. Keep in regular contact with your child's teacher, and ideally keep a diary charting your child's progress, so you can measure any change. For example, you may find that in January, your child required help to sustain attention after every maths problem when doing their homework, but by April, he could do ten questions continuously without support to stay on track.

It is important that your child does not begin to feel negatively about himself because of his difficulties. Keep an eye open for any "negative self-talk" such as "I'm no good at following instructions". Make sure you notice any successes, however small, and celebrate these. One great way of supporting your child's view of himself is to keep a "Brilliant Book". This is a book in which all successes are recorded. Your child chooses and decorates a special scrapbook. Inside, write down all the good things (e.g. "Bobby got 9 out of 10 in his spellings today!") and draw pictures together for the book. You can also stick in photos and certificates.

Strategy	I want to try this (Yes/No) – tick if yes
Watch and wait	
Brilliant book	

Strategy 2: Practise and reward. For some children, working on listening and concentration skills directly can help them improve. You could design a reward programme to help him practise these skills. Each day, spend ten minutes working together on a game or activity which requires concentration and attention. Bring him back on track if his attention wanders. Give simple, clear instructions. Your child should receive a reward (such as a token which they can collect, and eventually exchange for a prize). The reward is given simply for trying, regardless of how well he did in the task. Examples of games you could try include:

- "Freeze!": The child is allowed to pull silly poses, and when you shout "Freeze!" he has to sit very still for 10 seconds. If he achieves this he gets to make you freeze. The time can be gradually increased from 10 seconds.

- "Beat the clock": This can be used to achieve a necessary set of tasks such as getting ready for school the next day. Give your child a simple instruction, such as "put your homework diary in your bag". Then, counting down "3, 2, 1" give him a certain amount of time to achieve it (e.g. 1 minute). Set a timer. When he comes back to you, if he has managed to "beat the clock" he gets a 'high five' from you, and the next instruction is given. Five "beat the clocks" will earn him a reward. You can increase the length of the tasks (and the complexity of the instructions) as your child grows more and more skilled.

You may also wish to consider introducing your child to a musical instrument. Studies have shown that musical training in childhood improves children's cognitive functioning, including attention and switching between tasks. Children must consistently practise sustained concentration when learning an instrument, which strengthens this skill.

Strategy	I want to try this (Yes/No) – tick if yes
10 minutes on a fun concentration task each day	
Learning a musical instrument	

2. Thinking style and state of mind

Read this section if you think your child's thinking style, or her state of mind, might be affecting her ability to listen, pay attention or concentrate.

If a child develops negative thinking about her ability to listen and concentrate, it can sometimes create a vicious cycle ("I'm no good so I won't bother"), and can also affect his well-being.

Strategy 1: Introduce a Brilliant Book (see section 1).

Strategy 2: Teach self-compassion. Read chapter 5 on academic stress, and particularly the section in that chapter about Carol Dweck's "Growth Mindset". Children need to understand that just because they find something difficult at the moment, they may not always find it difficult. The brain can change and develop. Children also need to learn that being harsh or critical of themselves is unhelpful in so many ways. It is also illogical. Harsh or critical thoughts make us feel vulnerable and therefore set off the brain's "fight or flight" system, putting us in "threat" state. This then makes it much harder to pay attention and concentrate, because the brain is focussing on survival rather than learning. It can be helpful to use some ideas from compassion-focussed therapy here.

One practical suggestion is as follows: Talk to your child about her "critical voice", the one which tells her she is no good at concentrating. Then talk to her about her "kind voice". Ask her to draw these if possible. Then help her keep a diary. Every time the critical voice says something negative, help her counterbalance this with a kind voice such as "you will get better at this, everyone has things they struggle with and you are good at lots of things". Write this down. Review the diary every week, talking through the critical and kind thoughts.

Strategy	I want to try this (Yes/No) – tick if yes
Teach your child about the importance of having a "kind voice" as well as a "critical voice"	
Keep a diary of self-critical thoughts and help your child counterbalance these with kind thoughts.	

If your child is low in mood or tends to be anxious, this is likely to be having a direct effect on attention and concentration. Try these strategies:

Strategy 3: Understand why your child is low in mood, and consider if he might need help from a professional. Of course, this is not always easy. If there is a clear reason why your child is feeling low at the moment, such as a difficult life event or bereavement, then you do not necessarily need to do something about it. It could be a normal reaction to difficult circumstances. The chances are your child will eventually recover from this experience, and in the meantime he needs extra consideration and understanding from parents and teachers. Attention and concentration are bound to be affected, as the brain is in a vulnerable state and is likely to be largely in "survival mode" rather than focussing on learning. If this is the case for your child, a "watch and wait" approach is recommended, to see if things improve. If, however, your child's low mood has persisted and he has frequent negative thoughts about self, others and the world, he may need some help. Find a calm time to talk to your child about the way he is feeling, how often he feels down, and what it feels like. You could try using visual scales such as a "feelings thermometer". The child draws a picture of a thermometer. At the top of the thermometer draw a very happy face. This represents the happiest your child could feel. At the bottom draw a sad face. Then draw faces in between (you could have a total of 5 faces or 7 faces). This allows you to have a conversation with your child: Where are you today? What does that feel like in your body and in your mind? How often do you feel like that? If this gives you the sense that your child's low mood is not going to go away by itself, ask your GP to refer your child for further support (see Review section below).

Strategy	I want to try this (Yes/No) – tick if yes
Use feelings thermometer or other forms of drawing to understand more about your child's low mood	

Strategy 4: Read the chapter on Anxiety. If your child's anxiety seems to be affecting his listening, attention or concentration, read the chapter on anxiety (chapter 1).

Strategy	I want to try this (Yes/No) – tick if yes
Read the chapter on anxiety	

Strategy 5: Encourage a "soothing" learning environment at home, and at school. If a child is anxious about learning, consider Paul Gilbert's Three States of Mind. To sustain attention and concentrate effectively, a child cannot be in a threat state, but if they are feeling anxious, that is exactly the state they are likely to be in. The way to deal with this is to help the child to feel soothed so that they can relax enough to complete a piece of work, or even move to the driven state and feel highly motivated to complete this work. To encourage a child to get into their soothed state while trying to learn, it is very important that adults do not become cross with them. This is likely to trigger the fight or flight reaction. Where possible, when a child is trying to learn they should be able to sit in a relaxed and comfortable position. At home, you could provide a homework space that has soothing comforts, such as a soft blanket to put over themselves. You may have heard about research from the University of Bournemouth that has shown children learn better at school when they can wear their slippers in the classroom, rather than shoes.

The space where a child does their homework must be quiet and as free of other sensory experiences as possible, to give your child the best chance of being able to pay attention to the instructions, and keep concentrating until the task is complete. The TV should not be switched on, and even music can be distracting. On the other hand, if there is a lot of noise in the rest of your home, music can be useful to drown out other sounds, but classical music is best as it tends to be more calming and less distracting. Noise from siblings may be unavoidable, but consider trying to create a dedicated space for homework which is as far away from where others are playing as possible.

Strategy	I want to try this (Yes/No) – tick if yes
Make changes at home to ensure your child can be in a "soothed" state when doing academic tasks such as homework. For example, keep calm and avoid getting cross, place soothing and comforting items close to hand (such as a blanket)	
Speak to your child's teacher about making changes at school to ensure your child can move into a "soothed" state if anxious. For example, allocate a warm-natured, understanding adult to provide comfort and support if needed (could be the teacher or another member of staff), offer soothing activities (such as colouring) if required, consider allowing slippers in the classroom!	

3. Behaviour

Read this section if you have questions about whether your own expectations of your child are reasonable, or if you think your child might not have had much practise at following instructions, or might not understand that it is important to follow instructions. Also read this section if you feel your child struggles to get started or to sustain attention long enough to complete a task, or appears to give up easily.

Strategy 1: Reflect on your expectations, and adjust if necessary. If you think there is a problem with your child's attention or concentration skills, but others in your family do not, your expectations may be too high. Even if the school think there is a problem, could this be because the school has very high standards, or because other children in your child's class are unusually able? Have you seen progress in your child in the last few months? If your child is one of the youngest in the year group or was premature they may well develop these skills later. Even if they are not, there is a wide variation in the speed at which attention and concentration skills are mastered.

Strategy	I want to try this (Yes/No) – tick if yes
Adjust your expectations	

Strategy 2: Give your child lots of practise to build skill and confidence in listening and attention. Develop a routine of giving your child regular small tasks to carry out at home, giving them the best opportunity to be successful. This can be done in a very structured way. For example:

A. Remove distractions: Switch off TV, pause computer etc.

B. Say your child's name, ensure you are sitting or standing at their level, and look them in the eye.

C. Give them a single instruction e.g. "Please go and wash your hands."

D. Wait for them to think through the instruction (at least 5 seconds).

E. If they have been successful, provide lots of praise which is very specific such as "you listened to my instruction so well".

F. If unsuccessful, repeat A to E.

Strategy	I want to try this (Yes/No) – tick if yes
Give your child practise in following simple instructions to build skill and confidence in listening and attention. Use a familiar structure each time to give them the best possible chance of success	

Strategy 3: Give your child experience of cooperating with adults, by setting a goal and reward. This will help your child to learn the value and importance of cooperating, and give them practise at waiting for a reward. If your child is not very good at cooperating and tends to do his or her own thing, he is unlikely to be able to

prioritise an important instruction given by an adult (in other words, he is less likely to pay attention to such an instruction).

Here is an example of a clear goal and reward system.

Goal: To increase 7-year-old Emily's level of cooperation with adults, by practising listening and paying attention to instructions and carrying them out first time.

How it is achieved: a poster is designed which sets out what Emily needs to do, and what she will get if she does.

EMILY'S GOAL

EVERY TIME EMILY LISTENS TO MUMMY AND DOES WHAT SHE IS ASKED FIRST TIME, SHE WILL GET A SPECIAL "LUCKY DIP" MARBLE FROM THE BAG.

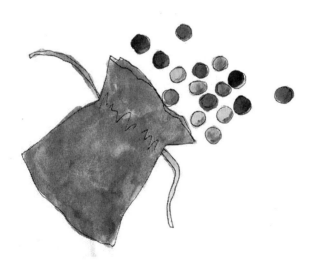

ONCE EMILY HAS EARNED TEN LUCKY DIPS, SHE ALSO EARNS A TRIP TO THE SKATE PARK.

The most important things to remember are to make the instructions into a visual poster so that everyone is clear on what your child needs to do, and to focus on only one goal at a time.

Strategy	I want to try this (Yes/No) – tick if yes
Give your child experience of cooperating, by setting a goal and reward	

Strategy 4: Break larger tasks or instructions down into small chunks, using rewards after each success

Homework tasks, or completing jobs at home, can seem overwhelming to children, even when their concentration, attention and listening skills are good. This applies particularly when the task is quite complex or is open-ended. A 7-year-old, for example, may not be able to follow the instruction, "Tidy your room". Instead, it could be broken down into smaller chunks with your support. For instance:

Step 1: "James, the first step is to clear your floor. Put everything on the bed and then we can decide what to do with it." *(James manages to achieve this.)* "Wow, well done James, mummy is going to be so impressed, and you have earned one reward token."

Step 2: "The next step is to put your books on the bookshelf. The big ones on the bottom and the little ones on the top. I will come back in a few minutes to check how you are doing". *(James manages to achieve this.)* "Fantastic, James. That's your second reward token earned!"

Step 3: "Next we need to sort your clothes out. Most of these are dirty. Pick each item of clothing up and see if it is dirty. If it is, go and put it in the washing basket. I will help you put away the rest." *And so on.*

Strategy	I want to try this (Yes/No) – tick if yes
Break larger tasks or instructions down into small chunks, using rewards after each success	

Strategy 5: Practise mindfulness each day with your child, to build attention skills

Mindfulness is a powerful tool. I wish that every child could learn it both at home and at school. Mindfulness teaches a child to focus on the present. That might involve noticing the sights, smells and sounds around him, or focussing on his breathing. It can be taught through guided audio tracks, video and books. There is growing evidence that mindfulness, when practised regularly (which could be as little as ten minutes per day), can help children with both attention and concentration skills. It can also help with many other important areas such as feeling calm and getting to sleep.

My favourite resources for teaching mindfulness in primary-aged children are:

- "Sitting Still Like a Frog" by Eline Snell (book & CD)
- "Still Quiet Place" by Dr Amy Salzman (CD)
- Headspace for Kids (app): www.headspace.com

Strategy	I want to try this (Yes/No) – tick if yes
Start to practise mindfulness for a few minutes each day with your child, to build attention skills	

Strategy 6: Build resilience by making a personal resilience poster

If your child has had listening, attention, and concentration problems for a long time, he may not have had the chance to build up his resilience; his ability to keep going, even when things get tough. If you haven't followed the instructions in the first place, it is hard to know how to keep going, and it can be easy to give up.

A resilience poster is a small but powerful tool which can be put on a child's wall and used again and again. It reminds a child of how he has dealt with difficulties in the past.

Here's how to do it:

A. Chat with your child about difficult times, perhaps during activities which he enjoys. For instance, "that time when you fell off the vault in gymnastics class", "the time you had an argument with your best friend Freddy". Collect as many examples as you can and make a list.

B. Start to talk about how your child managed to "move on" from what happened. What skills, ideas, personal qualities were involved? For instance: "I was embarrassed about falling at first but then after a few minutes I just thought it was funny. I was nervous about trying the vault again, but I decided to try it with an adult helping me". *Here, you could highlight how the child uses his* **sense of humour** *to bounce back, and manages to use his skills in* **asking an adult for help**, *in order to get over his nervousness.*

C. Make a poster, drawing or writing all the skills and ideas you have talked about. It can be as creative and as colourful as you like. It can be added to regularly. When your child has faced a difficult or challenging time, recap on the ideas in the poster.

Strategy	I want to try this (Yes/No) – tick if yes
Build resilience by making a resilience poster	

4. Environment.

Read this section if you think there may be things about your child's home life, school or lifestyle, which need to change in order to help him/her with listening, attention or concentration.

HOME LIFE:
Strategy 1: Set up a "dark den" or quiet place at home.

If you suspect that your child is feeling overwhelmed by sensory information, academic demands and social demands, and is showing signs of stress, they may enjoy and benefit from a place free from any of this. For some children, this is a little corner, tree house or play-tent, filled with relaxing things (e.g. a soft toy to cuddle, soothing music). For others, it is simply a chance to bury themselves under their duvet and read a book. When a child first gets home from school, this quiet space can be invaluable. In terms of how long your child will need to stay there, it will be different for every child. I have spoken to parents who have told me that an hour or an hour and a half is what their child needs in order to recover from the stresses of the day, but some children will not need as much as this.

Strategy	I want to try this (Yes/No) – tick if yes
Set up a "dark den" or quiet place at home	

Strategy 2: An increase in predictability and routines at home.

If you have noticed by reading this chapter that there are certain habits you would like to change, consider setting out these changes in a clear, consistent and predictable way, which will lead to a healthier routine for everyone in the home. The best way to set out good habits which children will accept and stick to, is to have regular routines. Creating a visual poster, or using pictures on a whiteboard, is a great way of creating a shared understanding of the routine. For example, on a weekday:

- 4pm home from school, snack and quiet time

- 4.30pm go outside and play

- 5.30pm homework or reading

- 6pm free time (could include time on electronic devices/ TV time)

- 6.30pm dinner/tea

- 7pm bath, relax

- 8pm reading time and bed

Strategy	I want to try this (Yes/No) – tick if yes
An increase in predictability and routines at home	

CLASSROOM SET-UP:

Strategy 3: Arrange a teacher meeting and talk through a checklist

A checklist may be based on the following, but individualised towards your child:

Key Principles:

1. Communicating precisely and clearly.
2. Decreasing distraction.
3. Nurture self-esteem by a) maximising opportunities for success b) communicating personal warmth and acceptance and c) providing positive recognition through praise and reward.

Specific ideas and strategies:

1. Children with attention difficulties are often *hypersensitive* to distraction. Seat them somewhere that minimises distraction, near a teacher who can easily notice if they are not attending. Intervene *without embarrassing* the child or disrupting the lesson. Agree cues or reminders to attend to the task, such as a gentle touch on the shoulder, which can calmly remind a child to re-focus.

2. Children can also be distracted by their own thoughts, so it is important for the task to be as stimulating and rewarding as possible.

3. Make sure instructions are concise and clear with as few subparts as possible. Back up oral communication with visual aids, e.g. simple step by step bullet points that children can underline or highlight as they do them. The use of visual hand gestures can remind a child to sit back down, or not to shout out.

4. Children will benefit from predictable, clear routines and structures to lessons. Create a simple visual daily schedule that the child can learn by heart.

5. Get children to use their own visual aids for remembering. E.g. mind maps, bullet points, images, interesting or funny mnemonics using a child's own interests.

6. Break tasks down into a small number of short steps. The emphasis is on reducing complexity.

7. The length and complexity of tasks should increase in accordance with ability and success in managing shorter tasks.

8. Children respond best to more specific and more frequent feedback on their performance. It can be helpful to have children do one or two small steps and then seek support to check they are on track.

9. Small and immediate rewards and praise are more effective than long-term or delayed rewards. Children need lots of regular and positive feedback for effort as well as achievement.

10. Rewards need to be tailored to the child's preferences. E.g. some children love working on the computer and others don't. Develop a rewards menu that is rotated frequently to avoid loss of interest.

11. Previewing and reviewing tasks helps children know what is expected of them and remember what they have learned.

12. Interactions with children need to be brief, calm and positive accompanied by proximity and good eye contact.

13. Children may perform best in pairs rather than group situations. Tables arranged in lines or a horseshoe are often better than tables arranged in small groups.

14. Lessons requiring most concentration and self-directed learning should be scheduled earlier in the day.

15. Tasks can be broken up in class with small physical breaks in between where children can move around or do a job to help the teacher, or sharpen a pencil, or help with the smart board etc.

These ideas were taken from "Attention Deficit Hyperactivity Disorder – A practical Guide for Teachers" by Paul Cooper and Katherine Bilton.

Strategy	I want to try this (Yes/No) – tick if yes
Arrange a teacher meeting and talk through a checklist	

OUTSIDE TIME
Strategy 4: Increase time in nature.

If you have a garden, or live near a park, this will be easier to achieve. The perfect times to do this are a few minutes before and after school, the former to set your child up for a positive day at school, the latter to help relieve any stress built up during the day. Even two minutes outside, walking, running around or playing football before school, will help. You could aim to increase this gradually.

Strategy	I want to try this (Yes/No) – tick if yes
Increase time in nature	

DIET
Strategy 5: Consider if your child is eating regular (or substantial) enough meals.

The most effective way to do this is by keeping a food and mood diary for a few days. Keep a note of what time your child is eating meals and snacks, and their mood, concentration and attention levels before and after eating. You may find that you need to increase the size of your child's packed lunch or increase the amount of protein and slow-release carbohydrates (for example, switch to wholemeal bread instead of white). It is also common to find that children need a healthy snack the moment they get home from school, as they are "running on empty". This should happen before any demands are made on your child (such as unpacking his school bag or getting changed), and before any questions about your child's day. He will be able to answer you more rationally and fully once his blood-sugar levels are restored.

Strategy	I want to try this (Yes/No) – tick if yes
Consider if your child is eating regular enough meals	

Strategy 6: Consider if your child is drinking enough.

Try to ensure your child has a refillable water bottle wherever he goes, and takes regular sips. This area is often overlooked.

Strategy	I want to try this (Yes/No) – tick if yes
Consider if your child is drinking enough	

Strategy 7: Reduce sugar and additives.

There is no guarantee that reducing sugar and additives will make a difference to your child's attention and concentration, but doing this will almost certainly have a positive impact on his overall health and will do no harm. Start with small goals, such as cooking from scratch a few times per week, and reducing fizzy drinks and squashes/cordials.

You may have heard about "exclusion diets". This is different from reducing sugar and additives. It involves a phase of cutting out a number of foods which may be contributing to your child's difficulties, for a few weeks, before gradually reintroducing them one by one and monitoring the effect. This should only be done with the guidance of a nutritional therapist or dietician.

Strategy	I want to try this (Yes/No) – tick if yes
Consider reducing sugar and additives	

Strategy 8: Consider if your child could be missing essential nutrients for attention and concentration.

If you suspect that your child does not eat enough of the types of foods described earlier, for essential nutrients like omega-3 or magnesium, think about which new foods you could gradually introduce, perhaps giving a reward for each new food tried. You may also wish to consider supplements, such as omega-3 oils (found in health food shops) which can be added to smoothies or juices. Magnesium levels can also be increased by adding Epsom salts to baths, or using a magnesium spray. Do not make major changes without discussing them with a dietician or nutritional therapist.

Strategy	I want to try this (Yes/No) – tick if yes
Consider if your child could be missing essential nutrients for attention and concentration	

EXERCISE

Strategy 9: Increase amount of aerobic exercise.

Not everyone is sporty, but everyone can find a type of exercise which they find fun. It could be:

- Bouncing on a trampoline
- Doing crazy dancing to a favourite piece of music
- Running around the block
- Playing in the park

If you can get your child "on board" by explaining to him why exercise is so important for his attention, concentration and learning, you may be able to devise a fun programme of activities together. A few minutes before and after school is best, and can be combined with "time in nature". If you invest a little money in the right clothing (a warm waterproof coat, some thermal wellies!) this can be done in all weather.

Of course, the easiest way to increase aerobic exercise is to walk, scoot or cycle to school. If walking try to keep up a brisk pace, so that your child is a little out of breath by the time he gets to school.

Strategy	I want to try this (Yes/No) – tick if yes
Increase amount of aerobic exercise	

Strategy 10: Introduce your child to a form of exercise that involves complex movement.

Ideas you could try include:

- Tae Kwon Do
- Judo
- Karate
- Gymnastics
- Dance
- Cheerleading

Strategy	I want to try this (Yes/No) – tick if yes
Introduce your child to a form of exercise that involves complex movement	

SLEEP

Strategy 11: Prioritise sleep over everything else.

Often sleep comes very low down in the pecking order, given children's busy lives with homework and after school activities. If listening, attention and concentration are an issue however, you should sit down and reassess your priorities. It may be time to cut down on activities or have a look at how homework could be better managed.

At weekends especially, sleep may suffer. A child's circadian rhythms need a regular bedtime in order to maintain balance and send out the right chemicals at the appropriate time of day (e.g. melatonin at night, cortisol in the mornings). Try to keep bedtime and wake-up time the same even at weekends.

Strategy	I want to try this (Yes/No) – tick if yes
Prioritise sleep over everything else	

Strategy 12: Use this "sleep hygiene" checklist.

1. Try to ensure your child wakes up and goes to sleep at the same time every day.

2. When he wakes up, help him get as much direct light as he can. Ideally, spend some time outside. This will stop production of melatonin (which triggers sleep) and increase production of chemicals which wake him up such as cortisol.

3. Ensure he eats breakfast soon after waking, to raise blood sugar and aid the brain in differentiating between day and night. Ensure your breakfast contains protein (e.g. eggs, nuts) or complex carbohydrates for slow release energy, and try to eat regular slow release energy foods during the day.

4. Bedtime routine: Around one hour before you want to sleep, think about calming each one of the senses to give the correct message to your child's brain. For example, turn down the volume on TV or music, talk in a softer voice, dim the lights, consider using relaxing smells (e.g. candles, oils) or tastes (e.g. warm milk). Experiment with winding down strategies e.g. bubble bath, singing, massage, story time, colouring or creative play. Ensure this time is protected every day.

5. Avoid caffeine especially at night time as this will be too stimulating.

6. Stop your child using electronic devices at least one hour before bedtime (ideally do not allow them in the bedroom).

7. Try not to do anything too exciting or stimulating in the evening, as your child's brain may become over-active.

8. There is some evidence that certain foods, when eaten as a snack before bed, can increase production of melatonin, the sleep hormone. These include Montmorency cherries (you can buy cherry juice or capsules from health food shops), kiwi fruits and bananas.

9. If your child has worries, try helping him write or draw them in a book next to his bed before he goes to sleep. This can help him to put them aside until the morning.

10. Calm a busy brain by doing ten minutes of Mindfulness (see above).

Strategy	I want to try this (Yes/No) – tick if yes
Use "sleep hygiene" checklist	

SCREEN TIME
Strategy 14: Reduce screen time.

Monitor your child's screen time by keeping a diary for 1 week. Set a realistic goal for reduction of screen time if necessary.

Strategy	I want to try this (Yes/No) – tick if yes
Monitor your child's screen time by keeping a diary for 1 week. Set a realistic goal for reduction of screen time if necessary.	

5. Family and relationships.

Read this section if you think your child's family relationships, relationships with peers or teachers, are relevant to his listening, attention and concentration difficulties.

PEERS
Strategy 1: Encourage your child to mix with a variety of other children, including those who have good listening, attention and concentration skills.

Mixing with children who have strong skills will help your child to place importance on these areas. If this is not possible at school, consider other avenues, such as Cubs or Brownies, drama or music groups or choirs.

Strategy	I want to try this (Yes/No) – tick if yes
Encourage your child to mix with a variety of other children, including those who have good listening, attention and concentration skills	

TEACHERS

Strategy 2: Seek to help your teacher understand your child's needs, and build your child's skills in a positive and constructive way.

Share some of your plans and goals from this book. See what your teacher can do to support each one. Teachers generally respond best to a few concrete and specific ideas or suggestions. Hopefully, this chapter has provided exactly what you need!

Strategy	I want to try this (Yes/No) – tick if yes
Seek to help your teacher understand your child's needs, and build your child's skills in a positive and constructive way	

6. Brain development.

As many of the strategies described above are aimed at building skills and therefore developing your child's brain, no new strategies are listed here.

Let's catch up with Bobby and Ellen, and see how their parents planned to help them.

Plan – **Bobby**, aged 6 years.

Bobby's parents Jackie and Simon realised that Bobby's sleep needed to be tackled as he wasn't getting enough. This was making his concentration difficulties worse. They liked the sound of these suggested strategies:

- **Prioritise sleep over everything else.**

- **Use "sleep hygiene" checklist.**

In addition, he was struggling with concentration when his tummy was empty, so they felt it would be important to make changes to his diet, particularly straight after school.

- **Consider if your child is eating regular enough meals.**

Jackie and Simon realised that Bobby would probably sleep better if they could help him wind down, so they liked the sound of the following strategy:

- **Experiment with winding down strategies.**

They also realised that he was feeling overwhelmed by noise and other sensory information at school, so when he got home he needed a break from this:

- **Set up a "dark den" or quiet place at home.**

They felt that, though not a priority, Bobby wasn't doing as much exercise as he needed, and they thought he would benefit from learning a sport which would help him learn mental discipline as well as complex movement to build concentration:

- **Introduce your child to a form of exercise that involves complex movement.**

Last but not least, although Bobby's school were supporting him well, Jackie and Simon felt there were a few more things that could be done to help him:

- **Seek to help your teacher understand your child's needs, and build your child's skills in a positive and constructive way.**

- **Request a teacher meeting and talk through a checklist**

Plan – **Ellen**, aged 11 years.

Vanessa, Ellen's mother, now realised that using her iPad at night was contributing to reduced quantity and quality of sleep. She therefore felt it would be important to look at reducing screen time, especially at night:

- **Monitor your child's screen time by keeping a diary for 1 week. Set a realistic goal for reduction of screen time if necessary.**

She realised that Ellen was anxious about work both at home and at school, but especially at school. She realised she wanted to meet with Ellen's teacher to discuss Ellen's anxiety, because the teacher probably did not realise how anxious Ellen felt. Vanessa wondered if something could be done to help Ellen feel safer/soothed at school, such as having a member of staff she could talk to regularly. At home, she decided she would help Ellen learn to calm herself and wind down.

- **Encourage a "soothing" learning environment at home, and at school.**

Vanessa noticed that Ellen certainly had "negative self-talk", and felt there was something wrong with herself because she could not concentrate well. Vanessa decided she wanted to start a Brilliant Book with Ellen, and work on self-compassion.

- **Introduce a Brilliant Book**

- **Teach self-compassion**

Vanessa wanted to get Ellen moving before school, feeling that some form of exercise would help her concentrate during the day. Also, even though she would have preferred Ellen to eat hot dinners at school, she thought she might start giving Ellen packed lunches, so she could ensure Ellen was having enough to eat.

- **Increase level of aerobic exercise**

- **Consider if your child is eating regular enough meals**

As Ellen found it very hard to get started on tasks, Vanessa realised she was getting overwhelmed by multiple stages of instructions. She realised that it would be helpful for Ellen to learn to break things down into smaller tasks, with adult help to start with.

- **Break larger tasks or instructions down into small chunks, using rewards after each success**

She also felt that mindfulness would help Ellen to sustain her attention for longer.

- **Practise mindfulness each day with your child, to build attention skills**

Now you have pinpointed the problem, understood possible causes and planned some possible actions to help. The next step is to decide which of these actions are the most important, and work out exactly how to use them to help your child.

Let us think about Bobby and Ellen, and how their parents have turned ideas into action:

Bobby, aged 6 years.

Bobby struggles to stay still and fidgets when he is asked to sit in one place.

Bobby cannot follow instructions given by the teacher or his parents, especially at the end of the day, without extra prompts and reminders from adults. His teacher thinks he can understand instructions, but when tired he does not "hear" (attend to) them in the first place.

Bobby's parents, Jackie and Simon, noticed that other children were able to sit and concentrate for longer periods of time. *Developmentally*, Bobby was at a different stage. He was born in July, and had been six weeks premature, so this could partly explain why he was behind some of his classmates.

Jackie and Simon also realised that Bobby wasn't getting as much sleep as he needed. As it was so difficult to get him to wind down, Bobby was going to sleep at around 9pm, and waking in the mornings at around 6am. Nine hours is too little for a 6-year-old.

Jackie and Simon then looked at Bobby's lifestyle including diet and exercise. Although Bobby ate a healthy diet without too much sugar or processed food, they realised he was getting hungry, and this was affecting his ability to pay attention and concentrate. He ate cereal for breakfast, and took a packed lunch to school: sandwich, fruit and yoghurt. By the end of the school day, when his concentration was at its worst, Bobby was very hungry. They realised he needed to eat more, particularly protein and complex carbohydrates, and that he needed to eat immediately at the end of the school day, to help regulate his blood sugar. Jackie and Simon realised Bobby wasn't doing any "formal" sport or exercise, other than running around a lot in the playground and doing PE. He was a child who perhaps needed more exercise than others.

When Jackie and Simon spoke to Bobby's teacher, they also found out that noise easily distracts him, even though he makes a lot of noise himself. He showed signs of being stressed and overwhelmed. He struggled to calm down, to get into "soothing" state, so by the end of the school day his body and brain were exhausted. Bobby was still in this state when he got home, so when demands were placed on him (for example, he was asked to do something) his brain took him into the red, "threat" state and he became angry, feeling overloaded and exhausted.

CONTINUED ON PAGE 335

Bobby's parents Jackie and Simon chose the following strategies:

Prioritise sleep over everything else.

- Use "sleep hygiene" checklist.
- Consider if your child is eating regular enough meals.
- Experiment with winding down strategies.
- Set up a "dark den" or quiet place at home.
- Introduce your child to a form of exercise that involves complex movement.
- Seek to help your teacher understand your child's needs, and build your child's skills in a positive and constructive way.

Request a teacher meeting and talk through a check-list

Jackie and Simon managed to get a babysitter, so they could go out for a meal and discuss what to prioritise. They agreed that they would prioritise sleep followed by exercise. They planned to start the first strategy at the weekend:

Prioritise sleep over everything else.

They thought the following steps would be involved:

1. Clear our diaries (and Bobby's) in the evening for at least two or three weeks and agree to take turns helping Bobby at bedtime.
2. Talk to Bobby about the plans to help him get more sleep, and explain to him using pictures why sleep is so important.
3. From Friday evening, start to bring Bobby's bedtime forward by 15 minutes every night.

Once Jackie and Simon had got started with this goal, they had some early success and quickly moved on to their second goal:

Use "sleep hygiene" checklist.

They thought the following steps would be involved.

1. Look at the checklist and decide which items on the list are most relevant to us.
2. Prepare a to-do list of all the changes we need to make in advance and anything we need to buy (e.g. buy hot chocolate, relaxing bubble bath and a notebook for writing down worries).
3. Sit down with Bobby and make a large poster of our new bedtime schedule and morning routine, using lots of colourful pictures. Put this on the wall.

After a few weeks, when they could see Bobby was getting to sleep earlier and was less tired, they started to think about their next goal:

Introduce your child to a form of exercise that involves complex movement.

Simon heard about a children's Tae Kwon Do class starting the following term, and felt this would be perfect for Bobby, so he signed him up.

Ellen, aged 11 years.

Ellen finds it hard to get started with open-ended tasks such as creative writing.

Ellen finds it hard to complete her homework; to persist enough to get the task done before she loses concentration.

Ellen is easily distracted when doing open-ended pieces of work.

Ellen's anxiety is causing her serious problems with attention and concentration. Her mum Vanessa realises that she is anxious for much of the time at school, because her teacher is strict, and she worries about being told off. She is also anxious about going to secondary school. Her anxiety means she is in "threat" mode, on the lookout for danger, and therefore her brain is not prioritising paying attention to instructions or concentrating on a task.

Ellen's anxiety is also causing sleep problems, which are creating a vicious cycle. She struggles to wind down at night because her brain is still in threat state. She uses her iPad to relax, watching YouTube videos. Vanessa realises that the blue light from this may make things worse. Ellen gets around 9 hours of sleep but frequently wakes in the night, often having bad dreams. She wakes tired, which affects her attention and concentration skills further.

Ellen likes to play cricket in the summer for her village team, but doesn't do any exercise apart from PE in the winter. She eats well but doesn't like the hot diners at school, so often only has a little bit to eat at lunch time. Vanessa thinks hunger and lack of exercise might both be affecting her ability to pay attention to concentrate.

Ellen's mother Vanessa chose the following strategies:

- Monitor your child's screen time by keeping a diary for 1 week. Set a realistic goal for reduction of screen time if necessary.
- Encourage a "soothing" learning environment at home, and at school.
- Introduce a Brilliant Book.
- Teach self-compassion.
- Increase level of aerobic exercise.
- Consider if your child is eating regular enough meals.
- Break larger tasks or instructions down into small chunks, using rewards after each success.
- Practise mindfulness each day with your child, to build attention skills.

CONTINUED ON PAGE 335

Vanessa decided that she needed to tackle screen-time as her first priority:

Monitor your child's screen time by keeping a diary for 1 week. Set a realistic goal for reduction of screen time if necessary.

She decided on the following steps:

1. Keep a diary, starting tomorrow.

2. Find a suitable time to sit down and talk calmly with Ellen about the effects of too much screen time on her sleep, and my plans to reduce it at night time. Agree a plan and put it in writing (make a poster to put on the wall in the hallway). Agree a reward (Ellen will get a reward token each time she manages to stick to the plan, and she will be able to trade these in for a treat).

3. Get started with the plan, on a day agreed in advance with Ellen.

After a few weeks, she noticed a positive difference in the time Ellen was able to get off to sleep. Whilst continuing with the plan, she felt she would like to give Ellen some skills to manage her anxiety and build her attention skills:

Practise mindfulness each day with your child, to build attention skills.

She felt the steps towards this would be:

1. Invite my friend Bhavna over to talk to Ellen, as she knows all about mindfulness.

2. Download the Headspace app on my iPad.

3. Starting on Friday, make mindfulness part of the bedtime routine. Lie down with Ellen for ten minutes, once she is in bed but before she reads her book, and listen to one of the mindfulness tracks together.

Now it is time for you to summarise all the areas which could help explain your child's difficulties with listening, paying attention, or concentrating, and list the recommended strategies. Look back at your responses in the previous sections (S – Spell it out, U – Understand and P – Plan), and copy into the form below:

S
SPELL IT OUT

My child's difficulties are as follows:

....

....

....

....

....

....

....

U
UNDERSTAND

The following may be the reasons for my child's difficulties, or may be hindering improvement:

....

....

....

....

....

....

....

These strategies might help:

_____

_____

_____

_____

_____

_____

_____

Now it is time to **Energise** your Plan!

Hopefully you have a list of ideas you want to try. You also have a busy life as a parent. It is very important that you do not try everything at once. This will overwhelm both you and your child.

Take a look at your chosen list of strategies in the **Plan** section above. Which one of these may be the easiest to get you started? Which might start to make a difference quickest? Which do you think your child would like to try first? Having discussed the options with your partner (if applicable), your child and anyone else who is involved, choose just one strategy.

These strategies might help:

_____

_____

_____

_____

These are the steps I need to take to get started

1. ....

....

....

2. ....

....

....

3. ....

....

....

I will aim to start on ....

I will need to allow at least ....
(e.g. 1 month) to see if the strategy is working.

I will review our progress on (date) ....

These are things which might cause problems/prevent success:

....

....

....

....

....

So, once you have started with your first strategy, you can keep some notes regarding your success, which will help you when you come to **Review** (R).

Once you have given the first strategy a good go, and you feel you are ready to move on to something else, choose the next priority. Use the table below to keep track of the strategies you have tried.

Record of strategies tried

Strategy description	Steps needed to get me started	Date started	Date reviewed	Notes (how did it go?)
E.g. **1.** Introduce a Brilliant Book	E.g. 1. Take Matthew shopping to buy a scrapbook 2. Decorate the book 3. Set an alarm to stick things/write things in the book every day at 6pm.	2nd June	2nd July	Matthew loves it. It is slowly helping him to see he can do things and encouraging to him to stick at things. We will keep going.

By the time you have read to this section, hopefully you will feel that you:

Have been able to describe in detail your child's particular difficulties with attention, listening and concentration.

- Have been able to understand some of the reasons why s/he has these difficulties

- Have considered strategies which may help your child.

- Have tried some of these strategies, one at a time.

- Are things getting better? If so, great! Now consider:

- Of the strategies in my table, which shall I carry on doing?

- Which strategies will I stop?

- What else do I need to do, to maintain progress?

If things are not yet better, consider:

Are there good reasons why things might be the same or worse than before? For example, has your child just faced a big change at school, or a difficult life event which you were not expecting? Or are things happening in *your* life which affected things?

Alternatively, if you have tried your best and things are no better, could your child have a difficulty which you need professional help with? This is not a failure; some children have more severe difficulties, and need support from someone who is specially trained to understand and help.

Seeking further help from school.

If things are not better, try to see your child's teachers as your allies, and find out what sources of support they can offer. Schools often have resources they can tap into. They may be able to involve your child in a small group working on attention and concentration skills, for example. They may be able to have a specialist teacher observe your child (if this hasn't been done previously), and make some recommendations. Your child's school may also be able to help you if you feel you need to seek further help. They may be able to guide you as to which professional(s) to seek help from, and can sometimes make a direct referral, for example to an occupational therapist.

Seeking further professional help

Although the strategies in this chapter may help all children, some children may need extra help and support from professionals. Some may benefit from an assessment by a paediatrician or clinical psychologist, as they may have a neurodevelopmental (brain development) difference such as ADHD, requiring specialist support. Your GP will be able to refer you to one of these professionals.

If, like Ellen in our case example, you feel that anxiety is significantly affecting your child's attention and concentration, you may wish to ask the GP or school to make a referral to CAMHS (your local Child and Adolescent Mental Health Service). This team may be able to offer a course of therapy, such as cognitive behavioural therapy, which can be very effective in treating anxiety. They also offer parental advice. An independent child psychology service, such as Everlief (our clinic in Buckinghamshire) will also be able to support children with anxiety. You can find independent child clinical psychologists by looking at the British Psychological Society's "Find a Psychologist" page: http://www.bps.org.uk/bpslegacy/dcp, or by searching on the ACHiPPP (Association for Child Psychologists in Private Practice) website: https://www.achippp.org.uk/directory.

If you are concerned that your child has sensory difficulties which are affecting his concentration, attention and listening skills, an occupational therapist (OT) may be able to help. Some OTs work in the NHS, but there are limited resources. Your GP or school can make a referral. Alternatively, you could find an independent occupational therapist. Many occupational therapists have their own websites and can be found by doing an internet search for an OT in your area, but you could also try the College of Occupational therapists: https://www.cot.co.uk/find-ot/find-occupational-therapist.

If you would like to seek advice about your child's eating, or whether he is getting enough of the essential nutrients, you can find a local nutritional therapist through the British Association of Nutritional Therapists (BANT): http://bant.org.uk/bant/jsp/practitionerSearch.faces.

Review – **Bobby**, aged 6 years.

Bobby's parents reviewed their goals. After 3 months they were still managing to prioritise sleep and used the "sleep hygiene checklist". They felt this had made a massive difference so they decided to make sure sleep remains a priority. Unfortunately, Bobby did not take to the children's Tae Kwon Do class. However, they found a street dance class which he loved, and he now dances twice a week.

Though Bobby's concentration is now slightly better at school, his parents feel the next step is to request a meeting with Bobby's teacher and talk through some of the strategies which might help him further. They also decided to meet with a nutritional therapist to see if they could make some changes to Bobby's diet which might help his concentration further.

Review – **Ellen**, aged 11 years.

Ellen's mother Vanessa reflected that setting clear boundaries on screen time to reduce it, and making mindfulness a daily part of Ellen's routine, had made a massive difference to her state of mind. Vanessa felt she needed to continue to work through the list of ideas she had developed, such as encouraging Ellen to take up exercise. She felt these lifestyle changes would help her to manage her anxiety and stress throughout secondary school.

References

Adan, A. *Cognitive Performance and Dehydration.* Journal of the American College of Nutrition, Volume 31, 2012:2 Pages 71-78.

Adolphus, K., Lawton, C. L. & Dye, L. *The effects of breakfast on behaviour and academic performance in children and adolescents.* Frontiers in Human Neuroscience. 2013; 7: 425.

Berto, R. *Exposure to restorative environments helps restore attentional capacity.* Journal of Environmental Psychology, Volume 25, Issue 3, September 2005, Pages 249–259

El Baza, F., Ahmed Al Shahawi, H., Zahra, S., Ahmed, R., Hakim, A. *Magnesium supplementation in children with attention deficit hyperactivity disorder.* Egyptian Journal of Medical Human Genetics Volume 17, Issue 1, January 2016, Pages 63–70

Foster, R. *Why Do We Sleep?* TedTalk (TedGlobal 2013).

Kaplan, S. *The restorative benefits of nature: Toward an Integrative Framework.* Journal of Environmental Psychology, Volume 15, Issue 3, September 1995, pages 169-182.

Könen T, Dirk J, Schmiedek F. *Cognitive benefits of last night's sleep: daily variations in children's sleep behaviour are related to working memory fluctuations.* Journal of Child Psychol Psychiatry. 2015 Feb;56(2):171-82.

Miendlarzewska, E. A. & Trost, W.J. *How musical training affects cognitive development: rhythm, reward and other modulating variables.* Frontiers in Neuroscience. 2013; 7: 279.

Ratey, J.J. & Hagerman, E. Spark (2009). *Spark: How exercise will improve the performance of your brain.* Quercus: London.

Richardson, A. (2006).*They Are What You Feed Them.* Harper Thorsons.

Stevens, L.J., Thomas Kuczek, M.S., Burgess, J.R., Hurt, E & Arnold, L.E. Dietary *Sensitivities and ADHD Symptoms: Thirty-five Years of Research.* Clinical Pediatrics. 2010, 50:4.

Thakkar, V.G. *Diagnosing the Wrong Deficit.* The New York Times Sunday Review: The Opinion Pages. April 2013.

Weare, K. (2012). *Evidence for the Impact of Mindfulness on Children and Young People.* University of Exeter Mood Disorders Centre in association with the Mindfulness in Schools Project.

Wolraich M., Milich R., Stumbo P., & Schultz F. *Effects of sucrose ingestion on the behaviour of hyperactive boys.* Journal of Pediatrics. 1985 Apr;106(4):675-82.

Further Reading

Compassionate Mind Foundation (Professor Paul Gilbert): https://compassionatemind.co.uk/about-us

Headspace for Kids (app): www.headspace.com

Richardson, A. (2006).*They Are What You Feed Them*. Harper Thorsons.

Salzman, A. (2008). *Still Quiet Place: Mindfulness for Young Children* (CD)

Siegel, D.J. & Payne Bryson, T. (2012). *The Whole-Brain Child: 12 proven strategies to nurture your child's developing mind*. Robinson.

Snel, E. (2014). *Sitting Still Like a Frog* (book & CD). Shambhala Publications Inc.

Biographies

Dr Liz Dawes:

Liz is a clinical psychologist and a mum of two. She qualified as a clinical psychologist in 2011 and has been working with children and families in practice ever since. Liz specializes in working with children with autism and their families at Everlief and in her own private practice. She is interested in finding fun and creative ways to help children learn the social skills they need to survive primary school in readiness for adolescence. Liz has developed a group programme at Everlief for teaching children the skills they need to make and maintain friendships. She is now hoping to develop a group for teenage girls with Asperger's Syndrome.

Outside of work, Liz has two lively and wonderfully enthusiastic young girls, and a menagerie of pets. She enjoys running and reading, and in those rare quiet moments, bird watching in the countryside.

Nicola Gorringe

Nicola is a Chartered and HCPC Registered Clinical Psychologist with additional training and experience in Cognitive Behaviour Therapy. She qualified in 1995 and has been working with children and families in the NHS before she joined the Everlief team in 2013. Her NHS experience has mostly been in Child and Adolescent Mental Health Services, working with children suffering from anxiety, low mood, low self-esteem and anger problems. She has also worked with adults and has a number of years' experience working in the field of chronic pain and chronic fatigue with adults and children, as well as taking the role of lead clinician in a service for children with challenging behavior.

Nicola was a guest lecturer at the University of Hertfordshire Clinical Psychology Doctoral Training Course and has regularly supervised and taught other psychologists and mental health workers as part of her work.

Nicola's practice is very much influenced by Attachment and Social Learning models of child development. She is particularly interested in helping parents understand the emotional reasons underlying children's behavioural difficulties, aiming to help families develop warm, responsive and positive relationships that provide the foundations for self-esteem and emotional wellbeing from infancy through to adolescence.

Dr Katherine Hodson

Katherine qualified as a clinical psychologist in 2005, and has subsequently worked in a range of child and adolescent teams, including general CAMHS (Child and Adolescent Mental Health Service), a CAMHS crisis team and a specialist team for looked after children with complex emotional and behavioural problems. Katherine completed her diploma in advanced practitioner skills for eating disorders in April 2008, and was trained in the Multi-dimensional Treatment Foster Care programme in Oregon, America in September 2009. Katherine moved into private work in March 2013, when she joined the Everlief Child Psychology team.

Katherine enjoys working with children and adolescents who have a variety of difficulties, although has a special interest in: eating disorders, toileting issues, anger and anxiety. She offers private clinical supervision for other clinical psychologists, consultation sessions for local schools, and has additionally been a school Governor since April 2012.

Dr Lucy Russell:

Lucy is a clinical psychologist and mum of two lively children.

She qualified in clinical psychology at the University of Oxford in 2005, and worked in Berkshire CAMHS (child and adolescent mental health service), before leading an intensive therapeutic fostering programme (MTFC) in Reading. In 2012 she left the NHS to set up Everlief with her husband Mike.

Lucy works therapeutically with children presenting with a range of difficulties at Everlief, and particularly enjoys combining mindfulness with more traditional psychological therapies such as CBT (cognitive behavioural therapy). Lucy has trained to teach the Mindfulness in Schools Project's ".b" curriculum for children, and offers this in schools.

Lucy is fascinated by the links between mind and body. She has a special interest in nutrition and mental health, as well as the benefits of exercise for wellbeing.

In her spare time Lucy is passionate about singing, regularly participating in musical theatre productions. She also takes part in adult cheerleading. She was inspired to take up cheerleading by her cheer-mad daughter, Olivia.

Dr Jen Swanston:

Jennifer has over seven years of experience working with children, adolescents and families in a number of different services. These include generic child and adolescent mental health services and more specialist services, such as an outreach and crisis service for children with complex emotional and behavioural difficulties. As well as working within both Cognitive Behavioural and Systemic models, Jennifer has completed additional training in specific trauma based models (EMDR and NET) and parenting approaches to tackle challenging behaviour. Jennifer has a specialist interest in working with anxiety, trauma and anger issues. She is passionate about engaging young people and their families using creative and flexible approaches.

Jennifer started working privately in 2013 for Everlief Child Psychology and her own independent practice. She carries out expert witness work, specifically relating to child and family court proceedings. Jennifer is a guest lecturer at Oxford University and provides clinical supervision and consultation to a range of professionals.

Dr Susan Wimshurst:

Susan qualified in 2005 and works as a Chartered and HCPC registered Clinical Psychologist both within the NHS and the Everlief team. She has worked for the NHS, within a Child and Adolescent Mental Health Service (CAMHS), since qualifying. Susan joined the Everlief Team in 2012.

Susan played a lead role in setting up a service in Buckinghamshire, offering assessment and treatment of a wide range of problems in children, such as sleep problems, toileting and anxiety. She now works with children and young people with a range of more complex difficulties within a CAMHS team in Oxfordshire.

Susan has a particular interest in supporting children with anxiety-related difficulties, including specific phobias, social anxiety and obsessive-compulsive disorder (OCD). She also has a special interest in autism and has a significant role in offering parental support following diagnosis. Susan offers supervision to other clinical psychologists and has provided psychological consultation for television programmes involving young people with mental health issues.